Persuasives
to
Early Piety

Interspersed with
Suitable Prayers

by

J. G. Pike

Soli Deo Gloria Publications
...for instruction in righteousness...

Soli Deo Gloria Publications
P.O. Box 451, Morgan, PA 15064
(412) 221-1901/FAX 221-1902

*

Persuasives to Early Piety was published in 1834
by the Religious Tract Society in London.
This Soli Deo Gloria reprint is 1996.

*

ISBN 1-57358-036-8

PREFACE.

THE sole design of this little volume, is to urge the young to yield themselves to God. It interferes not with the minor distinctions that divide the followers of the Saviour; but inculcates that heartfelt Religion, whose importance they all unite in acknowledging.

The Author of the book has no expectation of its being applauded for elegance of language, or the beauties of imagination. He has not written seeking human applause as his reward; for what is human applause? the applause of a world whose duration is a span; — of a world that will soon vanish away like smoke; — of a world whose very existence may be next to forgotten by the soul, in the distant and interminable scenes of eternity. The minister of the gospel meets with the best commendation, not when the discourse he may have delivered from the pulpit or the press is much admired, much applauded, but when the sinner becomes dissatisfied with himself and his pursuits; when the prodigal says, "I will arise and go to my father;" when the penitent weeps in secret over the crimes that have been brought to his review. Such applause the writer covets, and for such he does not hesitate to pray. He freely confesses, that it is his desire to do something for pro moting the kingdom of Christ beyond the narrow limits of his own congregation, and the confined space of a few short years.

In composing the subsequent pages, it has been the Author's wish to imitate the serious plainness which prevails in the writings of some of those eminent men, who lived a century and a half, or two centuries ago, rather than the more polished but much less impressive manner of the present age. Gospel truth is now often held forth in so refined a style, that the offence of the cross ceases, the force of divine truth is lost; it is little better than the mere wisdom of words, and has not much more effect than sounding brass or a tinkling cymbal.

How far the writer of this little book has succeeded in his aim, must now be left to the decision of God. If he deign to employ it as an instrument of advancing his cause, it will be successful; but if he have nothing for it to do, the sooner it shall sink into oblivion the better.

CHAPTER I.

§ 1. My dear young friend, if a person could rise from the dead to speak to you, could come from the other world to tell you what he had seen there, how attentively would you listen to his discourse, and how much would you be affected by it! Yet a messenger from the dead could not tell you more important things, than those to which I now beseech you to attend. I come to entreat you to give your heart to GOD; to follow the divine REDEEMER *now;* and to walk in the pleasant path of early piety. O that I could, with all the fervour of a dying man, beseech you to attend to your only great concerns! for of how little consequence is this poor transient world to you, who have an eternal world to mind! — It is not to a trifle that I call your attention, but to *your life,* your all, your eternal all, your God, your Saviour, your heaven, your every thing that is worth a thought or a wish. Do not let a stranger be more anxious than yourself for your eternal welfare. If you have been thoughtless hitherto, be serious now. It is time you were so. You have wasted years enough. Think of Sir Francis Walsingham's words; "While we laugh all things are serious around us. God is serious, who preserves us, and has patience towards us; Christ is serious, who shed his blood for us; the Holy Spirit is serious, when he strives with us; the whole crea-

tion is serious in serving God and us; all are
serious in another world; how suitable then is
it for man to be serious! and how can we be
gay and trifling?"   Do you smile at this grave
address, and say, this is the cant of enthusiasm?
O, think, that those who laughed at these solemn
truths, when the last hundred years began, now
laugh no more! The friendly warning may be
neglected, and the truths of the bible disbeliev-
ed, but death and eternity will soon force on the
most careless heart, a deep conviction, that religion is the one thing needful.

Yes, my young friend, one thing is needful;
so said the Lord of life; needful to you, to me,
to all. The living neglect it, but the dead know
its value. Every saint in heaven feels the worth
of religion, through partaking of the blessings to
which it leads; and every soul in hell knows its
value by its want.   It is only on earth that tri-
flers are to be found; and will you be one of
them?   God forbid!

Read, I beseech you, this little book, with serious prayer. Remember that it is your welfare
which is sought. I wish you to be happy here,
and when time is past, happy for ever. Fain
would I persuade you to seek a refuge in the
skies, and friends that never fail. I plead with
you a more important cause than was ever conducted before an earthly judge. Not one which
concerns time only; but which concerns a long
eternity. Not one on which a little wealth or
reputation depends; but one on which your
eternal poverty or eternal riches, eternal glory
or eternal shame, a smiling or a frowning God,
an eternal heaven or an eternal hell, are all de-
pending. And it is your cause I plead and not

my own; and shall I plead your cause to yourself in vain? O my God, forbid that I should!

I know, my young friend, how apt we are to read the most serious calls as if they were mere formal things, of little more consequence to us than the trifles recorded in a newspaper; but do not thus read this little book. Believe me, I am in earnest with you; and read, I entreat you, what follows, as a serious message which I have from God for you.

Consider what will be your thoughts of the advice here given you a hundred years hence. Long before that time, you will have done with this world for ever. Then your now vigorous and youthful body will be turned to dust, and your name probably forgotten upon earth; yet your immortal soul will be living in another world, and far more sensible of joy or grief than it can possibly be now. Then, my young friend, what will you think of this friendly warning? How happy will you be if you have followed the advice it contains! Fancy not that it will be then forgotten. Calls and mercies forgotten *here* must be remembered *there*, when every sin is brought to the sinner's memory. If now you think me over-earnest, you will not then entertain the same opinion. If now you slight this humble effort for promoting your salvation, and carelessly, or contemptuously throw this book aside, or read it and forget it, then, if ten thousand worlds were yours, they would appear a little trifle, for another season of salvation like that you now enjoy; and which, perhaps, you now waste: but now is *your* day of grace; then, another generation will have theirs.

Think again, that while you are reading this

thousands are rejoicing in heaven, that they, in past years, attended to such earnest calls. Once they were as careless as you may have been, but divine grace disposed them to listen to the word of life. They regarded the warnings addressed to them; they found salvation; they are gone to rest; and now with what pleasure may they recollect the fervent sermon, or the little book, that, under God, first awakened their attention, and first impressed their hearts! About one hundred and fifty years ago, a gentleman went into the shop of a Mr. Boulter, a London bookseller, to inquire for some plays. Mr. Boulter told him he had none; but showed him Mr. Flavel's treatise of "Keeping the Heart;" and assured him, that it would do him more good than plays. The gentleman glancing at different pages, said, "What a fanatic was he who made this book!" Mr. Boulter assured him, he had no cause to censure it so bitterly. He bought it, but said he would not read it. "What will you do with it then?" said the friendly bookseller. "I will tear and burn it," said he. Mr. Boulter told him then, he should not have it. Upon this, the gentleman promised to read it. About a month after, he went again to the shop, and spoke to this effect: "I most heartily thank you for putting this book into my hands — I bless God that moved you to do it — blessed be God that ever I came into your shop!" and then he bought a hundred more to give to those who could not buy them. How much happier, my young friend, is he now, than he would have been if he had continued the same thoughtless creature as he was when he entered the bookseller's shop! Now, though to us his name is unknown, we have reason to believe he forms one of the company above; but had he continued to waste his fleeting years, he might, in hopeless misery, have been wishing in vain for those precious hours he had wasted on plays, and romances, and novels. Had he slighted Mr. Boulter's advice, he might now in hell have been lamenting his folly. Yes, think that while you are reading this little book, millions of wretched souls, in utter darkness and despair, are cursing that desperate madness, which led them to turn a deaf ear to such friendly warnings, once addressed to them. O my young friend, I beseech you, by the joys of saints in heaven, and by the terrors of sinners in hell, trifle not with this affectionate call!

Consider further — if you were going a journey, you would make preparations for it. Would you not, if going to travel only one or two hundred miles? and were you thus far from home, would not your thoughts be often there? and if obstructions lay in the way, that threatened to prevent your ever returning, would you not exert all your skill and power to remove them? And are you indeed only a stranger and traveller upon earth? Are you only going forwards through a little span of time to an eternal world? And there to find an endless abode, amidst the deepest sorrow or the most perfect joy? And do many things unite to hinder you from reaching the kingdom of heaven? Is this the case? Indeed it is. And will you go forward, thoughtless whither you are going? Thoughtless of what awaits you on your entrance on that unseen world, that unseen, un.

known, endless world of joy unspeakable, or of
grief beyond expression.

Were your soul intrusted to another's care,
would you not complain of his cruelty, if you
saw one begging him to seek its happiness, and
yet perceived him careless whether you were
saved or lost? Would you not cry out, "O unhappy creature that I am, to have my eternal
all intrusted to a wretch so cruel, that he will
see me sink into the pit of destruction, to spend
a dreary eternity there, sooner than give himself
any care or concern about my eternal happiness!" Would such be your complaint in this
case? O, be not then, by carelessness, more
cruel to yourself!

While therefore, in what follows, I would address you with affectionate earnestness, I once
more entreat you seriously to regard the plain,
but important truths I may present to you; and
forgive me that I am not earnest enough, when
speaking to you on things of everlasting consequence. Did we but feel the thousandth part of
the worth of an immortal soul, I might abhor
myself for writing so coldly; and you blush
and be confounded, at having ever needed
warning to seek its welfare. It is impossible to
be earnest enough with you: if you ever know
the worth of true piety you will be convinced
that it is. Did we see thousands asleep on the
brink of a precipice, and some every moment
falling and dying, could we too passionately
endeavour to awaken those not yet undone? O
my young friend, if you have been a careless
trifler with the gospel of Christ, danger infinitely worse, eternal danger threatens you! Awake,
awake! I beseech you, awake! Awake, before it

is too late! before eternity seals your doom! before God forgets to be gracious! Awake! as in the sight of God I call on you, awake! Act not the sluggard's part! say not a little more sleep, a little more slumber! Close not your eyes to sleep in sin again! lest

———— you should shortly feel,
The sleeper sleeps no more in hell.

Awake! I beseech you, and begin to mind that one thing, which is so needful to you; that food is not half so needful to the poor wretch perishing of hunger, nor help to him that is sinking in the sea, or scorching in the flames! Perhaps all I urge to gain your attention is urged in vain. And shall it be so? Will you slight your God, and make your own destruction sure? Will you be a more cruel enemy to yourself than even devils themselves could possibly be to you? Alas! if you will, what must be your condition soon? But let me hope better of you, and offer you one request — look up to God, and join with me in the prayer that follows; and then beg his mercy on yourself.

§ 2. A PRAYER FOR THE DIVINE BLESSING ON THIS BOOK.

Ever blessed and most gracious God, thy smile is life, thy frown is death. Thou hast access to every heart, and knowest every thought of every creature in thy wide dominions. Look down from thine eternal throne, and teach one of the meanest of thy creatures to supplicate thy mercies. Without thy love we must be poor in the midst of plenty; and wretched in the midst of worldly joy; whilst in thy love is pleasure, though in the midst of pain; and wealth in the midst of worldly poverty. He that knows thee and loves thee, though he die of want and hunger, is infinitely richer and happier than the king who rules the widest empire, but knows thee not. Thou art our only happiness, yet have we not sought good in thee. Thou art our bliss, yet have we bid thee depart. Thou hast the first and most reasonable claim upon our hearts, yet by nature those hearts are shut against thee. But if thou hast blessed him that indites this prayer, with the knowledge of thyself, bless those who may read or utter it with the same heavenly knowledge. Great God, thou only knowest what is man. A fallen miserable wretch; a wilful child and slave of sin; a deserving heir of wrath and woe. Thy heavenly pity has opened for him a way of life, but how few are they who find it! and, ah! no hand but thine can guide the sinner into that peaceful path. Hard is the heart thy goodness does not melt — no rock so hard. Cold is the heart thy kindness does not warm — no ice so cold. Yet, alas! great God, such is naturally every human heart. Such was his, whom thou hast inclined to write this little volume; and such his who reads it. But thou hast power to soften the rock, and melt the ice, and change the heart; and hast thou not the desire? Merciful Maker, hast thou not sworn, "As I live I have no pleasure in the death of the wicked, but that the wicked turn from his way and live?" Thou hast said, "Look unto me, and be ye saved, all ye ends of the earth;" and thousands, now in glory, have experienced thy saving power. The feeblest instruments can in thy hand perform the mightiest works. A pebble and a sling can bring down to the dust thy proudest foe. Now then, compassionate God, display thy power to save. Grant that some who read this book may yield to its persuasions, and earnestly regard their best concerns. By feeble instruments thou hast awakened many a thoughtless heart; and if this be the feeblest of the feeble, yet magnify thy power and mercy by making it to one soul (O, might it be to many!) a solemn and awakening call. Let some of its readers learn the end for which life was given; and O, let them not sleep the sleep of sin and death, till awakened by judgment and destruction! Gracious God, teach them that life is not given to be trifled and sinned away. By the power of the gospel, subdue the stony heart, and break the rock of ice. With a voice, effectual as that which shall wake the dead, bid the dead in sin arise and live. Bid the young sinner, that may read this volume, flee from the wrath to come. "O, let not sin and death resist thee!" Let not Satan successfully oppose thee. Let not the stubborn heart refuse thee admittance. But, God of mercy, by thy conquering Spirit, make this little book, which in itself is feeble as a reed, powerful to lead to penitence, prayer, and conversion, some youthful wanderer from the paths of peace. O thou who pitiest wretched men, teach the young readers of this book to pity themselves! Let them not by sin and folly make even immortality a curse. Let them not despise thy gracious calls, nor trample on thy dying love. Over them let not hell rejoice, and heaven mourn; but let the angels that dwell in thy presence, and the saints that surround thy throne, exult over some penitent awakened by this feeble instrument; some youth embracing the gospel of thy Son, and finding every good in him. Great God, grant this request. O, let the sorrows of the Saviour urge it! O, let the intercession of the Saviour obtain it! O, let the influences of the Spirit accomplish what is thus desired! for, blessed Lord, it is here devoutly acknowledged, that, without that Spirit, "books are senseless scrawls, studies are dreams, learning is a glow-worm, and wit is but wantonness, impertinence, and folly." And O may it seem meet to thy divine Majesty, to grant, that when the author of this book has finished his course, that then, though dead, he may yet speak in the following pages; and continue to call on the young to "remember their Creator in the days of their youth!" If this be a sinful ambition, compassionate God, for Jesus's sake, forgive it; but if it be a desire which thy Spirit has produced in the writer's heart, for Jesus's sake grant the request. Bestow thy Spirit, O God of love! Bestow those blessed influences, O thou Saviour of mankind, who hast received gifts for men! Bestow them, O Father and Lord of all, and bring some youthful sinner to the feet of thy crucified Son! Though it be but one, grant that one may go to him for life. But O, again permit the petition, that if it please thee, the persuasions and motives for early piety here presented to the young, may be effectual to the conversion of many; and that many who shall read them may be led to Jesus, and be found to have their names written in the book of life, when time shall have erased every name that is written even upon rocks below.

And now, O God of grace, hear this supplication, and teach the young reader with sincerity of heart, to join in that which follows. Grant this, great God, for his sake who died on Calvary below, who lives, and reigns, and pleads for man above; and whose is the kingdom, the power, and the glory, for ever and for ever. AMEN.

§ 3. A PRAYER FOR YOUNG PERSONS, IMPLORING THE DIVINE BLESSING UPON THEMSELVES WHILE READING THIS BOOK.

Great God, thou seest me, a young and thoughtless creature. Young as I am in years, yet far have I gone in sin. So far that thou mightest justly have said with respect to me, " Cut down that cumberer of the ground;" and had that dreadful sentence been long ago pronounced and executed, I must have owned it just. My years are few, but my sins are many; more numerous are they than my days or hours, more countless than the hairs of my head. Alas! blessed God, what a part have I acted! I have received life from thee, and employed it in neglecting, and sinning against thee. I might have died at my birth, have seen the light and closed my eyes in death, but thou didst watch over me in infancy, didst guard me in childhood, and hast brought me to the blooming days of youth; and how have I requited thee? Wretch that I have been to requite thy love with ingratitude, thy goodness with neglect. Distracted creature that I have been, to spend the flower of my years in grieving thee, my best friend; in pleasing Satan, my infernal foe; and in undoing my own immortal soul. O, make me sensible of my sin; teach me to bewail and loathe my folly; and help me to forsake it! Now let me begin to live that life, which on a dying bed I shall wish to have lived. Merciful God, thou hast spared me in mercy; let me not appear to have been spared in vain; but let my life, which has been too long spent without thee, now be devoted to thee. Pour out thy Spirit on me, for he alone can teach me what thou art. Give me to thy Son, and thy Son to me. Thou art permitting me in this little book to read a serious invitation to early piety. Teach me to regard the truths I read; and may I read them with a devout and attentive mind. May the persuasions and motives here presented to me, reach my heart; and may I, when I reach the conclusion of this book, be no longer the thoughtless creature I have hitherto been; but may I be found to have chosen that good part, which none can take away. But, ah! great God! what am I that I should speak of reaching the conclusion even of this little book! Though I have read its first pages, I know not that I shall live to read its last. Young and vigorous as I may now be, perhaps, before I can reach its end, my time may be finished, my eyes closed in death, and my soul called to meet thee, my long neglected and much injured God. O then, teach me to be wise without delay! Teach me what religion is, and enable me to choose it as my portion. Teach me what I am, and lead me to Jesus Christ, thy once crucified but now exalted Son. O, make me thine! O

Saviour, make me thine! O God of glory, make me thine without delay, and teach me all thy will! Then, whatever be the instrument that awakens my soul, thine shall be the praise, for it is thy work, and the glory is justly thine.

Hear me, O thou most merciful Father, and wash my sins away in atoning blood; hear me, and let my youth from this day be devoted to thee; hear me, for the sake of thy beloved Son; and now to Father, Son, and Holy Spirit, as to the King eternal, immortal, invisible, the only wise God, be glory and dominion, world without end. AMEN.

§ 4. Having, my young friend, sought God's blessing, allow me now to explain to you the plan I design to follow in this little work. As my object is to persuade you to devote your youth to God, it is needful for me to address you as one whom I may suppose to be negligent of that best of blessings, humble piety. I shall, therefore, endeavour first to show you what is your natural condition, (Chap. 2). After this, I would entreat you to accompany me while I descend more into particulars (C. 3), and set before you some of the more common sins of youth. I would then point you to the Lamb of God; and would represent to you the nature of true piety (C. 4). Pursuing this subject, I would (C. 5) affectionately warn you against those delusive supports, on which many rest to their eternal ruin. I would then urge on you the infinite importance of early piety, by showing you (C. 6) the worth of your soul. By referring you (C. 7) to the advice of the eternal God. By displaying to you (C. 8) the love of God and Christ. By setting before you (C. 9) the peculiar acceptableness of early piety. By enumerating (C. 10) some of its numberless advantages. By glancing (C. 11) at some of its pleasures. By conducting you (C. 12) to take a view of the happy conclusion of a life of religion; and attempting (C. 13) an imperfect description of that heaven and that eternity to which religion conducts the soul. But fearing, that in many instances, all the pleasing motives which these considerations yield, may be of no avail; I shall then present to you reasons for religion, drawn from very opposite sources. I would here show you (C. 14) that while you neglect early piety you are destitute of all real good. I would describe to you (C. 15) the unkindness and ingratitude visible in such a course to God, and its cruelty to yourself. I would show (C. 16) the vanity of youth; and (C. 17) the sorrows and dangers that attend the way of transgressors. I would remind you (C. 18) of the approach, to the most careless, of judgment and eternity; and (C. 19) would glance at the dismal abodes of eternal wretchedness to which youthful sins would lead you. I then (C. 20), if you have not chosen true religion, would affectionately beseech you to choose it without delay. But, knowing how many objections are started against early piety, I propose (C. 21) to answer some of the principal of these. Having noticed these, permit me to occupy a few more lines (C. 22), in entreating you, *without delay*, to make your choice; and then (C. 23) to conclude the whole with a few directions, and some brief addresses. May God make this little book promote his glory, and your eternal benefit. — AMEN.

CHAPTER II.

THE FALLEN, GUILTY, AND RUINED STATE OF MAN.

§ 1. I now, my young friend, address you on a subject unspeakably important; as no hope can be entertained of doing you lasting good, till you feel the truth of the statement, contained in this chapter; but if you be led by the Divine Spirit, to perceive that this chapter describes your own condition, there will then be a pleasing prospect of your becoming acquainted with those things which belong to your everlasting peace.

In reference to bodily disorders it is said, that to know our disease is half the cure: the same observation will apply to the disorders of the soul. If one deeply infected with a fever, or the plague, were so deluded, as to believe himself enjoying perfect health, or to think himself, at worst, but slightly disordered, and therefore to neglect the means for restoring health, how soon would death and the grave convince him of his sad mistake! Such delusion is seldom met with; but an infinitely more dreadful and more mischievous delusion, is as common as the light of day. Perhaps you labour under its baleful influence. Perhaps, if your life has been unstained by flagrant enormities, you imagine yourself a good-hearted young man, or an innocent young woman. Your sins are softened down under the name of youthful follies. The deep corruption of your nature is totally hidden from your view. You are in danger of dying eternally of the worst of plagues, and yet thinking that all is well. You are exposed to the wrath of a justly offended God, and saying to yourself, " Peace, peace."

§ 2. God forbid that I should wish to repre- sent your state, by nature, as worse than he de- scribes it in his word. If I had the wish I should scarcely have the power. Be patient then, and hear the worst. What are you? If guided by the opinions of a poor blind world, you might reply, "A frail imperfect creature, guilty of some sins, but yet with so many good dispositions and good actions to counterbalance them, that I may reasonably hope for happiness and heaven." My dear young friend, are these, or such as these, your views of yourself? If they be, no wretched madman, bound with chains, crowning himself with straw, and imag- ining himself a mighty and happy monarch, was ever more deceived. I repeat the question. What are you? Let the word of the God of truth reply. And what is its answer? It teach- es you that you are corrupt and polluted, and at variance with your God; having all the powers of your soul disordered; and exposed, justly exposed, to everlasting ruin; and so en- tirely depraved and undone, that without a change as great as a second birth, you cannot possibly see the kingdom of God.

Perhaps you exclaim,* " Shocking doctrine!" whilst, full of indignation, you are almost ready to throw this book aside, before you have glanc- ed at the proofs afforded in scripture, for the assertions I have made. If this be the case, I beseech you to remember I appeal to scripture,

---

* A few lines, with a little alteration, from Fletcher's Appeal.

not to your passions; to the declarations of God, not to worldly delusions. You may cry out at the sight of a shroud, a coffin, a grave, "Shocking objects!" but your loudest exclamations will not lessen the awful realities, by which many have happily been shocked into a timely preparation for approaching death.

Refuse not then to listen to the declarations of God, on this momentous subject: to refuse to hearken is to seal your own destruction.

§ 3. His word assures you, that every human being is born into this world with a corrupt and sinful nature. — God formed man "in his own image," innocent and holy; but fallen man begat a son "in his own likeness," corrupt and fallen like himself. The consequence is, man comes into this world with a sinful nature; for "who can bring a clean thing out of an unclean? not one." Such is the exceeding sinfulness of human nature, that the word of God strongly describes it, by declaring that we are "shapen in iniquity and conceived in sin." "Man is a transgressor from the womb, and goes astray speaking lies." The devil is elsewhere called the father of lies; and one of the earliest tokens of human depravity is, that a disposition to commit that abominable sin so soon appears in little children. — Man is born untamed and rude as a "wild ass's colt." "Foolishness is bound even in the heart of a child." "The imagination of man's heart is evil from his youth," "is only evil and that continually;" "he is abominable and filthy, and drinketh in iniquity like water." As he advances in life, do

Gen. v. 1. v. 3. Job, xiv. 4. Ps. li. 5. lviii 3 Job, xi. 12 Prov xxii. 15 Gen. viii. 12. vi. 5. Job, xv. 16.

his corruptions weaken? The words of the apostle answer, No: "We ourselves, also, were sometimes foolish, disobedient, deceived, serving divers lusts and pleasures, living in malice and envy, hateful and hating one another." "God looked down from heaven upon the children of men, to see if there were any that did understand." And what is the dreadful result of this examination? " Every one of them is gone back; they are altogether become filthy; there is none that doeth good, no, not one."

§ 4. This sinfulness of your nature, my young friend, is not partial; it is not confined to some of your powers or faculties; but, like a mortal poison, spreads through and pollutes the whole. "The whole head is sick, and the whole heart faint; from the sole of the foot even to the head, there is no soundness in it, but wounds, and bruises, and putrefying sores." The heart, which should be the best part of man, is now the worst. "The heart is deceitful above all things, and desperately wicked." Such are the windings of its corruption, that no eye but that of Jehovah can trace them out. It is *full* of evil; not merely tainted but filled with sin; and "madness dwells in it." From this corrupt fountain, flows as corrupt a stream. "Out of the heart proceed evil thoughts, murders, adulteries, fornication, theft, false witness, blasphemies, covetousness, wickedness," or malevolence, " deceit, lasciviousness," or immodesty, "envy, pride, foolishness," or levity. Not merely is the heart thus polluted, "but the lusts of men war in their members." The eyes, the ears, the

Tit. iii. 3.　Ps. liii. 2.　Is. ii. 5, 6.　Jer. xvii. 9.　Ecc. ix. 3.
Matt. xv. 19.　Mark, vii. 22.　Jam. iv. 1.

hands, the feet, the lips, are all defiled by different sins; and the tongue, that member which
was formed peculiarly for its Creator's praise,
"is now a world of iniquity; and is set on fire
of hell." Man is elsewhere represented as born
in that state which is called flesh; a name applied to this corruption of our nature. "That
which is born of the flesh, is flesh." And "the
works of the flesh," says an inspired apostle,
"are manifest, which are these, adultery, fornication, uncleanness, lasciviousness, idolatry,
witchcraft, hatred, variance, emulations, wrath,
strife, seditions, heresies, envyings, murders,
drunkenness, revellings, and such like." Such
is man when the corruptions of his nature have
opportunity for appearing; and has he any
deeds of righteousness to counterbalance this
exceeding sinfulness? O, let the evangelical
prophet answer: "We are ALL as an unclean
thing; and *all* our righteousnesses are as filthy
rags; and we all do fade as a leaf; and our
iniquities, like the wind, have taken us away."
So far are our best actions, in our natural state,
from helping, that even they are polluted and
loathsome; and sin, like a whirlwind unop-
posed, sweeps us on to perdition.

§ 5. But I foresee an objection, which some
may make to parts of this statement.

Perhaps you, my young friend, exclaim, "I
have not committed many of the sins here
named." Perhaps not. I am here showing
you your own lost condition, by referring you
to those sad fruits which your depraved heart,
unless by one means or other prevented, would
produce; and which in millions of cases have

Jam. iii. 6. John, iii. 16. Gal. v. 19, 21. Is. lxiv. 6.

been produced. The restraints of education, or other things, may in you have checked some of these corruptions; but this makes no alteration as to your natural sinfulness. If in spring you were to cast one handful of wheat into the ground, and lay another by in a drawer, would you, in autumn, say of that which had been laid by, this is not wheat, because it might not have put forth the blade and the ear? No, it would still be wheat, still be of the same nature as that scattered in the ground, though its situation had prevented its growing, and producing fruit like that. So it is with human nature: in some situations its corruptions may not be so visible as in others; in some situations those corruptions may not have the same nourishment as in others; or may meet with more restraints; like the grain of corn, which is buried so deep that it can scarcely push its blade above the surface of the soil. All this may take place. All this does take place, in thousands of instances; but human nature, in its radical corruption, is every where the same; like wheat which is wheat still, whether it vegetates in the furrow, ripens in the ear, or is treasured up in the barn.

§ 6. Allow me, my young friend, after this general view, to descend into particulars.

The word of God, in describing your natural condition, represents it as so *extremely sinful*, that while in it nothing which you do can be pleasing to God. "They that are in the flesh" (under the government of that corruption which is named flesh), "cannot please God." *So entire* is this corruption, that an apostle confessed 'I know that in me, that is, in my flesh, dwelleth no good thing." So completely is the soul indisposed by it for all that is really good, that men are "dead in trespasses and sins." How awful is their delusion, who are strangers to real religion, and yet flatter themselves that there is something good in them to recommend them to God. Their best actions flow from corrupt motives, and are in his sight but a kind of splendid sins.

§ 7. Man is not only so extremely sinful that he cannot please God, but *so blind*, that he is entirely ignorant of what is acceptable in his Maker's sight. Our Lord himself declares, that the design of his gospel is to open the eyes of men, "and to turn them from darkness to light, and from the power of Satan unto God." He assures us that he came to "preach recovering of sight to the blind." His most distinguished apostle affirms, "that even the followers of Christ were sometime darkness;" that he and they had been "delivered from the power of darkness;" and humbly confesses, "we ourselves also were sometime foolish, disobedient, deceived;" being blinded by those false hopes and delusions which blind thousands now. *So destructive* is this blindness, that men "know not the way of peace." *So entire*, that the sullen ox and stupid ass know more of their masters, than unenlightened man of his God. "The ox knoweth his owner, and the ass his master's crib; but Israel doth not know, my people do not consider." *So awful* is this blindness, that "the natural man receiveth not the things of the Spirit of God; for they are foolishness unto him." Even "the

Eph. 2. 1. Acts, xxvi. 18. Luke, iv. 18. Eph. v. 8. Col. i, 13 Tit. iii. 3. Rom. iii. 17. Is. i. 3. 1 Cor. ii. 14. i. 18.

preaching of the cross itself, is, to them that perish, foolishness." And *so wilful*, that " men love darkness rather than light, because their deeds are evil; and proceeding in their career of madness, " fools make a mock at sin." Is it possible, my young friend, to give a sadder representation of the natural blindness of the heart, than these passages give? Sin, which God declares to be the cause of misery, death, and hell, men treat as a matter of foolish ridicule and mad laughter; while that glorious plan of salvation, which so magnifies the wisdom and love of God, that it astonishes the angels of heaven, even this is folly in the view of poor unconverted men. The man who should laugh at a thousand swords aimed at his defenceless head, or pointed at his naked breast, were wiser than he who laughs at sin. Less foolish were the wretch who should treat as folly, a plan to deliver him from the condemned cell, the halter, the gibbet, or the fire, than he who thus treats the wondrous plan which God has devised, to save him from the flames of hell.

§ 8. Shall I stop here? The word of God does not. The sacred writers continue the deplorable account of fallen man, by declaring that he is not only polluted and blind, but under the influence of the worst foe of God and man. — The devil, on account of his extensive reign, is called by them, " the god of this world;" " the prince of the power of the air;" and he and the wicked spirits that have fallen with him, " are the rulers of the darkness of this world." The ungodly are of their " father

John, iii. 19.   Prov. xiv. 19.   2 Cor. iv. 4.   Eph. vi. 2. vi. 12,
John, viii. 44   Eph. ii. 2.

the devil;" "he works in the hearts of the children of disobedience;" "he takes away the seed
that is sown in the thoughtless heart;" he blinds
the minds of the irreligious; and where the
"gospel is hid, it is hid" through his hellish
influence. They are "in the snare of the devil,"
and are "led captive by him at his will." They
who neglect religion to follow the world, are
"turned aside after Satan;" and lest you should
imagine that these deplorable assertions refer
merely to the most openly ungodly, you are assured by the divine Saviour himself, that the
design of his gospel is to bring men "from the
power of Satan unto God;" and that "the
tares," or all who are not in reality the children
of God, "are the children of the wicked one."
The apostle Paul confesses that he and his
Christian friends once were of this number; the
apostle John as solemnly teaches us, that all
men are either the children of God or of the
devil; and that those who do not practise righteousness, and cherish love, "are not of God."

Adding other awful particulars to this mournful description: the Son of God complains,
that they "will not come to him for life;" that
they "love darkness rather than light;" that
they hated him, and will hate his friends.

§ 9. To give a darker finish to this dreadful
picture, the word of eternal truth declares, that
men are "lovers of pleasures more than lovers
of God;" are "alienated from the life of God,
through the ignorance that is in them;" are
"alienated from God and enemies in their
minds, by wicked works;" that they "know no

John, viii. 44. Eph. ii. 2. Matt. xiii. 9. 2 Cor. iv. 4.   2 Tim. ii. 26.
1 Tim. v. 15. Acts, xxvi. 28. Matt. xiii. 23. Eph. ii. 3. 1 John, iii. 10.
John, v. 40. iii. 19. xv. 18. 2 Tim. iii 4. Eph. iv. 18.

D

God ;" are " haters of God ;" are "strangers
and foreigners to him ;" and "without God in
the world." Hence, in a natural state, "there
is none that seeketh after God ;" "there is no
fear of God before their eyes." By their lives,
even if they dare not utter it with their lips,
they say unto God, "depart from us, for we desire not the knowledge of thy ways ;" and by
choosing worldly vanities in preference to the
favour and service of God, they, in fact, utter
the dreadful sentence, " What is the Almighty
that we should serve him ? and what profit
should we have if we pray unto him ?" The
apostle Paul, in giving the darkest touch to this
dreadful picture, declares, that "the carnal mind
is enmity against God." A more awful description of fallen man cannot be given, than
that contained in these few words. The carnal
mind is strictly the earthly or sensual mind ;
that which the moral and the profligate alike
possess, while loving the world and the things
of the world. It is not an expression applying
merely to the most abandoned, but one that
applies to every human being, let his outward
conduct be ever so fair, whose mind cleaves to
this earthly clod. The miser as well as the
spendthrift; the pleasing young man that is following earthly objects with all his heart; the
engaging young woman whose thoughts are
fixed on fashion, dress, and gaiety, as much
possess the carnal mind, as does the shameless
profligate, whose conduct they abhor; and the
sober tradesman, whose plans and schemes all
refer to this world, is as much under its influence as either of the others. All these have a

1/hes. iv. 5. Ro. i. 30. Eph. ii. 19. Ro. iii. 11. Job, xxi. 14. Ro. viii. 7.

worldly or carnal mind, and what is it? enmity against God, enmity itself. Can worse be said of devils? have even they a mind more inimical to God than the carnal mind? what can be worse than that which is *enmity* itself? The Most High calls on heaven and earth to wonder at the horrid crimes of men; and declares, "I have nourished and brought up children, and they have rebelled against me." The Son of God represents man as a wicked prodigal, who has treated with the basest neglect, ingratitude, and cruelty, the best and most affectionate of parents. A prodigal so destitute of filial love, that he acts the part of a madman, and prefers the swinish husks in an enemy's country to the comforts of his father's house. And one of the best of men confesses, "We have sinned, and have committed iniquity, and have done wickedly, and have REBELLED, even by departing from thy precepts, and thy judgments."

§ 10. The word of God further shows the depth of our fall, and the malignant poison of our sin, by the display which it makes of the greatness of the remedy provided for our deliverance. No less a person than the Son of God, the Lord of all things, appeared as a Saviour. More was done to redeem than to create the world; the Most High thus showing that redemption was a more difficult work than creation. We are also assured, that there is a display of the *exceeding greatness of God's power* in the conversion of a sinner; that all who are saved are "born of the Spirit;" that "all things are of God;" and that it is God that prepares the soul for death and eternity. But my young

Is. i. 2. Luke, xv. 19. Dan. ix. 5. Eph. i. 19. John, iii. 5. 2 Cor. v. 18.

friend, would all this be requisite if man were able to deliver himself? would he need the help of an almighty arm if he were not in himself deeply fallen and utterly helpless?

§ 11. An important inquiry connected with this subject, is — are we to understand this sad description, as a description of mankind at large, or only of the worst part of the human race? Let the word of God give the reply. Hear its solemn answer. "Death has passed upon all men, because *all* have sinned." "The scripture hath concluded *all* under sin." "We *all*, like sheep, have gone astray, we have turned *every one* to his *own* way." None then, it seems, naturally incline their feet to the ways of God. "Each wanders in a different way; but all the downward road." "The whole world lieth in wickedness;" lies like a wounded and fallen captive, the helpless prey of an infernal foe. "*All* have sinned, and come short of the glory of God." "They are all gone aside; they are all together become filthy; there is none that doeth good, no, not one." "They are all under sin, there is none righteous, no, not one." "There is not a just man upon earth that doeth good and sinneth not." "If one died for *all*, then were *all dead*." So completely do sin and man accord, that a course of sin and rebellion is termed the "course of this world;" and these humiliating truths are taught us, that "every mouth may be stopped, and all the world become guilty before God.' And who shall refuse to submit, for who can say, "I have made my heart clean, I am pure from sin?"

Rom. v. 12. Gal. iii. 22. Is. liii. 6. 1 John, v. 19. Rom. iii. 23. Ps. xiv. 3. Rom. iii. 9, 10. Eccles. vii. 20. 2 Cor. v. 14. Eph. ii. 2. Rom. iii. 19 Prov. xx. 19

If we refer this point to the decision of the best of men, they unite from their own sad experience to confirm it. — David humbly confesses, "I was shapen in iniquity, and in sin did my mother conceive me." Daniel, who became so peculiar a favourite of heaven, humbly deplores his rebellion against his Maker. Job, not less distinguished for his piety, said, "I abhor myself, and repent in dust and ashes." Isaiah exclaims, "woe is me, for I am undone, because I am a man of unclean lips." Paul, who rivalled them all in his piety, and in his usefulness outdid them, says, "I know that in me (that is, in my flesh) dwelleth no good thing." "We were by nature the children of wrath, even as others." "Or now put the question to the best of the human species, the watchful, diligent, self-denying Christian, and let him decide the controversy. Go with him into his closet, ask him *his* opinion of the corruption of his heart, and he will tell you, that he is deeply sensible of its power, for he has learned it from much self-observation, and long acquaintance with the workings of his own mind. He will tell you, that every day strengthens this conviction; yea, that hourly he sees fresh reason to deplore his want of simplicity in intention, his infirmity of purpose, his low views, his selfish unworthy desires; his backwardness to set about his duty, his languor and coldness in performing it: that he finds himself obliged to confess, that he feels within him two opposite principles, and that he cannot do the things that he would."*

After such a review, how just appears the observation, "The merely outward irregularities

Ps. li. 5. Dan. ix. Job, xlii. 6. Is. vi. 5. Rom. vii. 18. Eph. ii. 3
* Wilberforce.   D

of men bear no more proportion to the whole of their depravity, than the particles of water, which are occasionally emitted from the surface of the ocean, to the tide that rolls beneath."*

§ 12. Think not that I love to dwell on this melancholy subject. Far from it ; but I warn you of your state and danger, that you may seek deliverance. That divine book, which gives the awful description you have now read of your state, gives as an affecting account of the danger, to which, as a fallen creature and a sinner, you are exposed. By the God of eternal truth are you assured, that men are " by nature the children of wrath ;" " that he who believeth not is condemned already ;" and, " that judgment has come upon all men to condemnation;" that men as sinners are in a state of death; "that the wages of sin is death ;" the second and more dreadful death, which consists in being cast into the lake of fire. And that " the soul which sinneth shall surely die." That " destruction and misery are in the ways of men ;" and that " a day of judgment and perdition to ungodly men is approaching ;" for which " they are reserved." Even the compassionate God is declared " to hate the workers of iniquity ;" and to have his " face set against them that do evil, to cut off the remembrance of them from the earth ;" and it is his solemn assertion, that " there is no peace to the wicked."

As it were, if possible, to guard men from self-deception, on a point of such infinite importance, the strongest expressions are used, in the word of God, in asserting that all are thus

* Fuller. Eph. ii. 3. John, iii. 18. Rom. v. 18. John, v. 24. Rom. vi. 23. Rev. xxi. 8. Ezek. xviii. 4. Rom. iii. 16. 2 Peter, ii. 7. ii. 9. Ps. v. 5. Ps. xxxvi. 16. Is. lvii. 20

undone. "As many as have sinned without law (without the advantages of God's written word), shall also perish without law;" "and as many as have sinned in the law, shall be judged by the law;" and its judgment is, that "*every one* is cursed, who hath not kept all things that are written in the book of the law to do them." In other words, that every one, who, even by a single sin, has broken the commands of God, has become an accursed creature. Conformably with this, the apostles of our Lord declare, "that the wrath of God is revealed from heaven, not merely against some atrocious crimes, but, against ALL unrighteousness;" that "*every* transgression and disobedience shall receive a just recompence of reward;" that " God will render indignation and wrath, tribulation and anguish, to every soul of man that doeth evil;" and that " whosoever shall keep the whole law, and yet offend in one point, he is guilty of all;" as truly condemned and ruined by that single act, as he would be had he broken the whole. While these are the declarations of inspired apostles, their holy Lord affirms, that even a sinful word exposes the soul to the danger of hell fire.

§ 13. Not merely do the Lord's inspired prophets and apostles represent our natural state as full of danger, but they represent that danger as inexpressibly dreadful. They assure us, that "the unrighteous shall not inherit the kingdom of God." That "the wicked shall be turned into hell, even all the nations that forget God;" and that on them " God will rain fire and brimstone, and a horrible tempest;" that

Rom. ii. 12.   Gal. iii. 10.   Rom. i. 18.   Heb. ii. 2.   Rom. ii. 9. James, ii. 10.   Matt. v. 22.   1 Cor. vi. 10.   Ps ix. 17. xi. 6.

"it is a fearful thing to fall into the hands of the living God;" for "our God is a consuming fire." That "the Lord Jesus shall be revealed from heaven, with his mighty angels, in flaming fire, taking vengeance on them that know not God, and that obey not the gospel of our Lord Jesus Christ; who shall be punished with ever lasting destruction, from the presence of the Lord, and the glory of his power." Then while some awake to glory, others shall awake "to shame and everlasting contempt." Then in vain shall the "kings of the earth, and the great men, and the rich men, and the chief captains, and the mighty men, call on the rocks and the mountains to cover them, and hide them from the wrath of the Lamb." "Whosoever has not his name found in the book of life, will be then cast into the lake of fire:" and not merely will atrocious sinners meet this dreadful doom, but "the fearful and unbelieving," those who are too cowardly to follow Christ, or who disbelieve his gospel, "shall be cast into the lake that burns with fire and brimstone." "Then shall they eat of the fruit of their own ways, and be filled with their own devices;" while "the smoke of their torment ascendeth up for ever and ever."

The divine Saviour, who was a pattern of tenderness and compassion, instead of softening down these dreadful representations, confirms them in the most decisive manner. — Infinite pity dwelt in his heart, he wept over wretched men, yet he declared that he himself, on all the irreligious, would pronounce the dreadful sentence, "Depart from me, ye cursed, into ever-

Heb. xli. 29.   2 Thess. 1. 7.   Dan. i. 2.   Rev. vi. 15. xx. 15. xxi. 8.
Prov. i. 31.   Rev. xiv. 11.

lasting fire, prepared for the devil and his an-gels;" and he affirms that "they shall go away into everlasting punishment;" "into the fur-nace of fire, where shall be wailing and gnash-ing of teeth;" "where the worm dieth not, and the fire is not quenched." To avoid this, he bids. you count nothing too dear. "Fear not," says he, "them which kill the body, and after that have no more that they can do, but fear Him who after he hath killed hath power to cast into hell." Dreadful doom! "whose heart can endure, or whose hands be strong in the day that God shall deal with him!" who can dwell with everlasting burnings! who can en-dure devouring fire!

§ 14. While, my young friend, you are thus affectionately warned of your danger, even by the Lord himself, you are as solemnly assured by him, that multitudes plunge into this eternal ruin; and that no outward privileges will suffice to deliver you from its horrors. As it were to quicken your concern after everlasting blessings, the Lord Jesus declares that but a few, a happy few, obtain them. "Wide," says he, "is the gate, and broad is the way that leadeth to de-struction, and many there be which go in there-at;" and then he adds in the most impressive manner — "Strait is the gate, and narrow the way that leadeth into life, and few there be that find it!" "Many are called, but few are cho-sen." Presume not then, that there is little danger of missing the path to heaven, for there is much. The way is narrow. Presume not that most will be saved, and that therefore you

Matt. xxv. 41. 46. xiii. 42. Mark, ix. 44. Luke, xii. 5. Matt. x.
28. Ezek. xx. 14. Is. xxxiii. 14. Matt. vii. 13. 14. xxii. 16.

may go contentedly with the multitude. The multitude are travelling the downward road; and but few find the path that leads to glory and to God: O, cherish a pious concern to become one of that happy few!

§ 15. Perhaps, my young friend, you attempt to set aside all that I have urged, respecting the danger of your state, by pleading, "I am not guilty of any notorious crimes; lying, lewdness, sabbath-breaking, dishonesty, and a hundred other vices, in which thousands indulge, I never practised." If you knew yourself and the law of God better, you might perceive that you have, in your heart, committed many sins, of which you now think yourself guiltless, but if it be as you imagine, yet allow me to remind you, that the word of God declares you as much a condemned and ruined creature, for leaving undone what you should have done, as for doing what you should not. Though your life may be moral, yet if you do not from your heart submit to the Son of God, you do not obey the gospel. "And what shall the end be of them who obey not the gospel of God?" "They shall be punished with everlasting destruction from the presence of the Lord, and the glory of his power." Be not then deceived; not merely the openly profligate, but the unrighteous, all who are destitute of real piety, "shall not inherit the kingdom of God." "If any man have not the Spirit of Christ he is none of his." "If any man love not the Lord Jesus Christ let him be accursed." "He that believeth not the Son shall not see life, but the wrath of God abideth

1 Peter, iv. 17.   2 Thess. i. 7.   1 Cor. vi. 9.   Rom. viii. 9.   1 Cor. xvi. 22.   John, iii. 31.

on him." The blessed Redeemer has taught us that merely "making light of the gospel," is the way to eternal ruin. "How then shall we escape if we neglect (do nothing worse than neglect) so great salvation!"

§ 16. And now, my young friend, what are your views of your own state? Do you feel to be justly a child of wrath, or do you cling to the delusions, by which thousands are undone? When looking round, you see many amiable persons, who seem to want nothing but the one thing needful, do you ask, "Are these like the vilest sinners threatened with eternal wrath? or if they are, can these be deserving of it?" Search the book of God, and you will there surely find that they are; and that, without one thing more, all the amiable qualifications imaginable, will do no more to save them from eternal wrath, than a fine dress to save a man from destruction, if hurled from the top of a tremendous precipice. Perhaps you may have been an affectionate child, you may be tender and compassionate, dutiful and obliging, but will this save you? No, never.—Excellent as these qualifications are in their place, if these could have atoned for sin, and saved the soul, the Son of God need not have died. But the fact is, you may possess all these, and a thousand other amiable recommendations, and yet live in rebellion against your God; and thus, however fair your character may be in the sight of men, in that of God it may be as dark and as vile as the character of Satan himself. What is rebellion against God, but continued disobedience and neglect of his commands? And are you

Matt. xxii. 1, &c. Luke, xv. 12, &c. Heb. ii. 3.

not guilty of this? Perhaps, you think not.
Well, inquire a little further. Which is the
first and great commandment? Is it not, "Thou
shalt love the Lord thy God with all thy heart,
and with all thy soul, and with all thy mind,
and with all thy strength?" Have you kept
this? Has God had all your heart? Have all
your affections been fixed on him? Has he
been loved with all your soul and mind; and
thus stood highest in your esteem; and been
chosen as your supreme good and only portion?
If not, however fair and pleasing your outward
conduct may have been, you have yet been living continually committing the greatest of sins;
for you have lived breaking God's first and
great commandment every day of your existence. If to love God above all things is the first
and greatest commandment, to live negligent
of him must be one of the greatest of sins, and
indeed a sin that opens the way to every other.
O my young friend, could we see things aright,
every other sin, so far as it referred to man only,
would dwindle into comparative innocence, compared with neglect of the blessed Saviour and
our adorable God! The blackness of every
other crime would be as light, compared with
the more horrible blackness of alienation of the
heart from God, that first of sins, that root of
every other. This has been mine, this has been
yours! and, unless your heart be changed by
divine grace, even at this moment this sin is
yours. Though unstained with the other dark
offences, of the robber or the adulterer, yet this
blackest of all you have as well as they. Like
them you belong to a false apostate race, that
have forsaken their God, and gone away back-

ward. And how can you hope for heaven, if this darkest of crimes remains unrepented and unforsaken?

§ 17. Perhaps a familiar illustration may render this subject still plainer. Imagine two favoured villages, under a kind and beneficent government, uniting in a cruel and unprovoked rebellion. The inhabitants of one of these villages are profane, contentious, quarrelsome wretches; those of the other are decent, quiet, sober men. Careless of threatenings, and unmoved by kindness, they persist in their rebellion. In the former village, discord, blasphemy, and every sin abound; in the other, harmony, and mutual affection prevail. Now, my young friend, if the inhabitants of these two places were brought to trial for their crimes at the same bar, would there appear much difference between them? Would they not all be rebels, ungrateful rebels; though one party were a set of tumultuous quarrelsome creatures, and the other harmonious good-natured rebels? Would not the same doom justly await them all? And if the quiet villagers were to plead in their own defence, that though it was true, they had engaged in an unprincipled and ungrateful rebellion; yet that they were kind, affectionate, and useful to each other: would not this very circumstance be an aggravation of their guilt? Might it not be answered, " Among such disorderly wretches as those, rebellion was likely to happen; but from you, better things might have been expected." Apply this to the present subject. The openly wicked and profane resemble the former of these; the moral and benevolent, that yet neglect religion, may be compared to

E

the latter.   In many things they differ; but
agree in the worst, that they have rebelled
against their greatest and best Benefactor.   Are
not you, by neglect and disobedience, a rebel
against your God?   Have not you, at least, by
a careless life, said to him, "Depart from me;
for I desire not the knowledge of thy ways?"
Have not you lived as without God in the
world?   So that if there had been no God, you
probably could hardly have been more forgetful
of him, than you have frequently been?   Has
not this been the case? and if it has, will it
avail for you at the last to plead, that you have
been kind, tender, useful, and beloved among
your fellow rebels?

§ 18. Have I succeeded in convincing you,
that neglect of God, and want of love to him, is
so enormous a sin, that this only, if you had no
other, would be sufficient to sink the soul to the
lowest depths of hell?   If I have not, O, let me
urge it further upon you, in another familiar
illustration!   Suppose that a child, as soon as
he could discover any disposition, should show
an entire disregard to the most affectionate parents.   Fondly attached to him, and desirous
to secure a return of affection, they study all
they can for his advantage, and heap new favours on him; still he forgets them, and shows
them no regard.   They confer on him more
favours, more benefits still; yet he still forgets
them, and even discovers a growing aversion
for them.   At length they place him out in the
world, and do what they can to promote his
happiness there: he still forgets them; seems
insensible to all their affection; has no more
love for them than the stones beneath their feet;

and even treats them with dislike; snuns their presence; and banishes the thought of them from his mind. Would not such a child deserve to lose his parents' love, and to be cast off for ever? Suppose this ungrateful child, by abusing his parents' kindness, undone, utterly undone; but their kindness ends not. They make themselves poor, to place him once more in circumstances of comfort, and give up whatever they have most valuable for this purpose: yet still he goes on as ever; unaffected by their tenderness; unthankful for their favours; and with an increasing dislike to them. Could they still retain one parental feeling? Would not such a monster of ingratitude deserve to be forgotten for ever? Or could they be thought unkind, if they refused to admit this child, with the worst of dispositions in his heart, to dwell in the closest intimacy with them? Would the case be mended, if this ungrateful creature were affectionate and grateful to every one but his parents? and careless of none but those his best friends and tenderest benefactors? Would not this make his guilt the worse; as it would show that his heart was not without gratitude and affection, though too depraved to offer them where most justly due? Would it be unreasonable for the most affectionate parents to banish such a child from their presence for ever? My young friend, harsh as it may sound, if you neglect true piety, you are a more ungrateful child to God, than the most ungrateful child could possibly be to the most affectionate parents; for how little are the obligations of a child to his parents, compared with those of a creature to his Creator and his God! And as much greater as is the obligation; so much viler, so much blacker is the ingratitude of neglect. O, how great is the debt of gratitude you owe to God! It is on his world you live. All that is agreeable around you was made so by him. Here are you placed to prepare for an unutterably better state. Nor are you here forgotten by your God. Every moment of time, every breath you draw, every pleasure you feel, you owe to him. No day passes without its blessings. One favour has scarcely vanished before others appear. The end of one mercy is the beginning of another. Though forgotten, God is not forgetful. Though he may have been neglected by you for days and years, he spares you still, that you may turn to him. He has not cut short your days in the moment of sin; nor hurried you from the scene of guilty delight to the place of eternal torment. Though unthanked for his blessings day after day, he has continued to give them. — Consider, that every thing you enjoy is God's; and then think, can the worst of crimes against the best of earthly friends be half so heinous as ingratitude to God. The mercies I have mentioned are the smallest of his mercies. We are fallen creatures. You have destroyed yourself, but in him is your help. To save you from ruin he gave his beloved and adorable Son. Could he give more? Though he was rich, the Lord Jesus Christ for your sake became poor; that you, through his poverty, might be rich. Could he do more? You are a child whom God has placed upon earth and crowned with mercies; and because you were else undone for ever, he, to restore you from your fallen state, has, to every other gift, added that best and greatest, his beloved Son. Could a child, under God, indebted to his parents for life, indebted to them for all his comforts, and indebted to them for recovery from a thousand evils; owe them a thousandth part so much love and gratitude, as you owe to God? or could such a one be a thousandth part so guilty as you must be, if you slight all the unspeakable goodness of God, and all the infinite love of the dying Saviour? How horrible a state it is, through wilful sin, to become the enemy of God in this world, and then to be such for ever! to begin by neglecting a kind heavenly Father here, and to end by hating him, as the sinner will, beyond the grave! To hate him who is all that is excellent and amiable; and in whose favour only one drop of happiness can be found hereafter. How horrible, most horrible a state is this! yet this condition is yours, if you are not reconciled to God. Can you expect that he should glorify in his presence, and admit to his right-hand, those whose hearts are averse to his ways, or entirely negligent of them; who are loaded with mercies, but still forgetful of the giver? What though they shine in the view of their fellow rebels; what though they be adorned with a thousand charms of body or mind: yet God beholds the serpent that lurks beneath the rose; He sees the ungrateful hellish heart.

§ 19. An excellent writer, noticing the delu· sions of the world, observes, that " young people may, without much offence, be inconsiderate and dissipated; the youth of one sex may indulge occasionally in licentious excesses; those of the other may be supremely given up to vanity and pleasure: yet provided that they are sweet-tempered and open, and not disobedient to their parents or other superiors, the former are deemed *good-hearted young men,* and the latter, *innocent young women.* Those who love them best, have no solicitude about their spiritual interests: and it would be deemed strangely strict in themselves, or in others, to doubt of their becoming more religious as they advance in life; to speak of them as being actually under the divine displeasure; or, if their lives should be in danger, to entertain any apprehensions concerning their future destiny." He continues —

"*Innocent young women! Good-hearted young men!*" Wherein does this *goodness of heart* and this *innocence* appear? Remember that we are fallen creatures, born in sin, and naturally depraved. Christianity recognises no *innocence or goodness of heart,* but in the remission of sin, and in the effects of the operation of divine grace. Do we find in these young persons the characters which the holy scriptures lay down, as the only satisfactory evidences of a safe state? Do we not, on the other hand, discover the specified marks of a state of alienation from God? Can the blindest partiality persuade itself that *they* are loving, or striving "to love God with all their hearts, and minds, and souls, and strength?" Are *they* "seeking first the kingdom of God, and his righteousness?" Are *they* "working out their salvation with fear and trembling?" Are *they* "clothed with humility?" Are *they* not, on the contrary, supremely given up to self-indulgence? Are *they* not, at least, "lovers of pleasure more than lovers of God?" Are the .... of religion *their* solace or *their* task? Do *they* not come to these sacred services with reluctance, continue in them by constraint, and quit them with gladness? Are not the youth of one sex often actually committing, and still more often wishing to commit, those sins of which the scripture says expressly, "that they which do such things shall not inherit the kingdom of God?" Are not the youth of the other mainly intent on the gratification of vanity; and looking for their chief happiness to the resorts of gaiety and fashion, to all the multiplied pleasures which public places, or the still higher gratifications of more refined circles, can supply?"

And now, my young friend, with all the seriousness I can use, allow me to ask you, if you were this moment to be summoned before the throne of your Judge, and were accused of having lived negligent of God, and thus of having lived a life of dreadful sin; would you not be obliged to plead guilty to the charge, or, at least, to stand speechless and confused before your Maker? Does not your conscience tell you, that you must? and if it does, "God is greater than your heart, and knoweth all things."

PRAYER FOR A YOUNG PERSON CONVINCED OF THE TRUTH OF THE PRECEDING STATEMENT, AND HUMBLED FOR SIN.

Thou kind, compassionate, and ever-blessed God, teach me, a poor sinful creature, to approach thee; and grant, that through the Lord Jesus, I may find acceptance with thee. Shame and confusion of face should cover me, while I draw near to confess my sinfulness before thee. Open my blind eyes, to discern my real state.

Soften my hard heart, that it may feel its miseries, and tremble at its guilt. No longer let baneful delusions hide the truth from my sight.

Compassionate God, thou hast been kind to me; but I, an unkind, unthankful wretch to thee. Not many years have departed since I first drew the breath of life; but, alas! how have those years been spent? My youth has been crowned with thy mercies; and yet I have forgotten thee. I have loved; but not loved thee. I have had fears; but felt no holy fear of thee. I have sought to please others; but lived displeasing thee. I have had a heart sensible of the tenderness of friends and relatives; but insensible of thine. The trifles and vanities of time have engaged my attention; while thy infinite love has been passed unregarded by. The ox knoweth his owner, and the ass his master's crib; but I have not known my God. The most savage beasts of prey have learned to love the hand that fed them; but, viler than the brute creation, I have forgotten the God in whom I live, and move, and have my being: and, Oh! poor blind creature that I have been! still I have claimed the name of Christian, and thought myself a child of God, and an heir of heaven.

No longer, great God, let such delusions blind my eyes; but help me, while I confess my folly, to feel what I am. I am the sinner which thy word describes. Like the lost sheep, I have wandered from thee; like the prodigal, forsaken thee. I have even rebelled against thee. I have been a lover of pleasures more than a lover of God. My heart is deceitful above all things; and has been the fountain whence every sin has flowed. I have by nature the carnal mind, which is enmity against thee: and, gracious God, the sad fruits of this enmity have been my neglect of thy favour; my unconcern at thy displeasure; and my forgetfulness of thy love. I have resisted thy Spirit; but listened to the suggestions of Satan. I have slighted thy word; but have been guided by the maxims of a corrupt world. Thou hast bid me remember thee in my youth; but I have forgotten thee. Thou hast commanded me to love thee; but I have neglected thee. Thou hast encouraged me to pray to thee; but I have often restrained prayer before thee, or, when I professed to pray, have mocked thee with solemn sounds on a thoughtless tongue.

Thou hast been a tender Father to me; but I, worse than a rebellious prodigal to thee. Thou hast wooed me by thy compassion; and, by the gift of numberless mercies, hast, as it were, said, Now love me, now give me thine heart: and I have not heard thy voice; or, if I have, refused to give what thy love claimed. I have undone myself; and thou hast interposed to save me. Thou hast even given thy best-beloved and adorable Son to die for me; yet even this matchless mercy melted not my hard heart. Can I, great God, hide my infernal wickedness? I cannot. It is open to thy view; and ever glaring in all its horror before thine eyes. Shall I extenuate my transgressions and corruption? Shall I plead much ignorance?—but I might have known thee. Shall I plead the thoughtlessness of youth? I dare not; for thoughtless as I have been of thee, young as I am, I have been thoughtful about the trifles of a moment. Shall I—no, I dare not, say, thou art not worthy of my love; for had I ten thousand hearts thy love would deserve them all. Shall I plead that I have been kind, benevolent, and useful to my fellow-sinners? Ah, my God! the plea would but aggravate my guilt: I have been kind to them; but unkind to thee. I have loved them; but been averse to thee: though thou hast an infinite and everlasting claim on my regard. My heart has glowed with gratitude for their tenderness; but been cold and unmoved by thine: though theirs has borne no more comparison to thine, than a drop to the ocean, or a grain of sand to the world. Kind and much-injured God, I own my guilt before thee. "I have sinned against heaven, and in thy sight." I have sinned against thee. I have sinned against thy once suffering, but now exalted Son. I have sinned against thy Holy Spirit. I have sinned against my own immortal soul. God, be merciful to me a sinner! No tears of penitential grief can wash away my stains. Teach me to plead the Saviour's death, and cleanse me in his atoning blood. Create in me a clean heart; and renew a right spirit within me. Let no more of the precious days of my youth be spent careless of thee, as many have already been. Take my heart, and make it thine. Take my youth, and let it be devoted to thee. Take me now in the flower of life, and let me live to thee alone: that while I live, I may live to the Lord; and when I die, may die to the Lord; and thus whether I live or die, may be the Lord's. Grant these requests, O most merciful God! for the sake of thy dear Son; to whom I would flee as my only refuge; and to whom be the kingdom, power, and glory, for ever and for ever. AMEN.

CHAPTER III.

SOME OF THE SINS OF YOUTH ENUMERATED.

§ 1. It was endeavoured, in the last chapter, to show you, that you are, by nature, a fallen, depraved, and apostate creature. Now, great God, assist me, whilst I strive to convince my youthful readers, not merely of the corruption of their nature, but of the error of their ways. Display to them, whither the paths of sin lead; and bid them seek true happiness in thyself.

My young friend, I entreat you to follow me while I point out to you some of those sins which undo multitudes. Among these evils, a thoughtless, inconsiderate spirit, is in young persons, one of the most common, and one of the most fatal. While open impiety slays its thousands, this sinks its ten thousands to perdition. A time is coming when you must consider your ways. From the bed of death, or from the eternal world you must take a review of life: but, as you love your soul, defer not till that solemn period, which shall fix your eternal state, the momentous question; "How has my life been spent?" Look back on your past years. They are gone for ever. But what report have they borne to heaven? What is the record made respecting them in the book of God? Will they rise up in the judgment against you? Possibly you may not see many instances of flagrant crime: but do you see nothing, which conscience must condemn; nothing, which would fill you with alarm, if going

this moment to the bar of your Maker? Perhaps
you reply, "It is true, I cannot justify all the
actions of my youthful years; yet the worst that
I see, were but the frolics of youth." My friend,
do they bear that name in heaven? Does your
Judge view them in no worse a light? It has
ever been the custom of this world to whitewash
sin, and hide its hideous deformity; but, know,
that what you pass over so lightly, your God
abhors as sins — sins, the least of which, if unforgiven, would sink your soul to utter, endless
woe. "For the wrath of God is revealed from
heaven against *all* ungodliness and unrighteousness." The iniquities of youth, as well as of
riper years, are abhorred by him. The sins of
youth were the bitter things which holy Job
lamented; and for deliverance from which David devoutly prayed. "Thou writest bitter
things against me; and makest me to possess
the iniquities of my youth." "Remember not
the sins of my youth, nor my transgressions:
according to thy mercy, remember thou me, for
thy goodness' sake, O Lord!"

Take then another review of life. Begin with
childhood. In that early period, so often falsely
represented as a state of innocence, the corruptions of a fallen nature begin to appear; and
the early years of life are stained with falsehood, disobedience, cruelty, vanity, and pride.
Can you recollect no instances, in which your
earlier years were thus polluted with actual sin?
Can you bring to remembrance no occasion, on
which falsehood came from your lips; or vanity,
pride, or obstinacy, was cherished in your heart?
or when cruelty to the meaner creatures was

your sport? Shrink not from the review; though painful, it is useful. It is far better to see and abhor your youthful sins in this world, where mercy may be found; than to have them brought to your remembrance, when mercy is no more.

But you have passed the years of childhood; you have advanced one stage forwarder in your journey to an endless world. Has sin weakened, as your years increased? Have not some sinful dispositions ripened into greater vigour? Have not others, which you knew not in your earlier years, begun to appear? and does not increasing knowledge add new guilt to all your sins?

Among the prevailing iniquities of youth may be mentioned : —

§ 2. Pride. This is a sin common to all ages; but, it often peculiarly infects the young. It is abhorred by God. "The proud he knoweth afar off." "He resisteth the proud; but, giveth grace to the humble." "*Every one* that is proud in heart, is an abomination to the Lord." "He hateth a proud look." "A high look and a proud heart, is sin." "The proud are cursed." Pride is the parent of many other vices. It puts on a thousand forms; yet, unless subdued by religion, is found in the palace and the cottage. You may see it displayed in the character of the young prodigal: (Luke, xv. 19, &c.) Has not this sin, which God so much abhors, crept into your heart? Perhaps it has made you haughty, when you should have been humble; obstinate, when you should have been yielding; revengeful, when you should have been forgiving. You thought it showed spirit, to resent an injury or

Ps. cxxxviii. 6. James, iv. 6. Prov. xvi. 5. Prov. vi. 17. Prov. xxi. 4. Ps. cxix. 21.

F

insult; instead of patiently bearing it, like him you call your Lord. Perhaps it has filled you with dissatisfaction; when you should have been all submission. You have thought it hard, in the day of affliction, that you should be so tried; and even if you stayed the murmur against God from passing your lips, have you not felt it in your heart? Pride has probably led you to neglect the counsels of wisdom; and to turn a deaf ear to those, who wished you well for ever. Vain of the ornaments of apparel, have you not bestowed more thought on the dress you should wear, than on the salvation of your immortal soul? and been more concerned about the shape of a coat, or the fashion of a gown or a bonnet, than about life or death eternal? Perhaps you have been one of those, who spend more time in surveying their own image in a glass, than in seeking the favour of their God. Ah! did pride never lead you to this self-idolatry? Did it never, never fill you with vanity, from the fancy of your possessing a pleasing face, or a lovely form, or manly vigour? Ah, foolish vanity! when you must so soon say to corruption, "Thou art my father; and to the worm, thou art my mother and sister!" Yet, foolish as it is, was it never yours? "Where is there a face so disagreeable, that never was the object of self-worship in a glass? And where a body, however deformed, that never was set up as a favourite idol, by the fallen spirit that inhabits it?"

§ 3. One of the most prevalent, and most baneful kinds of pride is that, which I may term, the pride of self-righteousness. Our Lord, in the parable of the Pharisee and Publican, gives a most striking description of this sin. The

Pharisee boasts, that he was not like others; that he had not committed such flagrant crimes as they; and that he practised duties which they omitted. On this sandy foundation, his hope for eternity appears to have rested. Nothing like humility entered his heart; but, in all the pride of fancied virtue he approached his God. This is the exact spirit of multitudes in the present day; and where young persons have been re-strained from open immoralities, how commonly does it exist among them! It is pleaded, respect-ing them, " that they are not like many profligate youth around them; they have not given way to profaneness and lying; to drunkenness or dishonesty: but, they have been kind and duti-ful; tender and obliging; have good hearts; and are good young people." They may have lived all their lives careless of God and their souls; but, this is not taken into account: others com-mend them, and they are willing to believe these commendations. They please themselves with their fancied virtue; think themselves very good young persons: and, proud of this goodness, go forward to meet that God, who sees in them ten thousand crimes; and who abhors nothing more, than the pride of self-righteousness in a creature polluted by daily iniquities.

§ 4. Another common sin of the young is, disobedience to parents. "Honour thy father and mother; that it may be well with thee, and that thou mayst live long on the earth." This is the divine commandment. There is, it is true, one case in which even parents should not be obeyed; when their directions and wishes are opposed to those of God: "we ought to obey

God rather than men;" and to love the Redeemer more than parents themselves.   Parents are
commonly the tenderest of friends; and pious
parents among the surest guides, that the young
and inexperienced can have, to lead them to the
footstool of God.   Your interests are theirs.
Your welfare their happiness.   But ah! has
their kindness met with the return it demanded?
Who, my young friend, so much deserve your
obedience and affection, as those who gave you
being, and who watched over your helpless infancy?   The father, whose years have been spent in
care for you; the mother, who tended you at her
breast, and led you through the days of childhood.   Have they received this obedience and
affection from you?

Perhaps I address one, whose disobedience and
unkindness have wrung with grief the hearts of
fond and pious parents; and filled them with
sorrow instead of gladness.   Their desire has
been to see you walking in the ways of God.
For this, they have led you to his house.   For
this, their prayers have ascended in public and
in private.   This, by their early instructions and
later admonitions, they have warned you to regard as the chief end of life; as that only concern, which, beyond all others, should interest
your attention, and engage all your heart.   And
now they see you negligent of God and religion;
and mourn in secret, that the child they love, is
still a child of Satan.   Ah! young man or young
woman, if this be your case, God will bring you
into judgment, for all your abuse of precious privileges, and all your neglect of parental instructions; and the prayers, and the tears, and the

Acts, v. 29.   Matt. x. 37, 38.

admonitions of your parents, will awfully witness against you. Think not, that if affectionate and kind to them, you will much mitigate the sorrows of truly pious parents. No; they will still mourn at the thought, that the affectionate child, they fondly love, is not a child of God. It will grieve them to the heart to consider, how near you are to endless destruction; and how soon they must bid you an eternal farewell, when they go to that rest, in which they have no hope of meeting you.

Ah! my young friend, if you slight religion, pious parents may leave you, mournfully saying, in their dying hour, "Alas! our beloved child, we shall see you no more: for our God you have not chosen as your God; and our Saviour you have not sought as your Saviour; and the heaven to which we go, is a rest to which you have no title, and which, dying as you are, you cannot enter!" Yes; bitterly will they mourn to think, that with so much that is lovely in their view, there is, in you, nothing that is lovely in the sight of God; and that all which they esteem so pleasing in you, must soon be buried in the deeps of hell.

§ 5. Another sin, not peculiar to the young, but awfully prevalent among them, is, the waste of precious time. The word of God reminds us, that "time is short;" and commands us "to redeem the time." The value of time is beyond our comprehension or expression.

"What its worth? ask death-beds; they can tell:
A *moment* we may wish, when worlds want wealth to buy."

Time is given us to prepare for eternity; but, alas how are its golden hours sinned and trifled away! Many young persons act as if they thought, they had so much time before them, that they may

afford to squander some: when, perhaps, their
wasted youth is their all; all in which they will
ever have an opportunity of prepaing for eternity; all in which they can "escape from hell and
fly to heaven." One of the most common ways
in which time is worse than wasted, is, the em
ploying of it on romances, plays, and novels.
Novels are the poison of the age: the best ot
them tend to produce a baneful effeminacy ot
mind; and many of them are calculated, to advance the base designs of the licentious and abandoned on the young and unsuspecting. But,
were they free from every other charge of evil,
it is a most heavy one, that they occasion a
dreadful waste of that time, which must be accounted for before the God of heaven. Let
their deluded admirers plead the advantages of
novel-reading, if they will venture to plead the
same before the worthy Judge eternal. If you
are a novel-reader, think the next time you take
a novel into your hands, How shall I answer
to my tremendous Judge, for the time occupied
by this? When he shall say to me, " I gave you
so many years in yonder world, to fit you for
eternity: did you converse with your God in
devotion? did you study his word? did you at
tend to the duties of life; and strive to improve
to some good end even your leisure hours?" then,
then, shall I be willing to reply; " Lord, my time
was otherwise employed! Novels and romances
occupied the leisure of my days; when, alas!
my bible, my God, and my soul, were neglected!"
In this way, and many others, is time, that mos¹
precious blessing, squandered away. Does not
conscience remind you of many leisure hours;
hours, which, though thoughtlessly thrown away,

would soon, to you, be worth more than mountains of gold or of pearl?

§ 6. Wilful neglect of the soul and eternity,
is another common sin of youth. Young persons
presume on future life; and grieve the Holy Spirit, by delaying to regard the one thing needful.
They trust in their youth. God reproves the folly, and says, " Boast not thyself of to-morrow;
for thou knowest not what a day may bring forth:"
but, few will listen to the warning. Instead of
doing so, they flatter themselves that they shall
live for many years; and think sickness, death,
and judgment, far from them. Hence they neglect the soul; and seem to imagine religion unsuitable, or at least not needful for themselves.
The blessed God calls on them in his word; the
crucified Saviour bids them come to himself, " I
love them that love me, and they that seek me
early shall find me;" the ministers of the gospel urge the advice upon them; prayers are offered, tears shed for them: yet, many persist in their
own ways; and, whatever they do, will not remember their Creator in the days of their youth.
My young friend, has this been your sin and folly? O, if it has, remember how many ways there
are out of the world! how many diseases to cut
short your days! God gives you time enough
to secure salvation; but think not, that he gives
you any to spare.

§ 7. An inordinate love of sensual pleasure
and worldly gaieties, is another most prevalent
sin of youth. The word of God describes those
who live in pleasure, as "dead while they live;"
and classes with the most abominably wicked,
those who are "lovers of pleasure more than lov-

Prov. xxvii. 1. Prov. viii. 17. 1 Tim. v. 6. 2 Tim. iii. 4

ers of God." Though such are the declarations of
the Lord; yet, pleasure, pleasure, is the chief object of thousands of the young.   Some pursue it
in the gross and brutish paths of rioting and
drunkenness; of chambering and wantonness:
others, in less profligate ways; but with hearts not
less intent upon it.   The card-table, the dance,
the horse-race, the play-house, the fair, the wake,
are the scenes of their highest felicity.   My young
friend, has not this love of worldly pleasure dwelt
in your heart?   Perhaps you have not run into
scandalous and disgraceful excesses; but have
you not had a greater love to worldly pleasures,
than to God and religion?   If you have, you but
too surely bear that awful mark of being a child
of destruction, that you are a lover of pleasures
more than a lover of God.   Have not you been
present at scenes of sinful amusement and guilty festivity?   Have not you been as anxious as
others, for those sensual delights which were most
suited to your taste? and, while thus loving this
world, have not you forgotten that which is to
come?   Have not you been more pleased with
some shining bauble or glittering toy, than with
the blessings displayed in the gospel? and been
more earnest about a day of promised pleasure,
than about securing an eternity of pure celestial
joy?   Think not that I mean to insinuate, that
the Christian should be the slave of melancholy.
Far from it; none have so much reason to be
cheerful as he, who reads his title clear to heaven.
But, wide is the difference between the innocent
cheerfulness and humble joy of the Christian, and
the vain pleasures of a foolish world.   The truly
religious have their delights; though they know
that there is:

No room for mirthful trifling here,
For worldly hope or worldly fear
  If life so soon is gone;
If now the Judge is at the door,
And all mankind must stand before
  The inexorable throne.

Let conscience now answer, as in the sight of God; has the love of worldly and sensual pleasure been cherished in your heart? If your situation has prevented your freely following the delights of sense, has the love of them dwelt within? If it has; though you should not have had the opportunity of indulging your worldly taste once in a month, or a year, you are still, in God's sight, as much a lover of pleasures, as if these had occupied every moment of your time.

§ 8. Sabbath-breaking, though not confined to the young, is a sin that eternally ruins thousands of them. God calls the sabbath-day his own; but makes the profit of it ours: and sabbaths spent in holiness, devotion, faith, and love, are blessings which help the soul on towards heaven; while, broken sabbaths increase the sinner's load of guilt here, and of misery hereafter. At the beginning of time God set this blessed day apart for sacred uses; and his express commandment is, "Remember the sabbath-day to keep it holy:" Ex. xx. 8. He calls for the *day*. He does not say, keep holy the sabbath morning, or the sabbath afternoon, or the sabbath evening; but, the sabbath day. Though this awful commandment is thus positive and express; yet, no sin is more common than sabbath-breaking. Some profane the whole day; others a part of it. Some employ many of the precious hours of the sabbath, in attending to their worldly employments;

others make it a season for finery and gaiety. They go even to the house of God, merely to see or be seen. They idle away their sacred time, in trifling conversation, vain amusements, and silly mirth; or, waste the holy day, in rambling in the fields with companions as frivolous and worldly as themselves. Yet sabbath-breaking is the fruitful source of sin and misery. A sabbath-breaker is justly described, as "one who despises his Maker; rebels against the King of kings, defies his vengeance, provokes his wrath; disgraces the Christian name; tramples on the laws of his country; ruins his own soul; and poisons others by his fatal example." And how have your sabbaths been spent? Have you been one of the thoughtless young women, or loose young men, that, on the sabbath-day, in giddy, but truly pitiable parties, throng our streets, or wander in our fields? Have you been one, who has made that most blessed day no blessing to yourself?

§ 9. The apostle Paul, when enumerating some of the sins of mankind, concludes the dreadful list with that, of their taking pleasure in the sins of others: Rom. i. 28. This, though one of the most awful, is one of the most common of human iniquities; and abounds among none more than among the young. Young persons are often each other's tempters and destroyers. The lewd and profane, tempt others to lewdness and profaneness. The thoughtless and the gay, persuade others to imitate their levity and folly. As if it were not sufficient to have their own sins to account for, many thus make themselves partakers in the sins of others; and, as if it were not enough to ruin their own souls, many thus contract the guilt of assisting to destroy those of their companions and friends. Have you never thus led others into sin? Perhaps some, who are now lost for ever, may be lamenting, in utter darkness and despair, the fatal hour when they became acquainted with you. Have any learned of you to trifle with religion; to squander away their golden day of grace; to slight their God; and choose perdition? If not by words, yet, perhaps, by a careless and irreligious example, you have taught them these dreadful lessons.

§ 10. I have now named a few youthful iniquities; but, think not that these things are all. No; every sin to which our fallen nature is prone, has been found, not merely in those, who, by years, were ripened in guilt; but, in those also, who were beginning the journey of life. And, not to enumerate the darker crimes of the multitude, who drink in iniquity like water; where, my young friend, is the youthful heart, that never felt the rising emotions of those infernal passions, pride, envy, malice, or revenge? Where is the youthful tongue that never uttered a profane, or wanton, or, at least, an unkind, or slanderous word? Where is the youth, possessed of the forms of piety, that never mocked God, "with solemn sounds upon a thoughtless tongue!" Where is the youthful ear, that was never open, to drink in with pleasure the conversation of the trifling and the foolish? and where the youthful eye, that never cast a haughty, an angry, a wanton, or insulting glance? Are you the person? Can you appeal to the Searcher of Hearts, and rest your eternal hopes on the success of the appeal, that love, unmingled love to God and man, has always dwelt in your bosom;

that no resentful, envious, or unkind emotion, was ever, for a moment, harboured there; that a law of constant kindness has ever dwelt upon your lips; that only meekness, and tenderness, and goodness have glanced from your eye; and that your ear was never opened to hear, with pleasure, of a brother's shame? Can you make the appeal? Surely you cannot. Your own "heart condemns you; and God is greater than your heart, and knoweth all things."

A PRAYER FOR A YOUNG PERSON, SENSIBLE OF BEING, IN A GREATER OR LESS DEGREE, GUILTY OF THE SINS ENUMERATED IN THIS CHAPTER.

O Lord, the great, and dreadful God, whose mercies are numberless, I have sinned, and committed iniquity before thee. Permit me to approach thee; and enable me to come with all the humility of repentance, and all the ardour of gratitude. If I never prayed before, now may I learn to pray. Thou art the Father and the God of those, who rest in heaven: and O! show me thy forgiving mercy; and give me that interest in thy beloved Son, which shall prepare me to join their triumphant family. But a moment of time separates me from the dead! yet, alas! how unprepared am I for the solemn change of death: I see, I feel this dreadful truth; but, how much more visible is it, Lord, to thee! Once, careless and unconcerned, I felt no alarm at the thought of meeting thy pure and holy Majesty. Ah, sad insensibility! had I then been called to meet thee, I must now have been lifting up my eyes in hopeless misery. If, taught by thy word, I review my life, I see it a constant blot. I look

back to my childhood; and, behold, alas! how
soon the corrupt dispositions of my nature appeared! As my years increased, my sins gained strength; my heart became more estranged
from thee; and my life more sinful in thy sight.
Thou lovest humility; but, I have been proud.
Thou hast commanded me to revere the authors
of my being; to listen to their counsels; and, by
tenderness, to requite their affection: but, how
often have I slighted their instructions; forgotten their kindness; been undutiful to them, and
in them to thee! Thou hast directed me to view
life as a dream; and, as my great concern, to
seek first thy kingdom and righteousness: but,
I have presumed on future days, and wasted
those thy mercy gave me. I have minded the
things of time; and forgotten those of eternity
Instead of seeking my happiness in Jesus, and
in thee; I have sought delight amidst the follies
of time, and have grovelled upon earth, when I
should have been soaring to heaven. I have
loved — O most patient God! may I dare to
confess it; yet, confess it or not, thou knowest
the horrible sin — I have loved the shadowy
pleasures of this world, more than I have loved
thee. O, that this stony heart might break while
I acknowledge my guilt! I have sunk lower than
the brutes that perish: they, formed for this
world, fill up aright their places in it; but I, cre-
ated to know thee, to serve thee, to love thee, and
to enjoy thee for ever, have yet grovelled in the
dust.

Thy word directs me to redeem the time; but,
Oh! how many precious hours, hours which the
dying would give worlds to purchase, have I sinned and idled away! Alas! the hours that I

have wasted on frivolous books, while thy blessed word has been neglected! The hours I have
squandered in trifling conversation and foolish
mirth, while not one word of my Redeemer, or
thee, or thy goodness, has dropped from my lips.

Thou, O Lord, hast commanded me to hallow
the sabbath; but, I have wasted many of those
sacred days. When thy children have been reaping immortal good; I have been heaping up
wrath against the day of wrath. Those blessed
seasons, which might have been a foretaste and a
preparative for an eternal sabbath in thy heavenly courts, even those to me have been days of
thoughtlessness, sin, and folly. Or, if I have gone
to thy house; yet, how often have pride, vanity,
and worldly pleasures filled my thoughts, even
there, and I have departed from thy sacred
courts, unmoved by thy terrors, uncharmed by
thy love. When I look back upon my sabbaths,
what a dismal blank do they appear!

To thee, O Lord God, belong mercies and
forgiveness, though I have rebelled against thee.
Thou hast not been in all my thoughts. By
my ungodly life, I have said to thee, " Depart
from me, for I desire not the knowledge of thy
ways;" and though thy beloved Son, once crucified for my sins, has claimed my heart, I have
refused to listen to his call. And, yet, I have deceived myself; have deemed myself almost innocent; have thought my life righteous; and
treated humble piety with contempt and scorn.
True wisdom I have counted folly, and folly prized for wisdom. Merciful Lord, my lips, my
tongue, my eyes, my ears, my hands, my head,
have all sinned against thee; but, Oh, my heart!
the heart I deemed good, what madness has

dwelt there! There hidden lay the seeds of every sin. There have those corruptions abode, which hell takes pleasure in viewing, but which heaven must mourn to see. There anger has burned. There pride has swelled. There envy and revenge have rankled. There vanity, indolence, discontent, ingratitude, and all the detestable brood of human vices, have shown their hateful forms. There too has reigned love for the present dying world, that love which leads a legion of iniquities in its train. And shall I now plead, that I am innocent? Shall I now declare, that my heart is good, and my transgressions few? Merciful God, forgive the blindness which deluded me with thoughts like these. No, O my injured Father, the smallest sin against thee is huge as the frowning precipice, dark as the shadow of death, and horrid as the depths of hell; and the smallest of my crimes have been as much committed against thee, as the more profligate actions of some, who never enjoyed the mercies with which I have been favoured. O my God, as a sinner, I would cast me at the feet of Jesus! I cannot hide my guilt from thine eyes; let me not hide it from my own. Thou hast seen all my sins, hast called on me again and again, and hast beheld the world and Satan preferred to thyself. Surely love like thine might have melted a rock of adamant; yet, it melted not my heart. Canst thou yet show mercy? Thou dost! O wonderful love! shall I abuse it still? O, rather may my pulse cease to beat, and the warm blood to flow through my veins! Lord lead me to the rock that is higher than I! Lead me to the atoning blood, which washes all sin away. Lead me to Christ crucified. Forgive, for his dear sake, the past; and O, give strength and grace for the future! I have lived long enough, alas, too long! to the world, to Satan, and myself; now let me live to thee. Now, for Jesus's sake, guide me from sin to holiness; from folly to wisdom; from death to life; from vain delight to real joy; and, finally, through the Lamb that was slain, advance me from earth to heaven, there to praise, bless, magnify, and adore redeeming love, through ages without end.

O gracious Lord, hear my requests, for Jesus's sake. — *Amen.*

CHAPTER IV.

THE NATURE OF REAL RELIGION BRIEFLY DESCRIBED.

THAT religion is the chief concern of all, is the declaration of the Most High; and early religion is what he solemnly requires. "Remember now thy Creator in the days of thy youth, while the evil days come not, nor the years draw nigh when thou shalt say, I have no pleasure in them." It is as much as if it were said, "Mind religion while you are young. Let that engage your earliest care. Let that possess the first place in your heart; for it is worthy of it. In the days of your youth, those best days, prepare to meet your God. While young, make him your friend ; seek an enduring mansion in the skies; and thus, to every other source of cheerfulness, add those last and best, your heavenly Father's care, and your gracious Saviour's love." The blessed Redeemer, who spake as ne-

Eccles. xii. 1.

ver man spake, affectionately declares the importance and value of real piety. "One thing is needful." "What shall it profit a man, if he gain the whole world, and lose his own soul?"

Most persons will acknowledge the excellency and importance of religion; yet, few are its real friends. "Few there be that find it." Many are entirely careless of it. Others have the form without the power. Others play the hypocrite's part; they "speak fair words and act foul deeds, lift their eyes to heaven and turn their steps to hell." Religion is not, like many worldly advantages, a blessing that descends from parents to children, from heir to heir. The child of the most pious parent is, by nature, as destitute of the dispositions which constitute religion, as the child of the most profligate. It is not, like the endowments of body or mind, as wit, beauty, strength, a blessing that we naturally possess; for, the dispositions of the mind, by nature, are altogether opposite to those of religion. Nor is religion a blessing that can be acquired without opposition and difficulty. The command of Christ is, "Strive to enter in at the strait gate." These words import, contending in the most resolute and earnest manner, and, as it were, *forcing* a way through whatever may oppose.

§ 2. Many, my young friend, are the sources whence this opposition arises. The corruptions of your own heart will oppose the entrance of divine truth into your soul. The false and deceiving opinions of the world would teach you, to look on real religion as enthusiasm, and to treat it with aversion and contempt. The evil Spirit, that great enemy of God and man, by every de-

Luke, x. 42. Mark, viii 36. Matt. vii. 14. Luke xiii. 23

lusion which he can present to your mind, will endeavour to prevent your submitting to Jesus Christ; and often but too successful are his exertions. "The god of this world hath blinded the minds of them which believe not; lest the light of the glorious gospel of Christ, should shine unto them."

And now, while I endeavour to describe to you what religion is, let me beseech you to unite your prayers with mine, that you may indeed be taught of God; and let me beseech you to attend as seriously to the plain and affectionate truths, that may be presented to you, as you would do if lying on a dying bed, and there earnestly inquiring how salvation might be found.

§ 3. Religion consists in such a practical knowledge of our own guilt and misery, as leads us to abhor sin and ourselves; and in such an acquaintance with the blessed God, and the adorable Saviour, as leads us to believe on Jesus for salvation, and resting all our hopes upon his atonement and righteousness, to trust our eternal all to his care; and to yield up ourselves, body, soul, and spirit, to the Father as our Father, to the Son as our Saviour, and to the Holy Spirit as our Sanctifier.

§ 4. The foundation of religion is laid in a knowledge of our own guilt and depravity. As sickness teaches the patient to prize the physician's aid; as slavery leads the captive to seek for liberty; and condemnation makes the criminal cry for mercy: so the knowledge of our own condemnation and guilt, prepares the soul for the reception of Jesus Christ. Are you ac-

2 Cor. iv. 3, 4.

quainted with this ?   Are you sensible that you have rebelled against a God of love? and are you penitent for your transgressions? You cannot else escape destruction. The Lord has declared, "Except ye repent, ye shall all likewise perish." "God now commandeth all men everywhere to repent." This repentance consists, not in a transient sorrow for sin, but, in such a sense of its evil, vileness, and ingratitude, as begets in the soul abhorrence of it, and an anxious desire for deliverance from its power and punishment.

§ 5. If knowledge of yourself, and of the evil of sin, has humbled you in the dust, and led you from the heart to exclaim, "God, be merciful to me a sinner;" then, permit me to add, that a most essential part of religion, is an acquaintance with the Lord Jesus Christ. Not a mere speculative knowledge of his excellencies, like that which even an infernal spirit may possess; but, such a practical knowledge of his power and grace, and such a belief in him, as subdues the soul, and leads the penitent sinner to make Jesus his hope, his trust, and his all. The substance of the gospel message respecting Jesus Christ is, — that his nature is divine: "He was in the beginning with God, and was God." That his own compassion and his Father's love, led him to assume the nature of man: "He took on him the form of a servant, and was made in the likeness of men;" "Though he was rich, for your sakes he became poor, that ye through his poverty might be rich." That his great object was to atone for sin: "He was wounded for our transgressions, he was bruised for our iniquities; the chastisement of our peace was upon him, and with his stripes we

Luke, xiii. 3. Acts, xvii. 30. John, i. 1. Phil. ii. 7. 2 Cor. viii. 9.

are healed." That this wonderful plan, for the redemption of a ruined world, was the effect of the love and wisdom of God: "God commendeth his love towards us, in that, while we were yet sinners, Christ died for us;" "We have redemption through his blood, the forgiveness of sins, according to the riches of his grace, wherein he hath abounded towards us, in all wisdom." And, that Jesus Christ is now exalted at the right-hand of power, to intercede for his flock; to guide, guard, and protect them; to receive them at the hour of death; and hereafter to appear as the Judge of all, when he will pass on all mankind the sentence that shall fix their eternal state, and when he will perfect the happiness of all his humble friends.*

§ 6. The important doctrine of Christ's atonement for the sins of man, may receive a plain and familiar illustration, from the history of Zileucus, an ancient lawgiver. Among his laws was one, which declared, that the eyes of an adulterer should be put out as a punishment for his sins. It so happened that the king's own son was the first convicted of the crime. The justice of the lawgiver called for the execution of the sentence: the pity of the parent pleaded for its remission. What was to be done? The king at length determined, that his son should lose one eye, and he himself would lose one. Thus should the sin be punished, though he himself would bear part of the punishment due to his guilty child. You here see such a stern regard to justice, as would convince the whole nation, that the law could not be broken with impunity; and, yet, such fatherly compassion, as

___

Is. liii. 5. Rom. v. 8. Ephes. i. 7, 8.   * New Test. many passages.

should melt the heart of the half-pardoned offender into deep repentance and self-abhorrence.

In the case of man, and in your own case, sin has deserved eternal punishment. Its *wages* (that recompence which it has deserved) *is death.* The justice of God called for the execution of the sentence; but, his wisdom devised a plan of mercy for a rebellious world, and his compassion induced him to adopt the plan. It was, that his beloved Son should suffer for man, and bear the curse instead of him: Gal. iii. 11. Thus would sin be punished; and thus might the sinner be *entirely* forgiven. Thus did God give to his whole intelligent creation an awful proof, that sin, in his dominions, could not escape unpunished. Yet, while showing his infinite hatred of sin, he showed his infinite love to ruined man, in thus appointing his beloved Son to stand in the sinner's place; and in thus punishing in Christ the sins of man, that the penitent sinner might go free.

§ 7. An acquaintance with this divine Saviour is absolutely needful for you. He is set forth as the only foundation for the sinner's eternal hopes. His is the only name by which a sinner can be saved; and he is the only way of access to God. The way of salvation is, believing on him from the heart. "Believe on the Lord Jesus Christ, and thou shalt be saved." "He that believeth, and is baptized, shall be saved." But, my young friend, permit me affectionately to caution you against deceiving your own soul with the shadow of belief instead of the substance; for, in one sense, "the devils believe and tremble." Believing in Jesus is termed, in scripture, "believing with the heart." There is the consent of

Acts, xvi. 31. Mark, xvi. 16. James, ii. 19. Rom. x. 10.

the heart to this plan of salvation, as well as the persuasion of the mind. Believing on Christ is described as a *receiving* of him. If you believe, you will receive him as your Lord, your hope, your Saviour, your all. Believing is also described, as being a *persuasion* of divine truths, and an *embracing* of them. If you believe on Jesus, you will be persuaded, on God's authority, that he is what the scriptures represent, an all-sufficient Saviour; that he has done what the scriptures declare; that he has laid down his life for you; and persuaded of these truths, you will embrace this great salvation. Believing is represented as a *going* to Christ; it is such a conviction of his power and grace as is attended by the going, as it were, of the soul to him for life and salvation. Look then to him. Rest your eternal all on his righteousness and death. Let this become your plea for obtaining mercy and heaven, that Jesus loved you; that Jesus died for you. Go in the solemn moments of retired devotion, and entrust your all to Jesus. Can you not there say to him, to whom darkness and day are alike, "Lord, I adore thee as my Saviour; thou didst die for my sins, and I commit my eternal all to thee. Wash me in thy blood; wash not my feet only, but also my hands and my head. Thy gospel I embrace. All that thou discoverest, let me believe; all that thou teachest, let me learn. Thy example I would follow. All that thou lovest, let me love; all that thou hatest, let me hate; and all that thou commandest, let my faith, working by love, urge me to obey. Be thou my all; thy death and righteousness, my hope;

John, i. 12. Heb. xi. 13. John, vi. 35.

thy life, my pattern; thy word, my rule; thy glory, my aim; thy love, my heaven."

A well-placed trust in Jesus Christ will be found a sure support for hope, and peace, and joy, when all other dependences sink in eternal ruin, and all other hopes are blasted in black despair. The soul, committed to his care, will be safe through its little stay among the objects of time and sense; and, what is far more important, will be safe and happy when the graves are giving up their dead, when the world is fleeing from the majesty of its Maker's face, and when creation is perishing in final flames.

§ 8. But perhaps you ask, "May I thus approach the Lord? may one so vile draw near to him with confidence?" You may; his word declares it. Come, says the compassionate Jesus, "Come unto me, ALL ye that labour and are heavy laden, and I will give you rest." "Him that cometh to me I will IN NO WISE cast out." "He is able to save to the uttermost, all that come unto God by him." "Whosoever will, let him take the water of life freely." "Come, for all things are now ready." "The blood of Jesus Christ his Son cleanseth from all sin." A poor heathen was once directed to make atonement for his sins, by driving iron spikes through his sandals; on these to place his naked feet; and in them to walk about four hundred and eighty miles. He began his painful journey; but, halting under a tree, a missionary came, and preached in his hearing from, "the blood of Jesus Christ cleanseth from all sin." While he was preaching, the man rose up, threw away his torturing san-

Matt. xi. 28. John, vi. 37. Heb. vii. 25. Rev. xxii. 17. Luke, xiv. 17. 1 John, i. 7.

dals, and exclaimed, "This is what I want!" and became a living witness, that the blood of Christ does cleanse from all sin. The same way for mercy is open to you. If salvation is what you want, you may find it in him who has saved thousands, and who will save thousands more. Many a promise and many an invitation, unite to declare, that you shall not apply to him in vain.

§ 9. Numbers profess a regard to Christ, whose hopes are in reality built upon themselves; and they imagine, that when they have done as well as they can, Jesus will make up the rest. But, that knowledge of the Saviour, in which so much of religion consists, leads to very different views. If you enjoy this, Jesus Christ will be your all. You will, as a lost, helpless, condemned, and wretched creature, come to him for life. Your whole trust will be in him: abhorring yourself, you will flee to him as your sole dependence. You will indulge no hope, from imagining that your sins are few or small; but, will own them deserving of divine wrath. You will no longer rest on the deluding, but absolutely false notion, that you have done as well as you could, and that therefore God will accept you; but, you will be humbled as a guilty creature at your Maker's feet. Nothing past, nothing present, nothing future of your own, must in the slightest degree, be the ground of your dependence; but, as stripped of every thing, as in yourself destitute of all good, you must look to the Lamb of God. A dying minister, eminent in his day, once said to a visitor that was taking leave of him, "Sir, I am every day expecting my death; but, I desire to die like the thief, crying to the crucified Jesus for mercy. I am nothing; I have nothing; I can do nothing, except what is unworthy; my eye, and hope, and faith, is to Christ on his cross. I bring an unworthiness, like that of the poor dying thief, unto him; and have no more to plead than he. Like the poor thief, I am waiting to be received, by the infinite grace of my Lord, into his kingdom."

§ 10. But, my young friend, do not mistake the nature of the gospel; or imagine, because the soul is saved solely through the obedience and death of Christ, upon its believing in him, that, therefore, holiness of heart and life is an unimportant thing. "Without holiness no man shall see the Lord." When Jesus invites the humbled soul to him, he adds, "Take my yoke upon you, and learn of me." He says, "Ye are my friends, if ye do whatsoever I command you." "If a man love me, he will keep my words." The true Christian's faith is represented, as "faith which works by love;" and without the fruits of holiness, "faith is dead, being alone." The Son of God says to his friends, "Let your light so shine before men, that they may see your good works, and glorify your Father who is in heaven." The apostle Paul argues, that true Christians are dead to sin; and declares, that the Son of God gave himself for them, with this design, "that he might redeem them from all iniquity, and purify unto himself a peculiar people, zealous of good works." If you, from your heart, receive the Lord Jesus Christ, as your Redeemer, you will also submit to him as your sovereign Lord; you will love the commandments of God, as just and holy; you will yield up yourself, body,

Heb. xii. 14.   Matt. xi. 29.   John, xv. 14.   John, xiv. 23.   Gal. v. 6.
James, ii. 17.   Matt. v. 16   Tit. ii. 14.

H

soul, and spirit, to the Lord Jesus Christ: that whether you "live, you may live to the Lord; or whether you die, you may die to the Lord." While religion leads you to trust the Saviour's death, it will lead you to copy his life.

The great principle of real holiness, implanted in all who truly embrace the gospel, is, that they are now no longer their own; but, "bought with a price," the price of "blood divine," and, therefore, bound "to glorify God in their body and spirit, which are God's," being now restored to him, their rightful owner, and become the property of God. From such a dedication of the soul and body to Christ, flows holiness, far superior to all the mere moral goodness (as it is termed) of the world. They who are given up to Jesus, wish to lose their own will and adopt his; to think, and act, and move, as he would have them. Hence, their desires after increasing and perfect holiness; for, they belong to him who is holiness itself. Hence, their love to a better world, and their deadness to this; for, they follow him, who cared nothing for this world, but whose home was heaven. Hence, their lives can no longer be devoted to the pursuit of trifling vanities; for, they are not their own, but have nobler objects to mind: they have a heaven to reach; a God to glorify; and a Saviour to honour, a Saviour, whose command to every one of his disciples is, "Follow thou me." "He has left us his example, that we should follow his steps."

Take, my friend, a brief survey of his character, whom the Christian is ordered to follow. Love was the distinguishing trait in the charac-

Rom. xiv. 8.   1 Cor. vi. 20.   1 Pet. ii. 21.

ter of Jesus Christ. Love to God, in the highest degree; love to man; love to friends; and love to enemies. — Love to God swallowed up every other passion in his breast. It was his meat and drink to do his heavenly Father's will; as it were, his refreshment and support, not his labour and fatigue. Here was one mark of his perfect love; and submission to the will of God was another. In the hour of his extremity his language was, "The cup which my Father hath given me, shall I not drink it?" "not my will, but thine be done!" Frequent communion with God in prayer and praise, displayed also the heavenly love that glowed within his heart. — The same gracious disposition appeared in him towards mankind. He never laughed at human follies; but, wept for human sins and woes. He laboured for the happiness of men. In the midst of poverty, in spite of opposition, in the prospect of death, he continued his labours; unhindered by calumny, reproach, or ingratitude. He lived, striving to make happy some of the sons and daughters of Adam; and he died, to open for them that way to heaven which none shall ever shut. Such was his love to man. — To his friends how tender! Read his discourse to them, and his prayers for them, in John's Gospel, C. 14, to C. 17, and there behold the expressions of his love. — To his enemies how kind! Let his behaviour witness this, when he shed tears for them who shed his blood; or when upon his cross he prayed, "Father, forgive them, for they know not what they do." He was meek when insulted; calm when provoked; ready to forgive an injury, and not to revenge himself up-

John, iv. 34; xviii. 11.   Luke, xxii. 42; xxiii. 34.

on the injurer. No selfish passion dwelt within his breast. Though rich, he had become poor, that through his poverty he might make many rich. He lived and died for others. His maxims were like himself, or like those of the heaven from which he came; not like those of the earth on which he abode. "Do good to them that hate you." "All things whatsoever ye would that men should do to you, do ye even the same to them." "It is more blessed to give than to receive." "Lay not up for yourselves treasures upon earth; but, lay up for yourselves treasures in heaven." Wherever the precious gospel is embraced, and Jesus followed, a change, most truly glorious and divine, will take place. Under its heavenly influence man becomes a "new creature; old things pass away, and all things become new." Let the passionate come to Jesus; and mildness, in their breast, will take the place of anger. The covetous will grow liberal; and from loving to grasp all they can, will love to part with the utmost in their power. The proud become humble. Drunkards learn sobriety; and liars love the truth. Thieves become honest. Sabbath-breakers improve the sacred days they wasted once. The prayerless learn to pray, and find their duty and their pleasures united in devotion. The hard-hearted change their natures for compassion. The implacable learn to forgive, as they hope to be forgiven. The earthly-minded renounce the things of earth, and seek their treasures in heaven. The man who trembled almost at a shaking reed, becomes, in his Redeemer's cause,

2 Cor. viii. 9.   Matt. v. 44.   Matt. vii. 12.   Acts, xx. 35.
            Matt. vi. 19, 20.   2 Cor. v. 17.

fearless as a lion. And they who have been addicted to what are commonly esteemed the most incurable vices, under the influence of true religion, change pollution for purity, wickedness for holiness, and the likeness of devils for the likeness of God. It is true, these glorious victories of divine truth and love often pass unnoticed by the world. No trumpet sounds the Christian's fame. No herald tells of his deathless victories. He often lives and dies, honoured by his God, and happy in him, though little known by man.

> "Full many a gem, of purest ray serene,
> The dark unfathom'd caves of ocean bear;
> Full many a flower is born to blush unseen,
> And waste its sweetness on the desert air."

There are few situations in which Christians can show those bright specimens of glowing piety, which dazzle the eyes of others: but, that steady, humble, constant piety; those secret desires for holiness and heaven; that private, daily converse with God in prayer; that cheerful, firm dependence on the atoning Saviour; and those attempts, in the retired scenes of domestic life, to live as apostles would have lived, if placed in a like situation — all this flows from following Jesus, as surely as water flows from a fountain. All this is the effect of being not our own, but of having Christ live in us, and being given up to the Lord. If we were wandering in an unknown country, and having lost our way, had entrusted ourselves to a guide; should we not renounce our own judgment, and our own will, and be so at our leader's disposal, that we might almost be said to move with his feet, and to see with his eyes? Such is the case in religion. We have lost our way to a better world; and, if Christians indeed, shall commit ourselves to Jesus's care, to be saved by him, in *his* way, by grace alone; yet, to go where he bids; to do what he enjoins, to live as he directs; to love what he loves; to hate what he hates; to shun what he commands us to avoid; to sit at his feet and learn of him; and to "follow the Lamb whithersoever he goeth."

§ 11. Closely connected with the knowledge of the Son, is the knowledge of the Father; indeed, so closely, that they cannot be separated. "This is life eternal; to know thee, the only true God, and Jesus Christ, whom thou hast sent." Jesus was "God manifest in the flesh." In him shone such a lively picture of the Father's excellencies, that "he who hath seen him hath seen the Father." Yet, it is proper to remind you, that Jesus is your way to God. The design of Christ is, to bring you to the Father, and reconcile you to him. He is the mediator, or intercessor, by whom you may find acceptance with your most compassionate but much-injured God. The glorious perfections of God claim your most devout reverence and admiration. Such is his infinite majesty, that this vast world, with all its islands, all its continents, all its nations, is in his sight as the small dust on the balance, or the drop of a bucket. Before him,

"Worms, angels, men, in every different sphere,
    Are equal all; for, all are nothing here."

Such is his power, that in an instant he could create a thousand worlds, and in another instant could destroy them all. Such is his knowledge, that he knows whatever has been, through the eternity that is past; and whatever will be, through

John, xvii. 3. 1 Tim. iii. 16. John, xiv. 9. John, xiv. 6. 2 Cor. v. 18, Is. xl. 15

the eternity to come. He is acquainted with the actions, words, and thoughts, of every one that ever lived on the earth; he sees what now are ours, and what will be those of all the nations that are yet unborn. Such is his love, that, for the sake of saving a lost race, he gave up to humiliation, sorrow, and death, his best-beloved Son, the Lord Jesus Christ, the partner of his throne, "the brightness of his glory, and the express image of his person." "Thousand thousands minister unto him, and ten thousand times ten thousand stand before him." It is against this great and dreadful, though gracious God, that you have rebelled; but, the blessed Jesus would lead you back to him. If you obey the gospel, God will become your Father. To him you will yield up what you have and are, as a reasonable sacrifice. In him you will seek your happiness; and in his presence your eternal rest. To know him, to love him, and to enjoy his favour, will be the highest ambition of your soul.

"Give what thou wilt, without thee we are poor;
And with thee rich, take what thou wilt away."

Every mercy comes from God; and every mercy should lead you nearer and nearer to him. The first and greatest of the commandments is, to love him. Sin, indeed, has made you live, not to God, but to yourself; selfish and lower views have ruled in your heart: but, if, by the gospel, you are led back to God, he will be your happiness, and his glory your aim. It will be your desire to be conformed to his will; your pleasure to please him, so that truly, "you'll live to pleasure, while you live to God." Your interests, and those of your Creator, will be no longer disjoined

Heb. i. 3. Dan. vii. 10.

and opposite, but again united. Your wish will be, that his will may be done *in* you; that his will may done *by* you; and that his will may be be done *with* you.

§ 12. A very important part of religion is, a knowledge of the Holy Spirit. Men, when first awakened to regard divine things, often imagine, that their own endeavours are to produce in them those graces which real religion displays. The word of God, on the other hand, represents them, as formed by the Holy Spirit. The Holy Spirit is promised to them that ask for his aid. The Christian is "born of the Spirit." The Spirit is sent, to "convince the world of sin." By the power of the Holy Spirit, "the love of God is shed abroad in the heart." By him hope abounds in the believer; his mind is enlightened; he is sanctified and strengthened by the Spirit of God. By the Spirit he is taught to cry, "Abba Father;" and "love, joy, peace, long-suffering, gentleness, goodness, faith, meekness, temperance," are the fruits of the Spirit.

All the graces of the Christian character, all the parts of holiness, are thus produced by the Spirit of God; and while you are assured, that "without holiness no man shall see the Lord;" you are taught, to look to God for his Spirit to form your heart anew. While it is to be your aim, to glorify God in all things; your dependence for ability to do so, is to be on the promised Spirit. Yet, think not, that, on this account, sloth and negligence in religious matters will be excused. The abuse, which Satan and the world would have you make of this evangelical doc-

Luke, xi. 13. John, iii. 6. John, xvi. 8. Rom. v. 5. Rom xv. 13. Cor. ii. 12, 1 Cor vi. 11, Ephes. iii. 16. Gal. iv. 6. Gal. v. 22. Heb. xii. 14. John, vii. 37, 39.

trine, is, that if the work is thus God's, you need not trouble yourself respecting it. A sure guide, the Lord himself, makes a widely different inference. That he "works in you, both to will and to do," is made by him the reason, why you "should work out your salvation with fear and trembling." When the husbandman in spring scatters his seed on the ground, he cannot make one corn produce a blade, nor one blade produce an ear; but, God, by his secret working, makes the seed vegetate, clothes the field with green, and, in the appointed weeks of harvest, loads it with waving ears of ripened corn. Who produced this harvest? Not man, but God. Yet, would God have produced it if the husbandman had neither ploughed nor sowed his field? He would have had no crop to reap if he had pleaded; "The work is God's, so I need not labour." As it is in this case, so it is in religion. The work is God's, and his shall be the praise; yet, man must use the means, and labour for his own salvation. He can no more change his own heart, than he can make the hard earth bear fruit; but, let him use the means which his Redeemer puts in his power, and God WILL give the blessing, for he has promised to do so. But, if, because salvation is of grace, and holiness by the Spirit of God, men neglect the means, and labour not for their own salvation; they have no more prospect of eternal happiness, than a husbandman would have of reaping an abundant crop, who never concerned himself with sowing a single grain. If you turn to God, and believe on Christ, you will be " a temple of the Holy Spirit;" and should not his temples be holy?

With him working in your heart, how inexcusable would you be to continue the slave to sin!

Thus you see what religion is. It consists not in a round of outward forms, though, if it be enjoyed, outward privileges will be prized and improved; it consists not in the strictest mere morality, though, if it influence the heart, holiness must surely follow: but, in such a knowledge of God in Christ, as makes believers his and not their own.

§ 13. If religion be chosen by you, you will determine, in God's strength, to abide by your choice to your latest day.   While the almost Christian halts between the world and Jesus, those who really flee to him, do so to be his decidedly.   "The world will laugh at me," may the young Christian say: "well, let it laugh; if I may but enjoy the smile of God, I can bear the senseless laugh of men!   The world will frown on me: well, let it frown; it frowned on my Master before me, and the disciple is not greater than his Lord!"   If you flee to Jesus, you will flee to him to be his, not only decidedly, but for ever.   You will view religion as a blessing, chosen once, but chosen for life.   You will value it as the one thing needful, compared with which, suffering or delight, life or death below, are nothing.   You will view his gospel as a blessing, most valuable in itself, and most important to you, though there were not another person on the face of the globe.   As a blessing so inexpressibly valuable and momentous, that you would prize it, though it were neglected by every human being but yourself, and though all the nations of the earth should unite to deter you from embracing it.   Such was the spirit of the martyrs. Their religion was not a blessing valued merely when the sun of prosperity shone ; but, one to which they clung when the storms of adversity and persecution beat upon them, and when the hour came that Christ or li e should be resigned. Though not called to martyrdom, yet, that high degree of value for Christ, which animated them, must dwell in your heart, or your religion will be an empty name ; for, the Lord has declared, " He that loveth father or mother more than me, is not worthy of me; and he that loveth son or daughter more than me, is not worthy of me ; and he that taketh not his cross, and followeth after me, is not worthy of me." " Whosoever he be of you that forsaketh not all that he hath, he cannot be my disciple."

§ 14. You have already, in one or two instances, been referred to the parable of the prodigal son; permit me to refer you to it more at large, as affording a beautiful description of real religion. In its first part (Luke, xv. 11 — 16), you have a picture of man while destitute of real piety; a picture, my young friend, of what you yourself have been. The prodigal loses all affection for his father ; wanders from him ; squanders his all, as if distracted ; and plunges deep in sin and misery. You have wandered from a kinder Father ; and, as you were shown in Chapter II, have acted, towards God, the prodigal's part. His sin was followed by misery ; and, unless you repent, your's must be by eternal ruin. But he repented. In the second part of the parable, verses 17 — 19, is contained a lively description of the nature of real repentance. He came to himself ; he felt

Matt. x. 37, 38.　　Luke, xiv. 33.

his misery ; he was humbled for his sin and folly ;
longed for the meanest place in his father's house ;
and arose to seek forgiveness. Such is repentance.
The once careless sinner, the thoughtless trifler
comes, as it were, to his right mind ; he sees that
in neglecting humble piety, and wandering from
his God and Saviour, he has acted as if bereft of
sense and reason ; he abhors his sin ; he is humbled for it ; he longs for a place, though it be the
meanest in the family of God ; religion, which
he once scorned, is now the object of his anxious
wish ; and, in sincerity and truth, he turns from
the ways of sin to seek his God.   The reception
the prodigal met with, verses 20 — 24, displays the
nature of the gospel.   No sooner did he sincerely repent and apply for mercy, than he found
it.   His father welcomed him to his bosom ; and
received him as his son again.   Yet, observe, he
had done nothing to deserve his favour.   It was
not of works (through any works of his); for, he
had returned to his parent a wretched, destitute
outcast :   yet, no sooner did he return, than he
was fully and freely forgiven ; his transgressions
were blotted out ; and he restored at once to his
father's favour.   Such is the grace displayed to
you in the gospel.   It is as free ; it is as full.
No works of yours can deserve the favour of
your God ; you have none that are worthy of
his regard.   What had the prodigal?   But, he
was immediately and freely forgiven ; so will
you be, if you come to God by Christ.   You are,
in a spiritual sense, as destitute, as wretched, as
guilty as he ; but, mercy as great is ready, at
once, upon your believing from the heart on
Christ, to forgive you, and save you, and make
vou a child of the Most High.   Observe one

particular more. The prodigal, thus freely pardoned, was admitted again as a son into his father's family. What would be his conduct there? Surely every motive of gratitude and love, would urge him to obey his father's will: but, the motive would not be, that he *might* find mercy, for he *had* found it; it would not be, to gain admission into his father's house, for he had gained it: far nobler motives, the motives of love, would influence his conduct. Such is the obedience, which I have described as the fruit of religion. Evangelical obedience springs from love, that love which faith produces. The true Christian serves God, not to gain admission into his Father's family; for, when he came to Christ he gained this blessing: but, he renders to him the obedience of a child, thankful for a thousand favours. "He is justified by faith alone, yet not by a faith which is alone, but which contains the seeds of universal obedience;" and having found mercy of the Lord, he lives to God. The difference between the state of mind in a person hoping to gain heaven, by his defective obedience, and that of the person, justified by faith, is well described in the following lines of one of Cowper's hymns:

"Then all my servile works were done
   A righteousness to raise;
Now, freely chosen in the Son,
   I freely choose his ways.

"What shall I do, was then the word,
   That I may worthier grow?
What shall I render to the Lord?
   Is my inquiry now.

"To see the law by Christ fulfil'd,
   And hear his pard'ning voice,
Changes a slave into a child,
   And duty into choice."

I

§ 15. Having now described to you what reli
gion is, it may seem almost superfluous to add,
that early piety consists in your thus becoming
a disciple of Christ in your youthful days. If
this be your wisdom and happiness, you will give
your youth to God.   You will listen to him, saying, "Wilt thou not from this time cry unto me,
My Father, thou art the guide of my youth?"
and the language of your heart will be, "Blessed God, by thy help, I will.   I consecrate the
morning of my life to thee.   I owe thee as much
as eternity can acknowledge.   Take then, O take
the little, yet the best, that I can offer; the prime,
the flower of my days.   Most young persons a-
round me are ruled by the maxims of a corrupt
world;   sinful nature governs them;   evil companions lead them astray;   and Satan urges them
to perdition: but, Lord, I will listen to thy voice.
Be thou my guide through all the slippery paths
of youth.   I cry to thee as my Father; I seek
thee now as such ; and let me love and obey thee
as a friend, to whom my welfare is dearer than it
is to myself."

If early piety, my young friend, be yours, in
youth you will forsake the world, and dare to stand
up for God and religion.   While thousands of
the young are building all their hopes upon this
fleeting scene; yours will be fixed on things unseen and eternal: while they are trifling with
the Saviour's love, you will gladly listen to his
voice, and learn of him.   Yes, in youth, you
will accept the proffered Saviour.   To him you
will flee, and to him may you say, "Dear Lord,
my youth is thine.   I gladly yield to thee the
best of my hasty life; gladly for thy sake renounce
a deceiving world.   For, O! what didst thou not

yield up for me! It is but a few false vanities that I resign, when resigning the world for thee; and while I part with a little dross, in thee I shall find inestimable treasures. Blessed Jesus, thou didst part with real happiness on my account. Brighter glories, than thy angels wear, thou didst resign for me. Thou didst forego on my account, nobler joys than those to which I aspire in thy presence. Take then my youth. Too much of it has already been lost; but, Lord, accept its remains; and let not another of my days be spent in the service of a world, that murdered thee; or of thy great enemy and mine. "Love so amazing, so divine," as is thy love, demands my youth, "my soul, my life, my all."

Thus, my young friend, if true piety is yours, must you renounce all that religion opposes; thus change your object, your master, and your way; and thus devote yourself altogether to him, who died on your account. Without this, to hope for heaven, is as distracted as it would be, if you threw yourself from the top of a precipice, to hope that you should not fall. It is hoping against hope. The word of God is plain, that, without conversion, there is no salvation.

§ 16. Many persons eminent for piety, when devoting themselves to the Lord, have done so in a written form of solemn self-dedication; and many pious divines have recommended this practice. The following is a short form of this kind, a copious and excellent one is given in Doddridge's Rise and Progress of Religion in the Soul.

Great and ever blessed God, I humbly approach thee, to engage myself to thee in a covenant that I hope shall never be forgotten. Feeling that everlasting salvation is of more consequence to me than a thousand worlds could be, and knowing that I am under infinite obligations to yield up myself to thee, I solemnly declare, that I take thee as my God.

I sincerely renounce this present evil world: I will not seek my portion in it; and its sinful customs, vanities, and delights, I give up; while in the world, it shall be my part, to live as not of it, but as a traveller to a heavenly country.

I solemnly take thee as my Father; in thy favour and love I will seek my happiness, and in thy presence my rest. I yield up myself to thee, to be disposed of according to thy will, and to be governed by thy laws.

I receive the Lord Jesus Christ as my Saviour; I confess myself an unworthy and miserable sinner; I look upon thee, O Lord Jesus, as sent by God to suffer for me; as my atoning Saviour I receive thee, and would rest all my hopes on thy atoning death and perfect righteousness; and I give up myself to thee, to be thy disciple and to follow thee.

As solemnly would I give up myself to the Holy Spirit as my Sanctifier; praying that his divine illuminations may enlighten my mind, and his powerful influences completely change my heart. By his teaching I would be taught, and his influence I will seek.

Thus I give up the world for thee, O my God: and solemnly yield up myself, body, and soul, and spirit, to thee, O Father, as my Father; to the Son, as my Saviour; to the Holy Spirit, as my Sanctifier: and now, with thee for my witness, I confirm this holy engagement.

And, O blessed God, I enter into it *solemnly;* for, I do it as in thy sight.

Fully; for, I make no secret reservation, but would be entirely thine.

Freely; for, no constraint compels me, but it is the choice to which thy grace has led me.

Deliberately; for, I have considered what I am now doing.

And *for ever;* for, this is the choice to which, by thy help, I will adhere till death removes me to meet my God.

PRAYER FOR A YOUNG PERSON, DESIROUS OF COMING TO GOD AND CHRIST FOR HAPPINESS.

Blessed and glorious God, thou art the happiness of heaven; and saints and angels find eternal good in thee. All thy family, in those mansions above, are satisfied in thy likeness, and drink of the river of thy pleasures. Thin is the veil which separates me from the eternal world; but, wide the gulf that would have divided me from their society, their pleasures, and their praise. A guilty child of man, I knew thee not. Corrupt and averse to good, I sought thee not. Ignorant and blind, I walked in darkness; and, yet, I thought I saw. Enslaved as the wretch that is bound in fetters of iron, and helpless as he who has lost every limb, I still knew not my captivity, and felt not my helplessness. Thus, gracious God, I might have continued, till the flames of hell had flashed before my departed and trembling spirit, if thy mercy had not interposed. But, O, eternal praises to thy name! that thou hast pitied, that thou hast helped a creature lost like me! Glory be to thee, that I hear of mercy! Glory in the highest, that thy Son has brought it to the world! For this shall thy praises be prolonged, through successive ages, till the last

trumpet shall summon thy children to the worship of a better world.   Surely the praises of
eternity will be too few for compassion like thine;
and the glowing offering of the hosts of heaven
cold, compared with the fervour of thy love.
Great God, I praise thee for mercy! I praise
thee for thy Son! Thou hast marked out the
way of life.   Thou hast shown the path of peace.
Thou hast assured me, that by thy grace he tasted
"death for every man;" that "he was wounded
for our transgressions, and bruised for our iniquities."

Now, O my God, let this blessed Redeemer be
my way to thee. Without thee, earth is but a
wilderness; and heaven, without thee, would be
no longer heaven. Thy presence can cheer the
darkest gloom; change night to day; and pain
to ease: sorrow to delight; poverty to riches; and
death to life. Thy presence can make the martyr's dungeon fairer than the monarch's palace;
and the sad stillness of the chamber of death
more pleasing than the voice of melody. Thy
love can make the dismal grave a more welcome
habitation, than the most cheerful dwelling
where harmony and affection abide. Thy love
is a treasure, compared with which the wealth
of worlds were poverty; and, O, a treasure,
which the enmity of worlds could never take
away! Thy presence darkens all terrestrial
glory, and makes earthly beauty charm no more.
To know thee, to love thee, and delight in thee,
is a heaven below, a heaven even in the midst
of conflicts and pain ; but, O, what a heaven is
theirs, who know thee, and love thee, and rejoice in thee in heaven itself! Great God, may
this happiness be mine! May I, a sinful child

of sinful man, a worm, a leaf, a shade, aspire so high! May I presume to call thee, the eternal JEHOVAH, mine! Ah! Lord, I may. Years ago I might; but, I slighted thee, and this unspeakable blessedness. O! well might my heart sicken, and my head grow dizzy, with shame and horror, to think of having slighted thee! But, now no more, O gracious Lord! I would act the prodigal's part no more. I come to thee; be thou my blessedness, or none will ever be mine. I come to thee; teach all my heart to bow before thee. Let love draw me to thy throne. Let faith repose on thy promises. Let submission make thy pleasure mine. Let me be a wanderer no more. Take the remainder of my youth, and let my life, longer or shorter, be all thy own.

And thou, O blessed Saviour, thou art revealed to me as the way to happiness, to heaven, and God. To thee I come for life, and help, and every good. Thy precious blood was shed for me. Thy righteousness is sufficient to clothe my guilty soul. I am nothing. I have nothing to present to thee, but what is unworthy of thy notice. My prayers, my praises, my holiest actions, need to be sprinkled with thy atoning blood. But, didst thou not come to save the lost! and I am lost. Art not thou the way, the truth, and the life! Be thou my life. Wash me in thy all-cleansing blood. Form me to thine image. Come, possess my heart, and by thy Spirit dwell in me. Guilty, let me flee to thy blood. Helpless, let me lean on thy arm; and worthy of destruction only, let me plead thy death before thy judgment throne. Act as my intercessor above; and make me thy humble friend below. I would sit at thy feet, and learn of thee; and, while I trust thy death, would wear thy image, and reflect, in some humble degree, thy lovely likeness. Like thee, may I be patient, humble, meek. Like thee, may I requite evil with kindness, and enmity with love. To thee may my life, my all be consecrated; and may death appear but a kind messenger, sent to fetch me to thyself. From this hour may my youth, my health, my strength be thine. May thy love animate me; thy precepts guide, and thy example direct me; thy promises cheer, and thy cautions warn me; thy hand support me; and, at the last, let me lean my dying head on thy compassionate arm, and find death swallowed up in victory. — Then may I praise thee in those brighter courts, for that grace which discovers to me the way of life, and which inclines me now to yield my fair but fleeting youth to thee.

But what, great God, am I! and what my resolutions and desires! Alas! I am weak as a reed, and my resolutions have been like the morning cloud or the early dew; yet, let me plead with thee, for thy promised Spirit. Hast thou not promised, that thou wilt give the Holy Spirit to them that ask thee? Bestow on me his sacred influences. With them water and refresh my soul. Let his holy motions incline me to every gracious act and desire. My soul is naturally like a dark and barren desert; but, blessed with his influences, the darkness will disperse, and the wilderness will blossom as the rose. He must teach me to know thee, or I shall never know thee aright. He must teach me to love thee, or divine love will be for ever a stranger to my breast. He must discover to me all the excellencies of my great Redeemer; for, without his teaching, all other would be in vain. Great and blessed God, give me thy Holy Spirit, and let me yield my heart to his sweet and gentle guidance. Let him lead me into all important truth. Let him fashion my soul anew; and create in me a clean heart; and renew a right spirit within me. By him, may all those dispositions that shall flourish in heaven, be formed within my soul during its abode on earth.

Father of all mercies, hear and grant my requests, for the sake of Jesus Christ. *Amen.*

CHAPTER V.

CAUTIONS AGAINST SOME DELUSIVE SUPPORTS, ON WHICH MANY REST THEIR HOPES TO THEIR ETERNAL RUIN.

§. 1. IT is extremely evident, from the word of God, that many fatally deceive themselves, with respect to their spiritual state. They say to themselves, *Peace, peace;* while God declares, *there is no peace* to persons in their condition. Like a captive, who dreams of liberty; but, wakes and sees the horrid walls of his dungeon around him: so they indulge the hope of heaven, till death puts an end to the deceitful dream; they awake in eternity, and find themselves for ever undone. Such is the deceitfulness of the human heart, that you cannot too solicitously guard against its delusions, and those of the world, that would blast all your hopes of happiness, and cover you with confusion and horror, when expecting joy and glory.

§ 2. One of the most common is, the belief, that all those are Christians who bear the Christian name, whose lives are virtuous, and whose deportment and temper are lovely. But, alas. all this is found in thousands, who know nothing of real religion; and, with respect to eternity, all these fair appearances and pleasing recommendations will avail not, if there be not true piety within. Perhaps this can scarcely be made more evident, than by referring you to the history of one, who possessed these qualifications in no common degree, but who still wanted the one thing needful.

In Matt. C. 19, Mark, C. 10, or Luke, C. 11, an instance of this kind is recorded. "When the Lord had gone forth into the way, there came one (a young ruler) running, and kneeled to him, and asked him, Good master, what shall I do, that I may inherit eternal life?" He was so moral a person, that he could say, with respect to many of the commandments of God (at least as far as his outward conduct was concerned), "all these have I observed from my youth." " And Jesus beholding him, loved him; and said, One thing thou lackest; go thy way, sell whatsoever thou hast, and give to the poor, and thou shalt have treasure in heaven; and come, take up the cross and follow me. And he was sad at that saying, and went away grieved. He was very sorrowful, for he was very rich." There cannot be a reasonable doubt, that this young man was in a state of sin and death, notwithstanding all that seemed so promising and fair; and, perhaps, this little history is recorded, to show how far a person may go in morality and a concern for religion, and yet fall short of heaven. There are but few.

in the morning of life, so amiable, and, according to worldly views, so good as this young man; and, yet, with much that was lovely, he was a stranger to real piety. He came running to the Lord, to inquire how he might reach a better world. Thus he manifested earnestness and humility. He was not ashamed to seek instruction, but went to Jesus with that most serious question, "What shall I do that I may inherit eternal life?" His thoughtfulness about eternity was the more observable, as he was rich, and exposed to the snares that accompany wealth. Justly has it been observed, "that his concern about his soul was not a sick-bed meditation, for he was in health; nor a melancholy qualm of old age, for he was young; nor was it the effect of his being discontented and out of humour with the world, for he was rich and prosperous." The manner often recommends the action; and there was much that was pleasing in his manner. Though possessed of wealth and honour, and coming to one that appeared poor and despised; yet, he used no haughty freedom, but approached his instructor with humility and respect. Besides all this, there was something more substantial in his character. Instead of running into licentiousness and riot, he had attended to the divine commandments. His life had been moral; he had been a dutiful son; was most probably affectionate and kind; and doubtless had secured the esteem of his friends; when even the Lord saw so much that was pleasing in him, that, beholding him, he loved him. But, when the blessed Saviour put him to the test, whether he would part with all for Christ and heaven, then his heart failed him: and he showed, that with so much that was lovely about him, he still was in reality a lover of this world; and if **any** man, young or aged, wicked or virtuous, "if any man love the world, the love of the Father is not in him." Yet, even the manner of his departure proved the interest he took in the question he had proposed; he went away grieved, and was very sorrowful. In short, he was such a one, that we may readily wish all young persons were like him; and, yet, he was such a one, that we must wish them to be much more than he was. In the general, you may learn from this affecting little history, that all which may gain the esteem of man, will be of no avail, as to the salvation of your immortal soul, if that true piety, which leads the soul to count all things loss for Christ, be wanting.

Having taken a brief view of this instructive case, let me lead your thoughts to a few more particular cautions.

§ 3. Guard against their dreadful delusion, who put a knowledge of some sacred truths in the place of religion itself. Many such self-deceivers abound in the world. They can discourse on the hallowed themes of the gospel; but, are strangers to its influence and power. To hear them talk, you might think them Christians; to see them act, you might suppose them heathens. The word of God declares, that all knowledge without charity (or love), is vain, and that its possessor is nothing. Fallen and infernal spirits probably know much more of some sacred subjects than the most eminent Christians in this life, yet they are devils still.

§ 4. Watch against resting your eternal hopes on outward privileges. You live in what is term-

1 John, ii. 15.　　　　1 Cor. xiii. 2.

ed a Christian land, but this does not make you a Christian; for a true Christian is a child of God "by faith in Christ Jesus." The young ruler was favoured with outward privileges. The inhabitants of Capernaum had enjoyed them; but sunk the deeper in hell through abusing them. And many, who ate and drank in the presence of Christ himself, and in whose streets he taught, will hear him say, "Depart from me, all ye workers of iniquity." The man without the wedding garment had been invited to the gospel feast; though his dreadful doom was outer darkness, where there is weeping and gnashing of teeth. Perhaps you, my young friend, have enjoyed all the privileges of a pious education; yet think not that these will take you to heaven. You must be born again. Your parents' prayers will not fix you in glory, if you do not learn to pray. Your parents' faith will not be accounted yours Though you should have had parents as pious, and as beloved by God, as Abraham himself; yet the language of the divine word is, "Think not to say within yourselves, we have Abraham to our father, for I say unto you, that God is able of these stones to raise up children unto Abraham;" and not merely is he able, but sooner would he do so than violate his word, by admitting an unconverted soul to heaven. Many parents will be found at the right-hand of Christ, whose children will never join them there; and many children who found the way to glory, though their parents lost it.

§ 5. Trust not, my young friend, your eternal hopes to the strictest attention to the outward

Gal. iii. 26.   Matt. xi. 23, 24.   Luke, xiii. 27.   Matt. xxii. 13.
Matt. iii. 9.

forms and duties of religion. Though you should say, All these have I observed from my youth; yet this observance is not a foundation on which to rest for eternity. O eternity, eternity! who can be anxious enough to build their hopes aright, when building for eternity! Perhaps, from your infant days, the house of God may have been your resort. Perhaps, few sabbaths could be named, on which you have not been there. Perhaps, in your chamber, or your closet, your morning and evening devotions have been regularly paid. Possibly, few days could be found, in which from your earliest childhood to the present period, you have missed this stated offering to heaven. Perhaps, you are disposed to ask, What more can I want? Alas! you may have done all this, and yet want every thing that most concerns you. You may want a new heart, and an interest in Jesus Christ. The Christian cannot live without prayer; but some attention to its outward forms does not make a Christian. God, it is true, may have had your words, but who has had your thoughts? Who has had your heart? Has he had these too? Have not these often been employed on other subjects, when, on your knees, you professed to be engaged with God? While some have passed months and years without prayer, you may have constantly attended to religious duties; but how little earnestness, how little sincerity, how little life, has there been in them! Consider how often, in private, you have knelt down and rose again, without a serious thought of God; how often, in public, you have listened with careless indifference: and then think, whether you, too, may not be said to have spent days and months without prayer; and whether you have not really resembled those, who live without God in the world. But if your devotions have been ever so fervent and sincere, still they are not the foundation for a sinner's hope. Jesus alone is that foundation.

§ 6. Trust not your eternal all to the greatest freedom from open vice, and to, what the world might term, an innocent life. You have already been shown, that there is no life so innocent as to give a well-founded hope of meeting God with comfort; that the young, as well as the aged, without a Saviour, are undone for ever; and that what the world esteems almost an innocent life, is, in the sight of God, a life of base ingratitude and iniquity. Perhaps, the open vices which ruin many, have not debased your character. Perhaps, the impious profanations of the swearer never escaped your lips. Perhaps, the excesses of the drunkard or the libertine have not polluted you. Perhaps, your tongue has usually uttered truth, and the arts of the liar have been unknown to you. You may have been free from these and other open vices; yet this cannot give you the faintest well-founded hope of acquittal at the great day of judgment, for you have sins, and it is impossible to express the evil of the smallest sin. Christ represents those whose sins are least and fewest, as owing to God ten thousand talents; none owe less, though some may owe more. Thus the most virtuous and the most abandoned, in the sight of God, approach much nearer to each other in guilt than you probably imagine. Trust not, then, to any fancied freedom from sin. It can hardly be urged on you too earnestly, that a single unpardoned sin is sufficient to damn a soul to all eternity. Did not one sin sink angels from heaven? Did not one, that would now be termed a little sin, turn Adam out of Paradise?

§ 7. Rest not your everlasting all upon the goodness or morality of your life. Morality is a lovely thing; it will adorn, but it cannot make a Christian. A person may be moral, yet a stranger to religion ; but cannot be religious, and not be moral. Various causes may produce morality of conduct, while the heart is altogether estranged from God. The young ruler, already mentioned, could say, respecting an outward attention to many of the commandments of God, All these have I observed from my youth ; yet he was perishing in sin. In his case, you see how moral may be the life, how lovely the deportment, how earnest after religion, the desires of one, who, after all, may fall short of religion, and thus fall short of glory. Has your morality been stricter than his? has your deportment been more amiable, or your desire after eternal life more earnest? If not, how can you hope for heaven on this ground, when he had all these, and yet was in the way to hell?

§ 8. If you should not rest your eternal hopes on any of these things, much less should you on any other amiable qualifications.

Many young persons are possessed of a variety of these, who are destitute of all true piety. Though they trifle with God and eternity, yet affection to relatives and friends seems to dwell in their hearts. Cheerfulness and good-humour beam from their countenances, and the accomplishments of science adorn their minds. All they seem to want is the one thing needful ; but wanting that, as to the eternal world, they want every thing. Only the recommendations of that humble piety, which makes Jesus all in all, would avail them there. The charms of religion only will bloom beyond the grave; those of person, of disposition, of deportment, will not long keep their power to please. Where true piety is absent, these are momentary attractions, that must shortly fade, and leave no trace behind. Very quickly the most sensible tongue will be as silent as the most silly. Loveliness and deformity will be alike in the grave; and those of the most amiable manners, and most engaging deportment, there be on an equality with the savage and the brute. The charms of beauty, of manners, of wit, may adorn the young in their hasty journey to an endless world; but religion only will prepare them for a heavenly home. Those may glitter on the casket; but only that will beautify the jewel. If then, my young friend, you would know your real state, examine not from what pollutions you may have been kept free; not what moral duties you have practised; not what religious ordinances you may have regarded; or with what attractions you may be adorned: but inquire, are you acquainted with the sinfulness of your own heart? Have you ever experienced repentance towards God? Have you ever committed your helpless soul to the Lord Jesus Christ? and sought your happiness and eternal good in him? If you are a stranger to all this, you are a stranger to religion.

§ 9. I may not improperly add, that if you would guard against deception on this most momentous of all subjects, you should endeavour to fix on your mind an abiding impression of the absolute necessity of real conversion. Consider, that without this you cannot be saved. The words of Christ are, "Verily, verily, I say unto thee, except a man be born of water and the Spirit, he cannot enter into the kingdom of God:" (John, iii. 5.) He does not say, except a man be virtuous in his habits, or moral in his life, or except he attend the outward ordinances of religion, he cannot see the kingdom of God; for all this he may mind, and never reach heaven: but, "Except a man be born of the Spirit, he cannot enter into the kingdom of God." He represents that divine change which passes on the hearts of all those that come to God by him, as essential to the happiness of your soul. By his atoning death, he removed the obstacles to your happiness that lay on God's part; and, by conversion, would remove those which spring from yourself. Be assured, on God's authority, there is no new-discovered way to heaven. The path is marked out. Repent, and flee from the wrath to come. Believe, and yield thyself to Christ.

§ 10. A MEDITATION ON THE SUBJECT OF THIS CHAPTER, CONCLUDING WITH A PRAYER.

And is it indeed true, O my soul, that the way of life is thus narrow! And can it be, that with so much to adorn the outward character, the heart may still remain in the gall of bitterness, and in the bonds of iniquity! Awakening truth! let it awaken thee. It is thy Judge that says, Wide is the gate and broad is the way that leadeth to destruction, and many there be which go in thereat. It is he that tells thee, that many are called, but few chosen. Wilt thou trifle with his word! Wilt thou deceive thyself, and hope against hope, when vast eternity shall be the measure of thy sufferings or joys, and when the smile or the frown of thy God awaits thee! Wert thou now going into his presence, where would the next hour find thee? O my soul, thou must appear before that Judge, whose eyes are as a flame of fire; who knows all thy secret sins, and from whom the minutest circumstance cannot be concealed: and what plea can I present to gain his pity? Shall I tell him that some knowledge of himself has been mine; that, unlike the perishing heathen, I called him Lord? but, has not he said, " Not every one that saith unto me, Lord, Lord, shall enter into the kingdom of heaven." Would not this plea for mercy aggravate my guilt, and cause even the heathen to rise in the judgment against me to condemn me! They knew him not, and could not love him; but I heard of him, and *would* not love him. Or should I plead the privileges I have enjoyed? Should I tell him of parents, now in heaven, whose prayers ascended to his throne for me? but, alas! my abused privileges double all my guilt. Should I plead with him that my life has been fair, my deportment lovely, my temper kind, my conduct just? but can all this extenuate my rebellion against him, and my forgetfulness of God? I know how vain, how very vain, it would be for a criminal arraigned for murder and treason, to plead in his defence, that though certainly guilty of these crimes; yet that he had never stolen a flower from his neighbour's garden, or an apple from his orchard: nor will it more avail me, when charged with ingratitude to my best benefactor, with rebellion against my God, to plead, in excuse for those vilest of sins, my kindness to my fellow-worms.

How solemn is the warning given me, from his sad condition, whose history I have been considering! How lovely was his deportment! how moral his conduct! how pleasing his early desire to find the way to life eternal! yet I have seen that *the one thing* he still wanted. And hast thou, my soul, that one thing? hast thou even as much to plead as he? Can I say with him, All these have I kept from my youth? Have I, in a humbler sphere, as seriously inquired the way to life and peace, as he did, in the midst of the ensnarements of riches and power? Far as he went, he did not go so far as to become a Christian altogether; and what am I, whose concern for religion has been so much less fervent, whose outward conduct so much less conformed to the will of God? What then wilt thou do, O my soul? canst thou bear to be banished from the realms of joy and love, and to hear thy now compassionate Saviour bid thee depart for ever?

O my God, never let me hear those awful words. Here I bow before thee, and have not one plea for mercy, drawn from any thing in myself, which would deserve thy notice. But stripped of every other, let this be my plea, that Jesus died for me a sinner. Thou hast taught me what to do; hast directed me to apply to him for life and peace. In him, thou hast laid a foundation on which I may build for eternity. There let me rest my all.

Wean me altogether from every other dependance. Search me and try me. If I deceive my own soul, discover to me the delusion, and save me from reposing my eternal hopes on any thing, except on the crucified Redeemer. Many, O Lord, are the devious paths of error; while strait is the way of life, yet, though strait, it leads to heaven. In that secure and peaceful path, O God, may I walk. May I be found in Christ. May I abide in him; and by this sacred connexion with him, be blessed in this life and for ever.

And thou, blessed Jesus, be thou my hope and peace, and may I find thee my Almighty Saviour. *Amen.*

CHAPTER VI.

THE WORTH OF THE SOUL A REASON FOR EARLY PIETY.

§ 1. The chief design of the preceding chapters has been to make you sensible of you need of spiritual blessings; and to give you a brief view of the nature of religion. Consider now more fully some of those reasons, which should induce you to embrace religion without delay. And may God enable me to set them before you with that affectionate earnestness and plainness, which become a dying creature, when addressing another who must soon be an inhabitant of heaven or hell!

One most weighty motive, to induce you to give your youth to God, is, that you possess an immortal soul. The body is the inferior part of your nature. Pass away a few short years, and it must mingle with the clods of the valley. By the body you are allied to worms and dust; by the soul, to angels and to God.

It is almost impossible to use words strong enough to express the worth of the soul. Such is its value that a glorious end were answered, if the earth and skies were maintained in being for ten thousand ages, merely to ripen one soul for immortality and heaven; and the labour of myriads of men and angels, through ten thousand thousand years, would be well employed, in directing one lost soul to a Redeemer. One of our poets, when glancing at the starry firmament, and comparing its glories with the soul, remarks with not more fervour than truth —

"Survey that midnight glory! Worlds on worlds!
Amazing pomp! Redouble that amaze!
Ten thousand add; add twice ten thousands more,
Then weigh the whole; *one soul* outweighs them all;
And calls the astonishing magnificence
Of unintelligent creation *poor*."

Another poet, with equal truth and beauty, says,

"The sun is but a spark of fire,
A transient meteor in the sky;
The soul immortal as its Sire,
                    Shall never die."

§ 2. Your soul is immortal. It derived its being from God. If religion be your choice, it will shine brighter than the stars of the firmament, when all those stars are gone out in eternal night.

A few years will finish all your delights, and hopes, and fears, below; then will your soul be fixed where it must live for ever. While you, my young friend, read these lines, the souls of millions are encountering all the sorrows, or are gladdened with all the joys of an endless world. For ages have the bodies of many of them been turned to dust; their very tombstones are mouldered away; but they all live in eternity, though forgotten here; they are hidden from your sight, but are more alive to joy or sorrow, than they ever were upon earth. Soon will the time arrive, when you must meet this solemn change of being; when you must converse with man no more, but must become a companion of angels or of devils. And, O, what is the worth of a soul! that may, through endless ages, shine in heaven, glorious as an angel of light; or which, covered with darkness, misery, and despair, must become a devil, in that lake of fire, where the fire never shall be quenched. O! in pity to your own precious and immortal soul, embrace, without delay, the gospel of your God.

§ 3. The worth of the soul is a subject, on which men of all descriptions have agreed; on which, the best and wisest have had their testimony confirmed, by the most careless and the worst. Martyrs have shown their sense of its value, by all their sufferings to secure its salvation. For this, thousands, as sensible as you of the comforts of life, have willingly forsaken "kindred, country, friends, and ease;" have been tortured on racks, or devoured by beasts of prey; been burned alive, or suffered torments far more intolerable than burning! "And others had trial of cruel mockings and scourgings, yea, moreover, of bonds and imprisonment; they were stoned; were sawn asunder; were tempted; were slain with the sword; they wandered about in sheep-skins and goat-skins; being destitute, afflicted, tormented; of whom the world was not worthy; they wandered in deserts and in mountains, and in dens, and caves of the earth." (Heb. xi. 37.) Impressed with the worth of the soul, many, with these dark scenes before them, have bid farewell to all the allurements of the world, to meet the roughest storms of persecution, face its dangers and sink into the grave beneath them. Yet while some were burning, others were coming forward to take their places in the true spirit of the English martyr, who, at the place of execution, kissed the stake and exclaimed, "Welcome the cross of Christ, welcome everlasting life." Does one of all these martyred myriads repent? Does one now imagine that he suffered more than salvation was worth ! Ah no, if they could now address you, they might tell you, that sooner than lose the soul, they would burn in flames a thousand times hotter; suffer torments a thousand times more protracted; prisons a thousand times more dismal; and meet death, in forms, if possible, a thousand times more terrible. And was it worth their while, to endure so much to reach heaven; and is it not worth yours, in earnestness, to seek ad mittance there?

§ 4. If, after the testimony of such distinguished witnesses, you should hearken to theirs, who have trodden a less brilliant and less suffering path to heaven, their testimony would be the same. Say to the dying Christian, "You are in those circumstances, which enable you to view this world and the next aright; what should I mind?" He, in purport, would reply, "Take care of your soul." A dying saint said, to some friends that visited him, "You come hither to learn to die. I can assure you that your whole life, be it ever so long, is little enough to prepare for death. Have a care of this vain deceitful world, and the lusts of the flesh. Be sure you choose God for your portion; heaven for your home ; God's glory for your end, his word for your rule ; and then you need never fear, but we shall meet with comfort."* Or ask the dying profligate, he who treated all religion as a dream, and the soul as a trifle, say to him, " What shall I chiefly mind ?" and would he not reply, " Take care of your soul, and avoid my folly ; for I have ruined mine." One unhappy man, who had lived in wealth and splendour, but had trifled with eternal things, a short time before death, said, " I had provided in the course of my life, for every thing except death, and now, alas ! I am to die, although entirely unprepared."† Another, who was eminent for his wisdom and learning, but who had been negligent of the great salvation, said, " It is lamentable, that men consider not for what they are born into the world, till they are ready to go out of it."‡ Another, who was distinguished for his talents, his ambition, and his success in gaining worldly honours, not long before his death, cried out, " O my poor soul, what will become of thee ! whither wilt thou go !"§

§ 5. Have you, my young friend, never been in that situation, in which the world appeared a dream, a cheat, a nothing ? Have you never lain upon the bed of sickness, and passed wearisome days and sleepless nights of languor or of pain ? Have you never been in such circumstances as to expect that a few days or weeks would end your mortal course, fix your body in the grave, and your soul in eternity ? and have you forgot what were then your views and feelings ? Did the world appear as enchanting to you then,

---

* Richard Baxter.
† Cæsar Borgia. ‡ Sir T. Smith. § Cardinal Mazarine.

as it does now ? Did the soul and its salvation
then seem a thing of little moment ? Rather did
not the world seem vanity of vanities ? Were you
now on a bed of sickness, or languishing and
dying, would not these be your views ? And
must not you, ere long, be in such a situation ?
And will you not then confess, that the only
thing that deserves your care is the immortal
soul ? O, why neglect it, when you might secure
its salvation ! Why put off entering the way of
life, till that way is shut for ever ? By the testimonies of others to the worth of the soul, and
by the convictions of your own mind, I beseech
you to secure its salvation, by applying, without delay, to the Son of God for life.

§ 6. Reflect on the interest taken in the welfare of your soul by those who are best acquainted with its worth. If you, my young friend,
were to behold a person in danger of death,
and to witness a whole kingdom filled with anxiety on his account ; to see the monarch stooping to the meanest offices of kindness ; all faces
filled with anxiety, all hearts with concern, for
this individual : you might justly believe him to
be one held in the highest estimation. Consider
then, I beseech you, the interest which all the
inhabitants of heaven take in the welfare of the
soul. Angels, those blessed spirits, to whom
all the glory of this world would seem a contemptible dream, are not uninterested where the
soul is concerned. " There is joy in the presence
of the angels of God over one sinner that repenteth." And as they rejoice at the conversion of
a soul ; so they watch, doubtless, with pleasure
over the steps of their future companions above.

Luke, xv. 10.

Sent by their Creator on errands of kindness, they descend to earth, and attend the soul in its progress towards heaven; and when its pilgrimage is concluded, become its convoy to the abodes of blessedness. O my young friend, shall these happy spirits take so much interest in the welfare of your soul; and will you yourself be careless?   Shall they be willing to minister to you as unseen messengers of love; and will you neglect that soul over which they would fain rejoice, whose mortal course they would cheerfully attend, and which they would gladly conduct to the bosom of Christ?

§ 7. But it is not merely the inferior though glorious inhabitants of heaven, whose conduct testifies the worth of the soul. God, the great and blessed God, has so loved the world, as to give his only-begotten Son to be a ransom for the ruined souls of men; and Jesus Christ, the brightness of his Father's glory, has suffered and died to redeem immortal souls from death. Raise your eyes, and view the creation of God. Behold the earth, the moon, the sun, the stars, and all the wonders of the spangled sky; and then consider, that for that soul which you have probably neglected, yet for that neglected soul, the Creator of this splendid train became a man of sorrows and acquainted with grief. O learn, my young friend, the worth of your immortal spirit, from what passed on Calvary in its behalf! See the God of glory resigning his best beloved to unbridled fury, stripes, and death; to the torturing cross, the bloody spear, and the dismal grave! See the patient Son of God, patient amidst enemies foaming with rage and breath-

See Ps. xci. 11 — Heb. i. 14 — Luke, xvi. 22.

ing out cruelty; see him there accomplishing what none but he could perform, and bearing a load of human guilt and sorrow, more vast and dreadful than any tongue can tell. See this, and learn the value of your soul more strongly than a whole creation could represent it to you. The creation is worthless, compared with its glorious Maker; but its Maker bled for us. O, that I could, with the earnestness of a dying man, urge upon you the worth of a soul ransomed by such a price! A soul lost is more than a world destroyed. Compared with this loss, the destruction of this vast world will be a trifle. Never did its Creator assume human nature, and die for its preservation from the final flames; but O, a spirit, an immortal spirit, a spirit for which Jesus died, if this is lost, what ruin, what misery is this! You gaze upon a dying world, and, engaged with its trifles, perhaps forget the immortal visitant within, forget that you have a soul which shall outlive the grasp of death, the bounds of time; but, O, forget its worth no more! Well might you wonder that such a treasure should inhabit a little piece of breathing clay. And can it be to you a matter of little moment, whether your immortal soul be saved or lost? Can you treat this as a thing of small importance, when the great God has stooped so low, and resigned so much, to open for you a way to happiness. He has withheld nothing that was needed to save you. No higher, nobler gift did heaven itself contain, than what he gave. Can you, will you, any longer treat that salvation with indifference, which the Son of God freely offers you, and which he purchased for you at the expense of nis throne, his happiness, and his life? O! danger, very, very, very dreadful, from which such a Saviour came to relieve us! O blessed, blessed salvation, which was obtained at so dear a rate! O precious, invaluably precious souls, for which such a price was paid! Such a soul is yours. You have one, for which the Son of God in torture died, and heaven lost its bright inhabitant. Such is the value which God has set upon your soul; but, my young friend, how have you valued it? Perhaps, if poor, you have laboured earnestly for to-morrow's bread, but never spent an hour's care on your immortal spirit; or, perhaps, if in easier circumstances, you have followed dress, gaiety, and pleasure, careless what became of your soul in that dreadful eternity, to which it hastes. O, act this wretched part no longer; but now make early piety your choice! Let not the blessed God be so anxious for your everlasting welfare, and you as careless of it.

§ 8. As thus, in the most affecting manner, the Father and the Son have declared the value of the soul; so also, my young friend, learn the same, from all which the blessed Spirit does for the salvation of sinful men. He strives with them. It is by his light that they discern the Father and the Son. Has not he exerted his power in your heart? Have not you felt those convictions of sin and folly, those devout impressions, and salutary desires, which really came from above? Has not the still small voice within, as it were, said to you, "Turn to God; forsake the world; your ways lead to misery, they will be bitterness in the end; follow religion and be happy." Have not you banished the warning, and quenched the holy thoughts and desires, thus given you from above? Yet has he left you? Has not your conscience been alarmed; and these sacred impressions repeated again and again? Why does the blessed Spirit thus strive with you? Why did he not take your first repulse, and leave you for ever? Why has he followed you with these salutary warnings? You did not seek them. Why has he made your heart at times almost begin to melt? Why let you feel the sting of sin? Why alarmed you at your situation? Why showed you your danger? Why induced you at times, if you would go no further, yet to wish you were a Christian? To wish that you were like some that you perhaps know? Why has the blessed Spirit bestowed all this care on a poor, thoughtless, ungrateful creature, whose heart has been shut against his gentle influence? Why, my young friend, but because he wishes you well for ever? God would not have you perish. Shall angels, shall the Father, Son, and Holy Ghost, all, all be filled with concern for the welfare of your soul, and will you slight that soul yourself?

§ 9. If, to all this evidence of the worth of your soul, I add more, it shall be, that even the malice of devils may teach you the value of your soul. You are taught, in the word of God, that Satan walketh about as a roaring lion, seeking whom he may devour. You are assured that he comes and takes away the seed sown in the careless heart; and that we have to wrestle with the rulers of the darkness of this world. The word of God represents his power as great; his influence is extensive; his devices are many.

1 Peter, v. 8.   Matt. xiii. 19.   Ephes. vi. 12.

Some he tempts to presumption, others to despair; and in a thousand different ways strives to keep the sons of men fast in his hellish chains.* But though the devil is a fallen and infernal spirit, you have no reason to doubt that he was once one of an exalted rank. He knows what heaven is, for he has lost it; he knows what immortality is, for he is doomed to it; and his artifices, his assaults, his watchfulness, his activity, in the dreadful work of destruction, prove how highly he values the immortal soul. It is a prize which he thinks worth his care and labour. No watchfulness seems to him too much for the accomplishment of its ruin. Though you may be inactive, he is activity itself. Though you may be negligent and slothful, in seeking the salvation of your soul, he is watchful and diligent in seeking its destruction.

A PRAYER IMPLORING A DEEPER SENSE OF THE VALUE OF THE SOUL, WITH A DEVOUT COMMITTAL OF IT TO THE SAVIOUR'S CARE.

O thou Almighty Father of Spirits, by thee this curious mortal frame of mine was formed, and from thee my immortal spirit came. Thou didst create man to bear more of the image of thyself, than any besides of these thy lower works. Thou didst breathe into him the breath of life, by which he became a living soul; while all thy other creatures here, are the creatures of a day. From thee have I received a soul, that must live through an eternity, as lasting as thy own. I know, O Lord, that it is appointed unto all men once to die; and I, ere long, must sink

* The young reader is recommended to read Brookes's Precious Remedies against Satan's Devices, a truly excellent little work.

beneath the stroke of death. These hands will forget to labour. These eyes will need the cheering light of day no more. This tongue will be silent. This heart will be filled with fear or love no longer. These limbs will become cold in death; none on earth will be concerned with me, nor I with them; but the worm will crawl and feed upon this flesh of mine, or corruption consume it, "till not one wretched trace remains resembling me!" But, O my God! that soul which thou hast made the tenant of this dying frame, must defy the power of death; must spring forward into new and unknown scenes; must behold the glories or terrors of the invisible world; while eternity, vast, boundless, joyful, or dreadful eternity, becomes the only limit of my suffering or happiness. With this prospect before me, let me prize my soul as a treasure, compared with which all the treasures of a thousand worlds were emptier than a bauble and lighter than vanity. O, let me feel its worth as I shall do on the bed of death! O, let me know its value as they have done who gladly bore prisons, and flames, and martyrdom, in every dreadful form, that they might but keep their immortal spirits safe beneath their Redeemer's care; and who thought all their sorrows well repaid, by landing on the peaceful shore of heaven! O, let me feel the value of my immortal soul, as they have done who trifled with theirs, till their day of grace was gone; and who then, in confusion, agony, and horror, bewailed their dreadful sin! Lord, may I learn from the joyful or sad experience of others, not to slight thy love! Thou hast cared for my eternal welfare, and thought no sacrifice too costly when the happiness of my immortal spirit was at stake. Let endless praises be paid thee for thy condescending kindness, praises as lasting and as fervent as thy love. Bless the Lord, O my soul. who redeemed *thy* life from destruction. And now, O Lord, may thy Holy Spirit, whose grace I have so often resisted, whose teachings I have so often slighted, may he possess this soul of mine, and make it a temple worthy of himself. Shed abroad thy sanctifying influences upon me, implant every grace within me, and train up my deathless soul for that holy and happy world, where I shall never be tainted with sin, or feel pain or sorrow more.

Blessed Jesus, thou hast died to set my spirit free from condemnation to eternal death : and take this precious jewel, and keep it safe beneath thy tender care. I cannot guard it from its ravenous foes. They seek its destruction ; but, almighty Saviour, they cannot tear the soul away that is lodged within thy protecting arms. To thee would I commit mine. It is the purchase of thy blood ! and thou wilt keep what I commit unto thee. Guard my soul from every foe, while I am a pilgrim here ; and, in my departing hour, may I see heaven opened, and expire with the dying prayer of thy first Martyr on my lips, "Lord Jesus, receive my spirit." *Amen.*

CHAPTER VII.

THE IMPORTANCE OF RELIGION FURTHER SHOWN, BY REFERENCE TO THE COUNSEL OF THE MOST HIGH, CONTAINED IN HIS WORD.

§. 1   ON all subjects in which eternity is

concerned, the word of God is our surest guide. Do not you profess to believe that word? By it your views should be regulated, as by it your conduct will be judged. A distinguished Christian, who is gone to his eternal rest, referring to the scriptures, justly says, "I have thought I am a creature of a day, passing through life as an arrow through the air. I am a spirit come from God, and returning to God; just hovering over the great gulf, till, a few moments hence, I am no more seen: I drop into an unchangeable eternity. I want to know *one thing*, the way to heaven; how to land safe on that happy shore. God himself has condescended to teach the way. For this very end he came from heaven. He hath written it down in a book. O, give me that book! At any price give me the book of God! I have it; here is knowledge enough for me. Let me be *homo unius libri*, (the man of one book.) Here then I am, far from the busy ways of men; I sit down alone, only God is here. In his presence I open, I read *his* book; for this end, to find the way to heaven." What this pious writer felt himself to be, you, my young friend, are now; a creature hastening to eternity, as fast as an arrow darts through the air, or as a shuttle through the loom: and will you not make that sacred book your guide? It teaches you that religion is true wisdom, and all else folly. That this is the *one thing needful*, the *good part*. It teaches you to seek this, whatever you lose by pursuing it; to embrace it, though at the expense of all you possess; to hold it fast, though that or life must be resigned. It teaches you, that in possessing the blessings of religion, you would possess every good ; and that the want of them is worse than hunger, poverty, or pain, prisons, or martyrdom. That if you enjoy the Saviour's love, it is a matter of very little importance what you suffer ; for here will be found enough to make amends for all : and that if you have not this, it signifies little what you possess ; for the want of this is the want of every thing tha⁺ is worth the thoughts or wishes of an immortal soul.

§ 2. The judgment of the blessed God, as to the importance of real piety, and of piety in youth, is solemnly given in his word. There his beloved Son and his inspired messengers speak in his name to you ; and, God of mercy ! give my youthful readers grace to listen to those admonitions of thine, that I would now repeat to them. Behold then, my young friend, "Behold the fear of the Lord, that is wisdom ; and to depart from evil is understanding. The fear of the Lord is the beginning of wisdom ; a good understanding have all they that do his commandments. Seek ye the Lord while he may be found. Call ye upon him while he is near. Let the wicked forsake his way, and the unrighteous man his thoughts. What shall it profit a man, if he gain the whole world and lose his own soul. One thing is needful. Seek ye first the kingdom of God and his righteousness. Enter ye in at the strait gate. Strive to enter in ; because strait is the gate and narrow is the way that leadeth unto life, and few there be that find it. Ye must be born again. Behold the Lamb of God. Believe on the Lord Jesus

Job, xxviii. 21.   Ps. cxi. 10.   Is. lv. 6, 7.   Mark, viii. 36.   Luke, x. 42.
Matt. vi. 33.   Matt. vii. 13.   Luke, xiii. 24.   Matt. vii. 14.
      John, iii. 7.   John, i. 36.   Acts, xvi. 31,

Christ. Fight the good fight of faith. Lay hold on eternal life. Be diligent, that ye may be found of him in peace, without spot and blameless. Let us labour, therefore, to enter into rest. Remember now thy Creator in the days of thy youth. I love them that love me; and they that seek me early shall find me. O, that they were wise, that they understood this, that they would consider their latter end! Fear not them which kill the body, and after that have no more that they can do: but I will forewarn you whom ye shall fear; fear him, who, after he hath killed, hath power to cast into hell; yea, I say unto you, fear him. Lay not up for yourselves treasures upon earth; but lay up for yourselves treasures in heaven, where neither moth nor rust doth corrupt, and where thieves do not break through nor steal."

§ 3. Are not these important admonitions the admonitions of your God? Religion is the blessing which they teach you to choose; a blessing which makes the poorest rich, and without which the wealthiest are poor. Notice a few scriptural admonitions more fully. The Lord Jesus gave it as his solemn and deliberate judgment, that *one thing is needful.* He made this impressive declaration to one who loved him, and whom he loved, "One thing is needful." Compared with it, all that man deems most important is an insignificant trifle: his wisdom, folly; his business and cares, laborious idling; his pomps and pleasures as vain as the plays of children, and his possessions as worthless as their toys. But one thing is needful. All that

1 Tim. vi. 12.   2 Pet. iii. 14.   Heb. iv. 11.   Eccles. xii. 1.
Prov. viii. 17.   Deut. v. 29.   Luke, xii. 5.   Matt. vi. 19, 20.

has agitated the generations of men for six thousand years; all that has engaged their hearts and employed their fleeting days, compared with this, is needless, is lighter than the driven chaff, emptier than the bursting bubble, and vainer than the flying shadow.

The same divine speaker said, "Labour not for the meat that perisheth, but for that which endureth unto everlasting life." He did not mean to forbid a proper regard to the duties of this life, but to command a far superior attention to the concerns of the soul; and he assigns an important reason for conduct which the world deems madness. Clothing and food, the body which they cherish, and even the world on which they are enjoyed, must shortly perish, and the time in which they are possessed is like the twinkling of an eye; but the blessings of salvation endure to everlasting life; and the soul that has these shall enjoy them through an eternity so boundless, that, compared with it, ages, as numerous as the drops of the sea, and one fleeting moment are alike: both so short, that placed by the side of eternity, their difference would be imperceptible, both would be nothing there. Similar to this is the commandment, "Seek ye FIRST the kingdom of God and his righteousness." Jesus had been speaking of food and raiment, those blessings so important to this life, and then he added, "seek ye FIRST the kingdom of God and his righteousness;" as if he had said, "Let thy earliest and thy chief care be to gain a title to the kingdom of God, and an interest in the Redeemer's righteousness. Prefer this not merely to worldly vanities and follies, but to the most important earthly bless-

M

ings; and be more concerned to possess this than the food that supports, or the raiment that protects, that feeble body of thine."

§ 4. While the divine Saviour thus teaches you to prize spiritual blessings, he directs you to view this world as vanity; to live above it; to expect and seek but little from it. The language of his word is, " The time is short, let those that have wives, be as though they had none; and they that weep, as though they wept not; and they that rejoice, as though they rejoiced not; and they that buy, as though they possessed not; and they that use this world, as not abusing it, for the fashion of this world passeth away." Is it possible, my young friend, in a more impressive manner to remind you, that as this world is a nothing, and the next every thing to an immortal soul, the next should be your choice? The happy and the afflicted, the aged and the young, the noble and the mean, are all travellers to eternity; and to them all, the time is short. It is so to you. Are you then possessed of the most endeared and affectionate relatives? have them as though you had them not; let not them or their affection p   ent your heart from rising to nobler friends above. Are you sorrowful? weep as though you wept not. Pursue eternal good with the same avidity, as if you had no sorrow to distract your mind. Are you happy? rejoice as though you rejoiced not; be like those, whose hope and comforts here are all destroyed, and who have not one pleasure left to draw their hearts downwards to the earth. Have you the treasures of this world? have them as though you had them not; employ them for the glory of God; and be as dead to them, as if you had nothing on this side the grave your own. Let neither the pains nor the pleasures of life, neither poverty nor riches, prevent you from seeking, with all your heart, durable riches and immortal glories. In the same chapter it is said, " Art thou called being a servant (in the original, a slave) care not for it." As much as saying, It is of so little consequence, in what situation a child of God passes through this fleeting world, that even slavery, dreadful as it is to human feelings, is a thing of little moment. It is no great matter, for so short a time, to live in poverty, hardship, and sorrow, when an eternity of light and joy, and peace and liberty, is just going to dawn upon the soul.

Thus, my young friend, you see it is the judgment of him who is eternal truth, that religion is every thing, and that all on earth is as nothing. Poverty or riches, health or sickness, food or hunger, slavery or liberty, life or death, all are trifles compared with that one most precious, but most neglected blessing.

The Lord Jesus Christ places the value and importance of real piety in a most striking light in the parable, or shall I say the history, of Lazarus and the rich man: see Luke, xvi. 19, &c.

Lazarus is described as poor, despised, afflicted, a beggar without one earthly friend. He has lived in poverty; and at last, unable any longer to glean his scanty pittance by wandering from door to door, he is laid at the rich man's gate, worn down with sickness. No kind relation, no benevolent friend cheers him. The crumbs which fall from his wealthy neighbour's table are his support; and these he earnestly desires, to satisfy the cravings of hunger. His tattered rags scarcely cover the spreading wounds in his disordered and dying body; and the dogs come and lick his sores. Is it possible to describe more complicated wretchedness? But he dies; and now he who had not one friend on earth, has angelic friends to conduct him to the regions of glory. Now farewell to poverty, to begging, to grief, to tattered rags, to painful wounds, to earth and all its sorrows. He, who had no abode here, finds an eternal abode in the mansions of bliss. He, who was an outcast upon earth, walks the golden streets of the new Jerusalem, and is become one of the host of saints, and " angels clothed in light." Near him, while upon earth, lived one, who enjoyed in abundance the pleasures, gaieties, and honours of a dying world. He knew not penury, or its sorrows, for he was rich; and every day had its sumptuous fare, and every season its splendid attire. But his all was in this world, he had nothing beyond the grave. At length he died. The skill of physicians, the tears of friends, and all the care and attendance which wealth commands, cannot ward off the stroke of death. He dies, and lifts up his eyes in hell. Which was the happy man? which the possessor of a real treasure? Surely you cannot hesitate to say, Lazarus. Yes, Lazarus. In his poverty he was rich; in his wretchedness he was happy; when he had nothing, he possessed all things; and when his misery seemed most complete, he was nearest to endless life and joy. What was it that made him so blessed? It was true piety. Without that, his poverty here had been the forerunner of deeper poverty hereafter; and poor on earth he had been poorer still in hell. When he was destitute of food, and friends, and raiment, and shelter, he had one thing left, and that the one thing needful. O my young friend, remember that if you were as poor as Lazarus, as afflicted as Job, as persecuted as Paul, the love of Christ would make you happy! And O, consider that without this you must be a miserable wretch, though you were to live in wealth, pomp, pleasure, and even royal splendour!

§ 5. Thus, my young friend, the divine Saviour represents real religion as an infinitely important blessing; his word also directs you to exert all the earnestness of your soul in its pursuit. You are exhorted to *labour for the meat which endureth unto eternal life; to labour to enter into rest; to strive to enter in at the strait gate; to give all diligence to make your calling and election sure.* He calls on you, to run with the perseverance of a racer; to sacrifice every good for this one, in the spirit of a merchant, who would sell his all to buy one immensely valuable pearl; to fight, with the resolution of a soldier determined to conquer or die; and even to suffer, with the constancy of a martyr, sooner than by neglecting himself to lose eternal life. In two most impressive passages, has the divine Saviour given this last exhortation: "Fear not them which kill the body, and after that have no more that they can do." The loss of mortal life, he teaches you to look upon as a little thing, if the soul is but safe. "And if thy hand offend *(ensnare)* thee, cut it off: it is better for thee to enter into life maimed, than having two hands to go into hell, into the fire that never shall be quenched; where their worm dieth not, and the fire is not quenched. And if thy foot offend

M 3

(ensnare) thee, cut it off: it is better for thee to enter halt into life, than having two feet to be cast into hell, into the fire that never shall be quenched ; where their worm dieth not, and the fire is not quenched. And if thine eye offend *(ensnare)* thee, pluck it out : it is better for thee to enter into the kingdom of God with one eye, than having two eyes to be cast into hell fire; where their worm dieth not, and the fire is not quenched :" (Mark, ix. 46.) How solemn an admonition, to make every sacrifice for eternal life, is contained in this awful passage ! Not merely does the Son of God command you to part with toys and trinkets for his sake; but, to esteem no sacrifices nor sufferings too great when life eternal is at stake. To cut off a right hand, then amputate a right foot, then tear out a right eye, would be to nature dreadfully severe: yet his direction is, if any thing which it would cost you as much pain to resign, as to do all this, should endanger your salvation, bear the pain; and whatever the body suffers, take care that the soul is not undone. Most of the Lord's hearers were the poor ; and to them the right hand is peculiarly important, as by its labour their support is earned ; and thus maimed, they might but linger out the remainder of a wretched existence. Taking these things into consideration, how solemn is the counsel of him, who spake as never man spake. It is as if he had said, "Salvation is the one thing needful ; and think nothing too precious to be resigned on its account: what though any thing as dear and important to you, as the hand that earns your food, the foot on which you pursue your labours, the eye which warns you of a thousand dangers, and which is the source of a thousand satisfac-

tions; what though any thing thus dear and useful, should ensnare your immortal soul, yet part with it; yes, part with it, though it cost you as much exquisite torture to do so, as it would to tear the tender eye from its socket, and to cut away the right hand and foot from the body they support and adorn. Part with the dear cause of destruction, though, through its loss, the rest of your days were even to be spent in misery and want. Yet mind not the miseries of an hour, to escape those of eternity; mind not all that a feeble body can endure, to escape the worm that never dieth, and the fire that never shall be quenched. Better, far better, were it for you, to go, if needful, through pain, and want, and wretchedness, to heaven, than through comfort, and ease, and prosperity, to hell." Solemn and awakening charge! O that it were felt by every heart! Awful, awful warning, repeated six times by a compassionate Saviour, that there the fire never shall be quenched.

Will you, my young friend, listen to his words? Will you, if you have not yet done so, now give your youth to God, and receive the blessed Jesus as your all in all? If you refuse, O may the God of mercy grant, that wherever you go in your mad career of business or of pleasure, the words of Christ may follow you, and still thunder in your ear, that in that dismal abode, whither sin and folly lead the soul, the fire never shall be quenched! Flee, then, from it! Flee for your life! Flee for your soul! If milder motives have not moved you, what can awaken you, if this warning of the Lord's cannot! Flee from the dear delights of sin, that are binding you over to perdition! They conduct

to that hell, where the fire never, never shall be
quenched. Flee from sins, that have ruled you
to the present hour! or they will shortly fix you
where the worm of remorse and despair can never, never die. Flee, or ere long the fire of hell,
flashing in your face, will tell you, that your day
of grace is past; and the worm that never dieth,
rising in your soul, will sting you with huge, inexpressible, and everlasting sorrows.

A PRAYER, IMPLORING GRACE TO PAY DEVOUT ATTEN-
TION TO THE SCRIPTURAL ADVICE CONTAINED IN THIS
CHAPTER.

O thou great and beneficent Father of all, while
I draw near to thee in prayer, stoop, for Jesus's
sake, to accept my feeble offering. Humiliation
should be mine in these solemn seasons, while
infinite condescension is thine. I have passed
but a few fleeting years in this world, yet, perhaps, have already seen many more than I shall
ever see again; and, O Lord, what folly, misery,
and madness, have marked much of my mortal
course! Instead of seeking first thy kingdom
and its righteousness, many of my early years
have been devoted to a thousand trifling vanities; and, negligent of laying up my treasures
in heaven, I have sought that felicity among the
follies of time and sense, which can be found in
thee alone.

Thou, O gracious Lord, hast an eternal, im-
mutable right to teach me what to choose, and
what to shun. Listening to thy word, may I
make true piety my early and immediate choice;
and may I have strength from thee to count all
things loss, that I may win Christ. If I should
have to pass over a painful path to heaven, still
let me tread that path, assured, that one hour of

glory there will compensate all the sorrows of the way. May I follow those who trod a thorny way before me, and who are inheriting the promises. Let me count no sufferings too heavy to be endured on his account, who bore the cross for me. When the world tempts me; when religion is despised, and this vile heart would be negligent of its blessings: then let me think of his dying love and of his various admonitions; then let me gladly make the most painful sacrifices, so that I may but escape the never-dying worm, and be a partaker in his righteousness, and an heir of thy kingdom. Impress deeply on my heart, that the *time is short;* and may I rejoice or weep, possess or want, as a traveller to eternity. May I, from this time, cry unto thee, *My Father, thou art the guide of my youth.* May the blessings be mine which rest on the humble, the poor in heart, and the peaceful. May I hunger and thirst after righteousness, and feel those desires, which nothing but thy love can satisfy, and may I be filled. May I consider my latter end, and when the solemn hour of separation from all mortal things arrives, then, O my God, look down upon me, and show a father's love. Cheer my departing spirit with thy smile. Let joys like those of Lazarus, then be mine. May ministering angels surround my astonished soul; and conduct it through the wondrous, but, by me, untrodden path, that leads from earth to heaven. There may I join the company, whose robes are washed in Jesus's blood; and there for ever celebrate thy love, and pay my grateful honours to the Lamb that was slain. Gracious Father, for his sake answer, and more than answer, these my humble prayers. *Amen.*

CHAPTER VIII.

THE LOVE OF GOD AND THE LORD JESUS CHRIST A REASON FOR EARLY PIETY.

§ 1. HISTORY relates, that one of those happy and triumphant saints, who passed through the sorrows of martyrdom, to the glories of heaven, just before he expired, lifting up his burning hands from the midst of the flames, exclaimed, " None but Christ, none but Christ !" In this, and ten thousand other instances, martyrdom itself was cheerfully borne, through love to the adorable Saviour : but whence sprung this fervent love ? The apostle's words reply, *We love him, because he first loved us.* My young friend, let me call your attention to this most pleasing and most powerful motive, for devoting your youth to God. Martyrs loved their God, because he had first loved them. — Martyrs died for their Redeemer, because he had first died for them; but consider, I beseech you, that all which was done for them, was done for you. That love which won their hearts, has been manifested for you as well as them. God in the gospel, is as kind to you as he was to them; heaven as open to you as it was to them ; and Jesus died for you as well as for them. Spend then, a few serious moments, in meditating on divine love. I have glanced at this subject before, but now entreat you to consider more fully the love of God, and the love of Christ.

§ 2. In the works of the Most High you may discern his love. The fruits we gather, the summers we enjoy, the harvests we reap, the air we breathe; are all proofs of the love of God. Your healthful days, your easy nights, your food, your raiment, your tender friends; all these are gifts from the God of love. He crowns successive seasons with his goodness; and seed-time and harvest, summer and winter, are fraught with his blessings. In infancy, childhood, and youth, you have experienced his kindness. Unnumbered mercies descended from him to you, before you could be conscious whence they came; and the streams of his kindness have continued full even to your present day; and should you choose him as your God and portion, then his kindness will endure while eternal ages roll. It is in the gift of his Son, the Lord Jesus Christ, that his divinest love is manifested. "God so loved the world, that he gave his only-begotten Son, that whosoever believeth in him should not perish, but have everlasting life."

§ 3. The gift of Christ is uniformly represented in the scriptures, as caused by the love of God. That blessed book assures us, that the divine Redeemer did all that he did, and endured all that he endured, in consequence of the love of God to a ruined world. The testimony of the Lord Jesus Christ to this momentous truth, is given in the words just quoted; his inspired apostles assert the same. "God commendeth his love towards us, in that while we were yet sinners, Christ died for us." "Herein is love, not that we loved God, but that he loved us, and sent his Son to be the propitiation for our sins." Does the motive of a giver, enhance the value of a gift? how then should you value Jesus, the best gift of God! In the gospel the infinite Lord of lords is displayed,

John, iii. 16.   Rom. v. 8.   1 John, iv. 10.

as stooping from the throne of his eternal majesty, to interest himself in your behalf; and love to helpless and guilty man, appears the directing motive even in the conduct of the Most High. *God so loved the world.*

§ 4. The love of God, to your immortal soul, is displayed in the greatness of the gift, which he gave for your redemption. Think of the Giver, and adore; think of the Gift, and praise and wonder. The brightest throne in glory was made vacant on our account; and Jesus, the delight of heaven, for us became a sufferer upon earth. He is with God, and is God; and is one with the Father, in a way which none can comprehend. On this subject, curious inquiry is fruitless; devout belief, in what God has declared, and humble adoration best become us. A worm or a mole cannot conceive the nature of the sun, or dive into the secrets of revolving planets, of stars fixed, or comets wandering for ages in the depths of the sky; but worms and moles might better attempt to unfold the mysteries of the starry firmament, than man try to unfold the more inexplicable mysteries, contained in the nature of Christ. Look on him as God with man; the well-beloved of the Father. By his hands the worlds were formed, and he is the same yesterday, to-day, and for ever. He framed the skies; yet, by his Father's appointment, bled for you. He was the object of his Father's infinite delight; yet such is the compassion of your injured God, that he gave even Jesus, his dearest treasure, to be the price of your redemption.

§ 5. The love of God, in giving his beloved Son for your salvation, is enhanced by his own

John, i. 1; x. 30. — Matt. xi. 27.

infinite excellencies. Join all the most noble representations of power and majesty, and all fall short of him at last. Heap together all the most splendid descriptions of glory and greatness, and apply them to the Almighty, and they will but dishonour him at best. If you imagine, as some philosophers dream, every star to be in reality another sun, and every sun attended by its revolving worlds; yet God, the great and glorious God, excels them more, than they united would excel one glimmering spark. Think of God, and what is man! Surely but the insect of a moment, on the atom of a day. Yet in redemption, to man the meanest, did God the highest stoop from his eternal throne. With an eye of softest compassion, he looked down, unutterably low, upon a perishing and guilty world; no help was seen, but his own arm brought salvation. In the gift of Christ also, we see the Most Holy stooping to visit the most polluted. The sun has its dark spots; but the God of heaven has not the shadow of a defect. He is as holy as he is high, as pure as he is powerful; while miserable man is polluted with all depravity, stained with every sin, black with every crime.

§ 6. The love of God was still further enhanced, by his knowledge of the deep abasement and cruel neglect, which awaited his beloved Son. Before Jesus left the bosom of the Father, he foresaw through what scenes his beloved Son would pass. He saw the Saviour on the cross, before the cross was formed; and heard his expiring groan, before that groan was uttered. A parent parting with his beloved son, may dismiss him more readily, if assured that everywhere a

kind reception would await him; but with regret, if conscious that nothing but sorrow and
distress would attend him. A stranger to the
world might have expected, that the blessed Jesus would have met with an infinitely welcome
reception here. It might have been supposed,
that desiring nations would have been ready to
hail his arrival; to offer him the throne of the
world, as some humble compensation for leaving his own; to echo the shouts of glory to God
in the highest, for peace on earth and good-will
towards men; to receive the illustrious visitant as
an object of universal admiration, esteem, and
love. But the Most High knew that the blessed
Jesus would not be thus loved, admired, and followed; he knew that gracious friend of sinners
would have for his attendants a few despised and
persecuted men; would be without a dwelling,
except the chance one which a few friends afforded, and sometimes in the most literal sense,
without a place to lay his head. He knew the
shouts which awaited his beloved Son were, *Crucify him, crucify him! away with him! not this
man, but Barabbas! his blood be on us, and on our
children!* This was the reception the blessed Sufferer met with from the world he came to save;
a reception foreseen by his heavenly Father,
who displayed his own boundless love, in be-
stowing such a gift on such a world. On a world,
too, of which the greater part would still make
their own destruction sure; and in spite of all
these miracles of love, would still prefer the dross
of earth to a dying Saviour and a gracious God.
Well might Christ say, God SO loved the world.
His compassion is beyond description. O, the
heights, and depths, and breadths, and lengths

of the love of God ; *It is higher than heaven, what canst thou know ! deeper than hell, what canst thou do ! the measure thereof is longer than the earth, and broader than the sea !* It is as vast as his own eternity. Could the extended sky be crowded with expressions, to declare the greatness of the love of God ; the extended sky would not contain the half. Could the ocean be emptied, drop by drop, and ages pass between every drop; could the world be destroyed, grain by grain, and ages pass between every grain; and could an archangel be employed, through all those ages, in unfolding the riches of divine love : the ocean would be emptied, and the world would be destroyed, before he had half finished his task. Here eternity alone can suffice.

§ 7. And now, my young friend, **what does** this love demand ? Can you give that gracious God too much, who gave his Son for you ? Can you *too soon* give him your all ? O, would you part with a father, a mother, a brother, a sister, a friend, to redeem even another friend from distress and ruin ? But your much-injured God has resigned his beloved Son to death, to redeem a world and you from perishing. He has done this, not for friends, but enemies ; thus has he commended his love ; for enemies, wilful, wicked, hell-deserving enemies. Shall all this be lost upon you ? Had some friend, by hazarding his life for you, snatched you from a burning house, or raging sea, how warm would have been your professions of gratitude ! But God has given Jesus to snatch you from more dreadful danger, even when he knew that his beloved Son would fall a victim to his compassion. How frozen is your heart, if such goodness does not melt it into penitence and love! Gracious Almighty, what can we render unto thee! we, bought by the blood of thy Son; we, redeemed by thy best beloved; we, whose sins he has borne, whose sorrows he has carried; we, rescued from the flaming pit of misery, not at the mere hazard of his life, but by that invalued life, and by sufferings more than human: what can we offer — but ourselves! By all this matchless love, I beseech you to be reconciled to God. O, harden not your heart against your best benefactor; be not your own worst enemy, when God would be your kindest friend. O, refuse not your youth to him, who has such infinite claims upon you! It has been justly said of ingratitude, that it is "of vices, first, most infamous and most accurst." It was the sin of Satan; but, O my youthful reader, how deeply will you be polluted with it, if you refuse to give your youth to God! His kindness to you through successive years, in infancy, in childhood, in youth, in health, in sickness, claims your heart; but, O, the gift of his Son! If you had ten thousand hearts, the love there manifested would claim them all; and will you deny him that one? Too long has it been shut against him, while sin and folly have triumphed in your breast; but shall it be shut against him still! Shall sin and folly still be preferred to a most kind compassionate God? Had you ten thousand lives, the love of God would demand them all! O, then, refuse him not that little span of life, which is all you will ever have in this world.

§ 8. From contemplating the love of God, the Father, pass on to view that of his Almighty Son. Though the Father gave his best beloved, yet Jesus came not by compulsion, but to be a WILLIN♥ victim.

> "Nothing brought him from above,
> Nothing but redeeming love."

His language was, "Lo, I come to do thy will, O God." He declared, "Therefore doth my Father love me, because I lay down my life that I might take it again. No man taketh it from me, but I lay it down of myself. I have power to lay it down, and I have power to take it again." "Ye know the grace of our Lord Jesus Christ, that though he was rich, for your sakes he became poor, that ye, through his poverty, might be rich." "Christ Jesus, who, being in the form of God, thought it not robbery to be equal with God; but made himself of no reputation, and took upon him the form of a servant, and was made in the likeness of men : and being found in fashion as a man, he humbled himself, and became obedient unto death, even the death of the cross."

Follow him in your thoughts, from his throne of glory, to "his poor manger, and his bitter cross," and mark the painful steps he trod; then may you feel that never love was like his love, and never sorrow like his sorrow. O, meditate on the compassion of a friend, before whose love that of the fondest earthly friend vanishes to nothing; your best, yet, alas ! perhaps, your most forgotten friend. He was the inhabitant of heaven before the world was formed. Eternal glories were his ; all the riches of heaven were his portion; and angels and archangels bowed at his feet. The happiness of the meanest of his disciples, in the heavenly world, is inexpressible. O, what then was the glory which the Son of God had with the Father, *before the world was*, when he thought it not robbery to be equal with God ! yet all this did he lay aside for you, for me. You have, perhaps, heard of this astonishing love, till it scarcely impresses or affects your mind ; but think, if you can, of something that may bear a humble comparison with it. Suppose that a person, not like you, but more happy, in a more exalted station, one who might unite the piety of Paul with the glory and wisdom of Solomon, should, from some disinterested motive, resign his happiness and honour, and assume the nature of a worm, like that to crawl on the ground, and hide in the dust ; would not this be love ? Could you do this ? Yet this would bear no comparison with the love of Christ. Could this be done, one creature would take upon him the meaner nature of a brother worm ; but when the Son of God appeared in the likeness of men, the Almighty Creator took on him the nature of the sinful creature. He came from a world where no sorrows enter, to a world of sorrow and distress. Born in poverty, he continued so poor that he could say, "The foxes have holes, and the birds of the air nests ; but the Son of man hath not where to lay his head." He was wearied with labours, and driven from place to place by the persecution of those very persons whose happiness he came to seek. He wept over wretched men, whom he saw ruining themselves for this world and the next. And, O my young friend, if you are unacquainted with his grace, were he upon earth again he might weep for you. He would see your danger, if you see it not. He would know the worth of your soul, though you know it not ; and would see, in all its horrors, the precipice whence you are falling, and the state of misery into which you are plunging.   After he had manifested his love to man, by his instructions, his tears, his prayers, his labours and his institutions, at length the last sad scene of his innocent life drew on; and now behold the man ! See him in the garden of Gethsemane, weighed down with inward sorrow.   " My soul," said he " is exceeding sorrowful, even unto death."   He was so overwhelmed with a horrid mixture of distress and anguish, that he prayed, if it were possible, the painful cup might pass from him ; but he added, " Father, not as I will, but as thou wilt."   He saw the world lying in wickedness, and ready to drop into eternal flames, and the iniquities of millions were meeting upon him ; but though oppressed by more terrors than any of his martyred followers ever felt, he would not give up his great work ; he would not let go a sinking world.   Again and again he prayed, and an angel appeared from heaven to strengthen him ; yet his unspeakable agony continued so dreadful, that his sweat was as it were great drops of blood falling to the ground.   Was there any sorrow like his sorrow ?   Stop not here ; he who went to Calvary for you, had not reached it yet.   See him betrayed by the kiss of a traitor. Behold the injustice, the insults, the ignominy of his mock trial.   The vilest malefactor probably would not have had such barbarous treatment.   Some spit in his face ; others cover his eyes, strike him, and scoffing, bid him prophesy who struck him.   Yet did not one repining word escape his blessed lips ; he was meekly suffering for his tormentors, and for *you*.   The heathen soldiers at length begin their part in this bloody tragedy.   They scourge him, dress him in a royal robe, plat a crown of thorns and place a reed or walking staff, as a mock sceptre, in his hand.   With cruelty yet unglutted, they take the staff and strike him on the head to give more exquisite pain by those blows, which might drive the thorns of the crown into his temples and his forehead; and now behold the man, clad in the robe of mock majesty; his head crowned with thorns, and streaming with blood; his face bruised with blows, his body torn by scourges : was ever love like his love!   He is condemned; and now see him carrying his cross, execrated and despised.   Dreadful was his path to Calvary, but he reached it at last; yet not to escape from his sorrows, these would only end with his life.   Behold him at the fatal spot.   See the cross formed, and him extended on it; yet even there he prays, "Father, forgive them, for they know not what they do."   Listen to the strokes of the hammer that drives the nails through his hands and feet.   Mark the gushing blood, the shattered bones.   See the cross raised from the earth on which it lay, and let down with a jerk into the hole in which it should stand, that this might torture more the tortured body that hung upon it.   Through six long hours of indescribable misery, behold the Divine Sufferer thus suspended, execrated by earth, insulted by his cruel foes; and even in appearance deserted by heaven, when he uttered that mournful cry, *My God, my God, why hast thou forsaken me!*   His Father seemingly deserted his best beloved for a time, that he might be able to receive you, a poor sinful wanderer, and make you his for ever.   At length he expired.   What a scene followed! rocks rending, graves opening, midnight darkness at noon-day. Was it an emblem of that everlasting darkness which shall overwhelm an ungodly world! Or would heaven hide the dishonours of its Lord! When he left his throne of glory he knew that all this was to befall him; he knew that he should be treated as if he were the worst of malefactors; he knew that the hand which

> "Formed the skies would bleed for you,
> But bleed the balm you want."

And he so loved our wretched and guilty race, that the view of all these dreadful scenes prevented not his coming. He came to save; and is able to save unto the uttermost.

§ 9. The love of Christ is displayed by the free and gracious invitations in his word. One or two of these may serve as specimens of many. He came to seek and save the lost. Let the proud pharisee scorn the penitent publican; but Jesus calls publicans and sinners to himself. Let the self-conceited philosopher look with contempt upon the unlearned and the poor, who disregard his cobweb speculations; but Jesus welcomes the poorest and most ignorant to his arms of mercy. "Come," saith he, "come unto me, all ye that labour and are heavy laden, and I will give you rest." "Him that cometh to me I will in no wise cast out." To those who feel the vast weight of their eternal interests, and their own ruined state, how welcome are these promises, and such as these! It is as much as if he had said, "Come unto me. Man may despise you, but I will receive you. Come, all ye who labour for salvation, and who are laden with sins and

Matt. xi. 28.   John, vi. 37.

sorrows.   Come, not one of you only, not a
thousand only, not a million only, but ALL.
Come from every nation; come in every age;
come from every rank of life; come from every
class of sinners; come, ye who, feeling the burden most oppressive, are almost driven to despair.
Come, all; for ye cannot come in such multitudes that I cannot help you; ye cannot come
so burdened that I cannot relieve you; ye cannot come so wretched that I will not save you.
Come then, and I will in no wise, on no account
whatever, cast you out."

§ 10. The love of Jesus does not stop here.
If you, my young friend, become truly his, it will
attend you through all the seasons of life, in the
hour of death, and into the eternal world. He
is, to his friends, the guide of youth, and the
support of age. Not changeable, like many
earthly friends; not frail, like all. The same is
his love to his disciples now, as it was to those
who first obeyed his gospel; for " he is the same
yesterday, to-day, and for ever." He is the
shepherd of his flock, and guards them with an
ever-watchful eye. He knows their wants, he
administers to their comfort, he hears their prayers, and feels their sorrows. Such is his feeling
for his friends, that they are represented as his
" flesh and bones." And when Paul persecuted
them, he said, " Why persecutest thou ME ?"
He proportions their trials to their strength, and
says to each, " My grace is sufficient for thee."
Nor does he permit those trials to befall the
weak Christian, which the strong only could
bear. " Had I felt " said one of his disciples,*

Heb. xiii. 8.   John, x. 11.   Ephes. v. 3.   Acts, ix. 4.   2 Cor. xii. 9.
* Richard Baxter.

"as strong assaults against my faith, while I was young, as I have done since, I am not sure it would have escaped an overthrow." He is the intercessor for his people in his Father's presence, is still engaged with their concerns; and is gone to prepare mansions for their reception; and soon will come to fetch his followers home. If you are his, he will support you through life, and uphold you when the awful hour of death draws nigh. If you partake of his love, having loved you, he will love you to the end. Though friends and kindred, the nearest and the dearest, die, the Christian has one friend, who is always near, and always gracious; and, when death itself is past, will find the Saviour's love greater than any heart conceived.

§ 11. Can you measure the heights and depths, the lengths and breadths, of all his love? It is impossible. Such love demands the return of gratitude and love. The affection and tenderness of parents or friends has made you love them in return; but what parents, what friends, ever showed so much concern for your happiness as the Son of God has done? They have not left a throne in heaven, suffered persecution on earth, and died a painful death for you: Jesus only has done this. Their kindness bears no comparison to his; and if theirs wins so much of your affection, does not his deserve far more? Yet if you do not give yourself to him, you will deny him all his love claims from you; and would you do this? What dreadful stupidity they manifest who pass through the world without ever thinking why they came into it! And what horrible ingratitude in treating with neglect

Heb. iv. 14—16.—1 John, i. 2.   John, xiv. 23.

the stupendous love of the dying Saviour! Can
you offer him too much, who gave up so much
for you? Can you love him too much, whose
love led him to endure an afflicting life and a
tormenting death for you? What an exchange,
my youthful friend, has he made with wretched
man! He bore our sorrows that we might share
his joys. He suffered on the world where we
dwell, that we might rejoice in his abode. He
took our guilt, that we might partake of his righteousness; groaned, that we might smile; wept,
that we might exult; was crowned with thorns,
that we might be crowned with glory; endured
the bitterest agony, that we might escape eternal
torments; died, that we might live; and came
from heaven, that we might go and dwell for ever
there. O then, remember, that when he was
agonizing in the garden, crowned with thorns,
torn with scourges, nailed to the cross, and writhing in misery there, that all this was on your
account, and not his own. Can you review his
sufferings, and yet refuse to yield your all to
him? Does love to parents, affection to sisters
or brothers, dwell in your heart? and is there no
room there for love to a far better friend than a
thousand earthly relatives united? Can you
think of the Redeemer's goodness, and yet treat
him with neglect? Would any one else do for
you what the Lord has done? Would the gay
world, that perhaps tempt you to slight him,
bear such sufferings for you? It is related of
Colonel Gardiner, that at the time of his wonderful conversion, he apprehended that there was
before him a visible representation of our Lord
Jesus Christ on the cross; and he was impressed as if a voice had come to him to this effect:

"O sinner, did I suffer this for thee, and are these thy returns!" If you, my young friend, have hitherto neglected religion and the Son of God, would he appear, might he not justly say the same to you? Is this your return for all that love of his which these pages faintly display to you? By ingratitude and neglect will you requite his dying love? Suppose he were to appear before you, and, with compassion in his eyes, and love in his heart, were to look on you, and say, "Young sinner, behold these hands, these hands endured the nails for you; will you, by preferring sin to me, open these wounds again? Will you undo what I died to perform? Behold this side, this side was pierced for you; will you pierce it deeper still by your neglect? Behold this head, this head was torn by the thorny crown for you; will you add fresh pangs to what I then endured, by forgetting him who never forgot you? Did I bear scoffs, the scourge, the cross, slow torture, inward and outward agony, and lingering death for you; and are sin and neglect your returns? O, what answer could you give to questions like these? Surely tears would start from your eyes, remorse tear your heart, and confusion cover your face. And do you think the blessed Jesus endured the less, or loved the less, because he is not here to tell you the greatness of his sufferings and his love? It cannot be; and will you then submit to him? or will you still harden your heart in ingratitude and neglect? Perhaps, if you were to declare what has been your past treatment of the gospel and religion, an honest confession would be, "I never thought on the subject." Alas, what a confession, when a vast eternity is at hand!

But O, again I ask you, can you, will you thus requite the Saviour of the lost? Can you look on him afflicted, tormented, suspended between heaven and earth, defiled with blood, and sinking beneath an intolerable load of sorrow; can you look back to Calvary, and continue to treat him thus? I know the world tempts you to do so; but will you let the world prevail? Did he leave heaven and the brightest throne in glory to encounter such horrors for you; and will you not give up, what the vain world can offer, for him? Let it do its best; were its riches, pleasures, honours, yours, are these things better than the heaven to which Jesus fain would lead you? He came to save the lost; will you refuse to let him save you? The graves opened and the rocks rent at his crucifixion; shall graves open sooner than your heart? and even rocks be softer? Were you to see a beloved friend ascend a scaffold on your account, then see his lifeless body bleeding, the eyes "that loved to look on you" closed in death, and all this for you, and in your place; you could not be unaffected. Again, I remind you, that for you your injured Lord bled, and bled not by a sudden, but a lingering death; and can you remain unaffected, because you see not the mournful spectacle, when you know that it was once seen, till heaven, indignant heaven, turned the day to darkness, and hid the bleeding Saviour? Unless you turn to him, as far as you are concerned, all this will be in vain. As to you, it will be in vain that he came from heaven, and became the poor man of sorrows. As to you, it will be in vain that his hands, his feet, his side were pierced, and that he became the sufferer of the cross, the victim of death. O, let him not have to say to you, " *You will not come to me that you might have life.*" Flee to him for salvation. O, give him your youth. Trust him with your soul. Make him your all in all; and in him be blessed for time and eternity. But if you refuse to do this, if you continue to slight his love, and to deny him all that such goodness claims; then, young sinner, expect hereafter no gentle flames, no tolerable damnation : for know, that the deepest and most wretched hell will not be more wretched than such iniquity will deserve. Your sin will be nothing less than preferring Satan, who tries every method in his power for your destruction, to that blessed Friend who bore such sorrow for you. You will be covered with a load of ingratitude, blacker, in one respect, than that which sunk the devil and his angels to the lake of fire ; they sinned against a gracious God, but, if you continue to slight the gospel, you will sin against a gracious God, and a suffering Saviour too. Even devils themselves may then rise up in the judgment to condemn you; and to declare those who could be insensible to such goodness, and indifferent to such a friend, in this respect at least, more horribly wicked than themselves.

§ 12. PRAYER FOR THOSE YOUTHFUL READERS, WHO, FEELING THE GREATNESS OF DIVINE LOVE, DESIRE TO BE THE LORD'S.

Compassionate Lord, what miracles of love hast thou displayed! How beautiful are thy works! how great the wonders of thy power! but O, in the gospel, how much greater are the wonders of thy love ! How numerous are those mercies, which hourly come from thee; but, O how

much the gift of thy Son surpasses them all!
Amazing love! that thou shouldst give such a
gift to such a world. O, let this love fill all my
heart, and engage all I am and have to thee! O,
let me view it as manifested to *me*, a sinner!
With wonder and gratitude, may I look on Jesus,
as given by thee, to snatch even *me* from perdition;
and may I be sweetly constrained to yield up
myself, body, soul, and spirit unto thee. O my
God, poor are my praises, cold is my gratitude.
I owe thee more for the gift of Jesus, than millions of tongues could utter, or millions of years
declare. I would lie abased before thee, for having offered thee so little. Oh my injured God!
my forgotten Saviour! my neglected soul! Had
I ten thousand hearts, thy love demands them
all; yet much of my life has passed, and angels
and men have seen me denying thee this one, poor
unworthy heart. Great God, could I feel the
evil of such sin aright, this heart would burst with
sorrow, and these eyes would weep till death
stopped the flowing tears; but, imperfect in every thing, I am imperfect in my penitence. Yet
let me feel so much as shall lead me to abhor
myself for past ingratitude: and cold as is my
heart, so far at least may it glow with love, as
shall lead me to lie cheerfully at thy feet, seeking all my good in thee. Farewell, earth! farewell, all the allurements of a dying world! my
God demands my heart; my God shall have it.
And, O thou blessed Lord, form me according to
thy will, and make me, in some good measure,
holy, harmless, humble, undefiled, and separate
from sinners. Guide me by thy counsel, and afterwards receive me to glory.

And, O thou compassionate Saviour, wha

praises, what gratitude I owe to thee! Why didst thou stoop beneath the grave, to save a sinking world! Why pass by sinful angels to visit sinful men! Why raise man to the heaven he never enjoyed, and not restore them to the heaven they lost! Why sink so low, to raise us so high! Why suffer for such a worm as I! *Even so*, Lord, *for so it seemed good in thy sight.* Blessed Jesus, thy divine goodness undertook, thy power performed this miracle of miracles, this more than wonder. No merits didst thou see in man. None wilt thou ever see. Never can we repay the debt of gratitude. Never love thee half enough. O gracious Saviour! O divine sacrifice! thou didst bleed, didst bleed for me; didst come to wash away my stains; to seek and save me who was lost. Let me live to thee; and in my life adorn thy gospel and glorify thy name. Let me die to thee; die with an assurance that I am thine; die, saying in my last hour, Beloved Saviour, through thy merits and thy death, a poor polluted worm, deserving hell, ascends to heaven. *Amen.*

CHAPTER IX.

EARLY PIETY PECULIARLY ACCEPTABLE TO GOD, AND PECULIARLY HONOURED BY HIM.

§ 1. THE affection of earthly relatives and friends, you doubtless esteem of much importance to your happiness; but there is one infinitely greater Friend, whose approbation is of more consequence, than that of all earthly friends united. The King of kings deigns to regard early piety as peculiarly acceptable to himself, and this is a weighty reason for its choice. If then you would be happy here, and happy for ever, useful on earth, and glorified in heaven, I beseech you to make this blessing yours. I beseech you to remember, that the esteem and love of mortal friends, if obtained in youth, and enjoyed through following years, and if ever so important for all the term of life, will sink into insignificancy itself, when death shall dislodge your soul from its feeble habitation, and eternity receive you to its endless abodes. But to possess that early acquaintance with Christ, that early piety, which is peculiarly pleasing to God, will most nearly concern you, long after you have done with the world; long after not one trace of you or yours remains on earth; long after the shroud, that dress of the grave, and the coffin, that dwelling of the dead, are mixed and lost in the dust that covers them; long after the graves have given up their dead, and the Judge fixed their eternal doom. Tell me, my young friend, of that worldly concern, which will be of any importance to you, when the year 2000 comes. Alas! you cannot. The world then as now, may be gay and thoughtless; but to you, long, long, long ere that period comes, there will not remain one bitter dreg of any worldly sorrow, nor one pleasing memorial of any worldly joy. The sun will shine as brightly then for others, the earth be as gaily dressed for them as now for you; but long ere that time arrives, those who are in vigorous youth or decrepid age, will be mixed in the same dust. The clods of the valley, almost for ages, will have covered both alike forgetful of a busy or a pleasurable world.   The grass of the field, for years and years, will have flourished and faded about the spot where you and I shall lie.   O vain, and passing world! how wretchedly are that youth, and health, and strength, misemployed, which are employed for thee!   Seek, my young friend, a better portion than such a world can give.   Pursue his favour, whose favour will be found better than life, when the world itself has passed away like a shadow, that vanishes when the sun goes down.

§ 2. Religion in any situation, or in persons of any age, is acceptable in the sight of the Most High, and is deemed true wisdom by him.   His word declares, "The fear of the Lord is the beginning of wisdom ; a good understanding have all they that do his commandments."   A person may be poor, ignorant, mean, and of small capacity ; yet, if guided by the counsel of God, this poor unlettered man shall be esteemed by his Maker, as *wise* and *of good understanding :* another may be great and noble, skilful in all knowledge, able to discourse in many languages, and the world may be astonished at his talents ; yet, because he knows not true piety, God would pronounce him a fool, a man of no understanding.   So precious is true piety in the sight of the Lord.

But while piety in any situation or age, is pleasing to the Most High, yet learn from the divine word, that youthful piety has peculiar charms.   No sight upon earth is more lovely, than to see young persons in the very bloom of life devoting themselves to the Saviour, who died for them, and ornamenting his religion by giving it their best years.   Religion may be regarded by the aged convert from sin and folly ; but it must be honoured by the young, or by those who were religious in the prime of their days. Early piety is peculiarly pleasing to the blessed Jesus. One of the last commands he gave to Peter, was, "Feed my lambs." The apostle John was his young disciple, but he was "the disciple whom Jesus loved." The case of the young ruler also in this view deserves attention. Excepting the apostles, he is the only person expressly mentioned in the New Testament as young who went to our Lord to inquire the way to heaven. He was a stranger to the Lord, and yet more is said of him, than of whole multitudes besides; for of him it is said, that "Jesus loved him." And though the Lord, notwithstanding all he saw so pleasing in him, afterwards spoke of him as a perishing sinner; yet even his want of real piety may show you how that blessing is valued by the Lord Jesus when possessed by the young. If, though not truly a child of God, the Lord was so much taken with him, how much more would he have won on Christ's affection, if to every other recommendation had been added, true piety!

——————— "That last and best,
Which more than doubles all the rest."

A parent may be pleased with another's child, but is more pleased with his own; and the Lord, who beholding that young man loved him, would doubtless have loved him more, if he had been his own disciple. Ah! had he listened to the call of Jesus, how high a place might he have possessed in his Redeemer's heart! Perhaps, the very first; for not even of the apostles themselves, is so much said of the Lord's loving them, before they became his disciples, as is said of his love to this young man.

§ 3. The marked and honourable distinction which God has placed on early piety, strikingly shows how peculiarly acceptable it is to him. He has made few, except those converted in early life, instruments of advancing, to any considerable degree, his glory upon earth. Late converts have generally crept, as it were, singly into heaven ; while many converted young have been employed by God, to lead their friends, their children, or many others to the abodes of bliss. As by early piety the young peculiarly honour God; so he condescends, in return, peculiarly to honour them. Run over the list of names which God has so honourably distinguished in his word, and observe they were converted while young. Abel, the first of martyrs, sought God in his youth. Enoch, celebrated for so glorious a translation to heaven, was removed thither, when (considering the length of life at that period) a young man. Noah, the father of a second world, when young served the God of heaven. Abraham, pronounced the father of the faithful, and the friend of God, while young set out for the heavenly country. Moses, who was *faithful in the Lord's house,* in his youth *refused to be called the son of Pharaoh's daughter,* and counted *the reproach of Christ greater riches than the treasures of Egypt.* Joshua, who made the noble resolution, " *as for me and my house, we will serve the Lord,*" had made the same, long, long before. Samuel, that much honoured prophet, when yet a child, said to the Lord, " *Speak, for thy servant heareth.*" Job, distinguished for his patience and his piety was pious in his early

life. Elijah, who was conveyed in a fiery cha-
riot to glory, was, most probably, the servant of
God in his youth. Elisha, on whom his spirit
rested, seems to have given himself to God betimes. Isaiah, the sweetest herald of the Saviour's approach, while young became the prophet of the Lord ; so too did Ezekiel and Jeremiah. Daniel, who walked with God even in
Babylon itself, and who found his God his pro-
tector even in the lions' den, had sought his God
in his early days. Shadrach, Meshach, and Abed
nego, whom God so honoured, that they passed
unhurt through the burning fiery furnace, were
all pious in their youth. Passing by others, we
come down to the Redeemer's days. Then John
the Baptist, the great forerunner of the Lord, in
early life began to deliver the message of his
God. The apostles of the Lord and Saviour,
there is much reason to believe, were converted
young. Thus was Peter ; thus was James. Paul,
once a persecutor, then an apostle and martyr,
was a young man when brought to the knowledge of the Son of God. So, too, was John, the
beloved disciple ; so too most probably all that
illustrious company. Timothy and Titus were
young, but faithful followers of the Lord ; and,
as if to show that in youth God should be glorified, the Son of God himself came into the
world, accomplished his great errand in it, and
returned to his Father's bosom, when he had
spent little more than three-and-thirty years upon its surface. If we turn to some female characters, which the scriptures commend to our respect and imitation, still will the same observation hold. Mary, whom, as the mother of our
Lord, all generations shall call blessed had

doubtless given her youth to God. Mary, who *sat at Jesus's feet, and heard his word,* who possessed that good part which none could take from her, appears to have early chosen that *one thing needful.** If we come to later times, still God seems, almost invariably, to have acted by the same rule, and seldom to have conferred distinguished honour, except on early piety. Baxter and Owen, Doddridge and Watts, Wesley and Whitfield, and hundreds more, that were in their day employed to lead thousands to heaven, were all converted young. Almost, if not quite, every living or departed missionary sought God in the days of youth. Carey and Ward, Brainerd and Elliot, Schwartz and Martyn, in youth were brought into the ways of peace. Thus also have the most eminently distinguished women. Lady Jane Gray, and Queen Mary the Second, the Countess of Huntingdon, who from a comparatively small fortune is said to have employ-

---

* In proof of the youth of some of these persons, observe, Abel was dead before the birth of Seth, which took place when Adam was but 130 years old. Noah is spoken of as a just man, who walked with God *before* the birth of any of his children, and Shem was born 450 years before his death. Abraham, when at God's command he left Haran, was 75 years old, which bears the same proportion to his age, as 30 would bear to the age of man in the present day. See respecting Moses, Heb. xi. 24. Joshua, see Exod. xxiv. 13; xxxiii. 11. &c. &c. Samuel, see 1 Sam. chap. iii. Job, see Job. i. 1; xliii. 16. Of Elijah's age, but little is said. Elisha seems to have been a young man, 1 Kings, xix. 20. Isaiah, the least possible term for the duration of his prophetical office, is 48 years; (see Lowth's Isaiah, Note 1.) and life being then about the present length, he appears to have entered while young on that office. Jeremiah exercised his prophetical functions at least 42 years, and seems to have been called very young to it. See Blaney's Jeremiah, Note 1, and Jer. i. 6. Ezekiel, see Preface to Newcome's Ezekiel. Daniel, Shadrach, &c. see Daniel, chap. 1. James, Peter, &c. See Doddridge's Remarks on the time when their Epistles were written; from their age at that time, it is easily inferred, that they were young when called by Christ. Paul, see Acts, vii. 58. Mary, the mother of Christ, see Luke's Gospel, chap. 2. Mary of Bethany, from the circumstances recorded respecting her, and from what ancient history says of her brother Lazarus, seems most probably to have been a young woman.

ed nearly a hundred thousand pounds on religious objects; the Countess of Suffolk, whose
piety has often been displayed for the imitation
of others, and many more; the lovely Harriet
Newell, and others who like her have trod the
missionary path, have all displayed the charms
and obtained the honours of early piety. When
God, my young friend, has thus distinguished
youthful religion, while he has set such honour
upon it, would you neglect it? Would you delay to seek it? Rather, I beseech you, yield
yourself a living sacrifice to him who says,
' *They that seek me early shall find me.*"

§ 4. We may discern various reasons why the
blessed Saviour should have a peculiar fondness
for his young disciples; and why the Most High
should take early religion as a mark of regard to
himself, that he will distinguish with particular
approbation at another day; that day when all
the dear delusions and gay vanities of this world
will appear wretched vanities indeed. One of
these is the decided affection to the Lord which
early piety displays. You suppose they love you
most, who are ready to do the most for you; and
depend upon it, the blessed Jesus judges by a
similar rule. Those who are most willing to honour him, and give him most, show most affection.
Now early piety is the best proof of this kind
which you can offer. If in God's strength you
resolve that the Lord shall have those blooming
years, which others spend in sin and folly, this
will manifest the most decided preference for
him. "I love my Saviour much," may be said
by one converted in old age; but "I have humbly proved I love him much," is a declaration
that must be left to those converted in youth.

They do not give their Lord merely the even ing of a day, whose best hours have been devoted to folly and to sin, but present him a better offering than it would ever otherwise be in their power to make.   As the blooming spring is the loveliest season of the year, so is youth of mortal life.   It is the season in which those graces should be implanted in your heart which may bring forth fruit to the glory of God.   It is the season for activity and vigour ; the time in which you might do much for God.   While your mind is not distracted with cares, nor your body worn with infirmities, nor your affections chilled by age; but while health, and cheerfulness, and all the vigour of life are yours, is the season in which to make the best offering to your God. God, when he ordained sacrifices of old, ordered that none which were blemished, should be presented to himself.   The creatures offered were to be the most perfect and vigorous of their kind ; and he reproved those who brought inferior ones.   So, my young friend, before your soul is loaded with the black crimes of many ungrateful and wicked years; before your powers are enfeebled with the infirmities of old age; devote yourself *a living sacrifice* to God. God, it is said, *loveth a cheerful giver*. If this is true, where gifts of much inferior value are concerned, depend upon it, that it is so in the present case.   The Lord loves the cheerful offering which the young make of themselves to him, in the bloom and vigour of their days, better than the offering of a few sad dregs of life, which is wrung, as it were, from the aged and infirm.   " He that soweth sparingly shall reap also sparingly ; and he that

Lev. iii. 1, 6, &c.   Mal. i. 8, &c.   2 Cor. ix. 7.

P

soweth bountifully shall reap also bountifully."
They that yield the most to God, shall, through
his abounding grace, reap the most bountiful
harvest f glory and joy; but who sow so bountifully s they who forsake the world while
young, and then offer to God all they have and
are? The affection of the young also is commonly the most fervent; it glows with a strong
er flame than that of age: and the young follow
ers of the Lord resign their hearts to the impres
sions of his love, when most capable of loving
him in return. They love him soonest; and are
we to wonder if he loves them best? Some, like
Manasseh, after long years of rebellion, are driv-
en by a heavy rod to penitence, and they are welcome; but where is the late penitence of Manasseh celebrated, as equally acceptable to God
with the early piety of Abijah, Josiah, Timothy,
or John? Abijah God took to himself; because
in him only *was found some good towards the Lord
God of Israel,* in the house of Jeroboam. Josiah
did right in the sight of the Lord; and God heard
his prayers, and promised that he should not see
the evils which were about to overwhelm his
wicked country. Over Timothy Paul rejoiced
as his beloved son in the faith; and John lean-
ed on the bosom of Jesus. He loves all who
humbly love him, but those best, who, beginning
soonest, love him most. If you would be truly
pious, apply to God for grace to be so betimes.
If you would have your piety peculiarly pleasing to the Lord, let it be the piety, the kindness
of your youth. Would you thank any one to
offer you a shell without the kernel? or a stalk,
when the flower were withered? or dross when

2 Cor. ix. 6.

the gold were gone? and would you offer to the Lord the poor remains of a life, spent in the service of Satan? and after having wasted your youth, your health, your strength, your prime, would you give to Christ the leavings of the devil? O, act not so base a part! But if you would be pious, be so in these your early days! Then will they be your best days. Every year that departs will bring on a happier; and the last will be the happiest of all, because the last will land you in that world, where there is nothing but happiness.

§ 5. Early piety is also peculiarly acceptable, as it not merely shows the truest love to Christ, but manifests most gratitude for the boundless love of God. His love calls for thankfulness more fervent than any imagination can conceive or tongue express; but, by devoting your youth to him, you may give the best expression of gratitude in your power. You may say, "Great God, I owe thee more than it is in my power to conceive, much less to declare. I have no way of testifying gratitude equal to my obligations; but help me to show all the thankfulness I can. The warmest will be cold; the most will be little: but such as I am take me, and by the offering of my youth may I show that I am thankful, though I can never be thankful enough." It has been said, that in the war which divided the United States of America from England, a British commissioner offered a great bribe to Mr. Reid, an American agent, and that he answered, "I am not worth purchasing; but such as I am the king of Great Britain is not rich enough to do it." My young friend, be assured, it will be an acceptable token of your gratitude to God, if you treat the world as he treated the British commissioner. Say to it, "Begone, vain world; I am a poor insignificant creature, but such as I am, thou art not rich enough to buy me from my God; I owe him such a debt as I shall never through eternity discharge, but what little I can offer him, that little with his help I will."

By early piety, you would also avoid adding to that load of ingratitude, which a continuance in sin would occasion. You would grieve the Holy Spirit less: alas! you have grieved him too much already. You would resist fewer of his calls: alas! you have resisted too many already. Supposing, which most likely would not be the case, but even supposing, that God should spare you, and his Spirit lead you to repentance twenty years hence; yet must it not be more pleasing to the blessed God, to see you now humbled as a penitent at the Saviour's feet, than to see you there, after resisting his Spirit, and adding ingratitude to ingratitude, through twenty more rebellious years of sin? O, then while you have the power of showing some humble thankfulness to God; while you may avoid a load of base ingratitude; while you have resisted fewer calls, and grieved the Holy Spirit less than you would otherwise do: be truly wise and make your God your friend.

§ 6. Another circumstance that may render early piety peculiarly acceptable is, its rareness; for though most that come to Christ come to him in youth, yet small is their number compared with the multitudes that are strangers to the grace of God. Among the great, how many families are there in which not one true Christian is to be found! among the poor the case is the same.

Look at the factories and mills, where twenty, thirty, forty, or even hundreds are employed; and among scores, perhaps but one or two will be found, that sincerely love and follow Christ. True religion was never in fashion upon earth. In youth, even when free from what the world calls vice, there is often little to be seen besides pride, vanity, and folly. That fair morning of life, which a few happily improve for the glory of God and their own eternal welfare, most spend, as if religion were no concern of theirs; as if they had no soul to save, no death to fear, no heaven to seek, no hell to escape. Many young followers of Christ have done their business for eternity, before others, their equals in age, began theirs for time; and have been ripe for an eternal weight of glory, before others began to think of everlasting things. Thus the rareness of early religion may well make it peculiarly pleasing in the sight of the blessed Jesus. He sees the greater part of the young utterly careless of his dying love, or even treating religion as a thing unsuitable to youthful gaiety; but he beholds a few, that are offering him their best years; and he beholds them with pleasure, and will remember the kindness of their youth. He who will remember even a *cup of cold water given to a disciple* out of love to himself, will never forget the humble resolutions of that young disciple who says to him, " Blessed Redeemer, I would be more thy friend; because thou hast so few that are thy friends at all. Few offer thee any of their time; so I would offer thee all the rest of mine. Few show any gratitude for thy living kindness, or thy dying love; but, O thou compassionate Saviour! take my youngest and best years, that thou mayest have all my life, since thou hast none of theirs."

§ 7. Early religion has frequently to surmount many discouragements, which may render it more acceptable to him, who tries in various ways the faith of his disciples. It is pleasing to him to see his young followers overcoming the world, and pressing onwards to heaven in spite of all that is done to hinder them. Young persons are most apt to be taken with the follies and vanities of the world. Its theatres, novels, romances, and other time-wasting and sinful pleasures, have frequently more charms for them than for those of riper years; and by them its laugh is often more dreaded. This, those who will be seriously religious, must not always expect to escape. Ridicule is one of Satan's grand weapons; when his servants cannot persuade others out of religion, they try to laugh them out of it: so that we need not be surprised, if we hear true religion ridiculed as fanaticism, enthusiasm, unnecessary preciseness, or canting hypocrisy. But to take up a despised cause; in the face of an irreligious world, to choose religion; to scorn alike the laugh or frown of men; and, in defiance of all discouragements from earth or hell, to give your youth to God, and glory in the cross of Christ: this is pleasing in the sight of the Lord. Far would I be from insinuating, that this is meritorious in his view. No, if you do this and ten thousand times more, you will still be *an unprofitable servant;* still, as one of the chief of sinners, must be saved by grace: yet, such conduct is pleasing to him, who does approve, and will reward the humble piety of his young disciples.

§ 8. PRAYER FOR GRACE TO COPY THE EXAMPLES OF EARLY PIETY, ENUMERATED IN THIS CHAPTER.

Blessed Lord, how many are those engaging motives, which urge me to yield my all to thee! With pleasure let me review those which have been presented to me; and not merely may the review afford me pleasure, but from it may I gather immortal benefit. Is it indeed true, O my God, that I have *now* the opportunity of making a more acceptable offering of myself to thee, than I ever hereafter shall be able to make? Is it indeed true, that in thy sight, and that of the blessed Jesus, early piety has such peculiar charms? Let me not doubt this, even for a single moment; but rather let me bless thee, for condescending so low, as to regard any thing in sinful man as pleasing to thyself. *Now* then, O Lord, make me a monument to the honour of thy grace. *Now* wash me in the blood of thy dear Son. *Now* adorn my soul with his spotless righteousness, and form me to his lovely likeness. Let Jesus, beholding me, love me. Let him see in me of the travail of his soul, and behold in me another young convert to his gospel. In these my early days, like Mary, may I *sit at his feet and hear his word;* and O, may a double portion of that spirit, which dwelt in thy children of old, descend on me. Like Abel, may I offer in sacrifice to thee, whatever I possess most dear and precious. Like Enoch, may I *walk with God.* Like Abraham, may I sojourn on earth, *as in a strange country;* looking *for a city that hath foundations,* laid by thy almighty hand. O, may I possess the precious faith which he possessed, and follow thee, though I should not know whither I am going! Like Moses, may I choose rather to *suffer affliction with the people of God, than to enjoy the pleasures of sin for a season.* May I esteem the reproach of Christ my greatest honour; and may I endure, as seeing thee who art invisible. Like Joshua, may I serve the Lord; and, with Samuel, say, *Speak, Lord, for thy servant heareth.* O, may I imitate the faith and piety of all that goodly company, who sought thee in their youth; who loved thee in their prime; and who are honoured by thee in the realms of endless day. If but few love thee in sincerity, let me be one of that happy few who make God their all. Should I find early religion the source of many difficulties; should it even expose me to the contempt and aversion of friends, whose esteem and love I now enjoy; yet, O my God, let not this move me; but may I gladly bear my cross for him, who bore a heavier cross for me. May I cheerfully go to him without the camp, bearing his reproach, and esteeming nothing dear compared with thy love; nothing valuable compared with an interest in Jesus. Grant this, O blessed Lord, for my Redeemer's sake. *Amen.*

CHAPTER X.

THE ADVANTAGES OF EARLY RELIGION.

§ 1. AMONG those things which have most influence on the minds of men, are profit and pleasure. While recommending early religion to you, think not that I wish to render you poor or unhappy. Far from it: I rather wish you to be truly rich, and truly happy, not merely for the little span in which earthly pleasures or riches are enjoyed; not merely for a period so short as ten thousand thousand ages, but for ever and ever. Where is that treasure to be found that will enrich you for eternity? Not amidst the wealth of this world. "Man knoweth not the price thereof; neither is it found in the land of the living. The depth saith, It is not in me; and the sea saith, It is not with me. It cannot be gotten for gold, neither shall silver be weighed for the price thereof." Where are they, that, but a few years back, possessed pleasures and honours, parks and palaces, crowns and kingdoms? All vanished from the world;

> —"And now, ye lying vanities of life,
> Ye ever tempting, ever cheating train,
> What are ye now, and what is your amount!"

While entreating you to pursue more solid good, I would recount to you some of the advantages of religion in youth.

§ 2. Early piety is comparatively easy. The total corruption of man's heart is such, that at every period of life, there are difficulties in turning to God in reality. At any time it is needful to *strive* to enter the strait gate; but it is much easier to turn to God in youth, than it is in later life; the heart is then not so hardened, as it is by a longer life of impenitence and sin. The mind is not so averse to instruction, as it is when prejudices have so darkened all its faculties as almost to exclude the heavenly light. When sin has long reigned triumphantly; when Satan has long led the sinner captive; it is hard to escape from his tyranny, and many have experienced this. The scriptures confirm the doctrine of the difficulty of conversion late in life. "Can the Ethiopian change his skin, or the leopard his spots? then may ye also do good, that are accustomed to do evil." In this sense we may apply, with dreadful propriety, the words of Nicodemus : *Can a man be born when he is old?* When is it that disease is most easily checked? Not when it has laid fast hold on the vitals ; but when its first symptoms appear. When is it that the mistaken traveller may most easily forsake the wrong, and return to the right path? Not when he has travelled for miles in a wrong direction, but when he enters that way. Were you rushing down a steep hill, when might you most easily stop? Not when you had nearly reached the bottom, but when you began to descend. So

> " 'Tis easy work if you begin
>   To fear the Lord betimes;
> While sinners that grow old in sin,
>   Are harden'd in their crimes."

In another view early religion is comparatively easy. There is reason to believe that God will sooner hear your prayers for mercy, and grant you peace and pardon, if you turn to him immediately, than if you refuse for awhile to listen to his calls. If you delay to turn, God may afterwards delay to manifest his forgiving love ; and may lead you through tedious scenes of doubt and pain, anxiety and fear, which, but for these refusals, you would have never known. An eminent Christian, who was converted by no means at a late period in life, after feeling disappointment that his mind was not relieved from its oppressive burden so soon as he had hoped, observed, " I have now learned how unreasonable was such an early expectation. I have been taught to *wait patiently* upon God who waited *so long* for *me*."

Before your sins are more multiplied, before your heart is hardened, before Satan gains a firmer hold upon you, O, turn to God! Make not work for future repentance. Harden not your heart now, lest God, in righteous judgment, should harden it for ever. Employ not your best years in shutting the gate of life against yourself; or in filling with difficulties the only pathway to heaven. If a person, with but *one* way from a precipice, were to employ himself for weeks and months in stopping up that way, or in making his escape by it tenfold more difficult, how great would be his distraction! If another, with *one* door opened, to let him escape from a dismal dungeon, were to spend the time in which he should flee from prison and the gallows, in fastening up that one door with bolts and bars, how great, how dismal, would be his folly! But, O my young friend, if you do not now turn to Jesus and to God, far greater will be yours! By continuing careless of the Lord, you will fill with difficulties that one way of escaping from hell, which is now comparatively easy; you will shut against yourself the door of mercy by which you should flee from destruction; and will make it tenfold more difficult for your own soul to escape the flaming sword of divine Justice the eternal prison which is never opened; and the fire that never shall be quenched.

§ 3. Another advantage attending early piety is, that it is that which is most honourable to God and to yourself; and it is that which has the fairest prospect of becoming eminent piety. Religion is honoured, when the young but faithful votaries of the Lord, are seen renouncing the world in the prime of their lives. The world seems to imagine that religion is only suited for gloom and age; but they show that it has charms that win the hearts of the sprightly and the young. The world seems to suppose that what Satan leaves, is all that should be devoted to God; but the young followers of the Lamb show, that such are the excellencies of his service, that it calls for their youth, their health, their prime, their all. How have the glories of religion been displayed by those young converts, who, after a short course of humble piety, have bid an early and yet joyful farewell to all beneath the sun; who have seen no charms in this deluding world sufficient to tempt their wish to stay; but who have calmly departed to eternal rest, before they had passed even sixteen, eighteen, or twenty years below ! Will not you, my young friend, make that offering to the Lord, which such have made? Will not you tell a deluded world that religion is better than life?

Early piety is honourable, as it is that which is most likely to become eminent piety. Faint at the best is the likeness of God on his children in this world. The greatest saint is only a penitent and pardoned sinner; but when faith, and hope, and love, and holiness appear in their fairest earthly form, then is religion honoured most; then even its enemies at times are constrained to bear testimony to its excellence. Such are the testimonies that the ancient heathens bore to the virtues of the primitive Christians. "These," said one, " are the men who speak as they think, and do as they speak." "Behold," said another, "how the Christians love one another !" Even the apostate Julian, their great enemy, commended their charity and benevolence. Who is it that bear most of these divine fruits? Is it the late convert? Ah, no! "Those that are planted in the house of the Lord, shall flourish in the courts of our God, they shall STILL bring forth fruit in old age:" (Ps. xcii.) It is the piety of those who knew religion in early life, that thus bears fruit in age; and having borne it long, still bears it then; and becomes eminent on earth, or is glorified in heaven. If, as many believe, there be various degrees of happiness and glory in the eternal world, who have so fair a prospect of reaching the higher, as those who begin the soonest? A person setting out on a journey at day-break, may travel further by noon, than he who sets out at noon would do by midnight. So in religion, they who yield their hearts to Christ in youth, may get much forwarder in the way to heaven by middle life, than they could do by extreme old age, if they were to put off the care of the soul to later years. Thus every way early religion has its advantages. If you now come to Christ, and should live to old age, he may make your piety more eminent here, and give a brighter crown hereafter; or if you should die, as many do, in the prime of life, you will have lived long enough to find the way to glory and God.

> "Long do they live, nor die too soon,
> Who live till life's great work is done."

Whatever may befall you, nothing would come amiss, when either life or death were a blessing; when a longer stay below might more mature the work of God in your soul, and a shorter one would remove you to speedier glory.

Q

§ 4. Early religion is not merely easy and honourable, but profitable piety. "Godliness is
profitable for all things, having the promise of
the life that now is, and of that which is to come:"
(1 Tim. iv. 8.) It brings its own reward; it will
advance your temporal, spiritual, and eternal
welfare. If you are rich, it would make you infinitely richer; would give you treasures, compared with which, the wealth of the world is
lighter than a feather weighed against mountains
of gold. If poverty be your lot, this would make
you partaker of those blessings, which constitute
an angel's wealth. Though poor on earth, you
would be rich in heaven. The soul that en-
joys the blessings of the gospel, may truly say
to its great Author,

> "Thou art my God, and all the world is mine:
> While Thou art sovereign, I'm secure.
> I shall be rich, till Thou art poor;
> For all I wish, and all I fear, heaven, earth, and hell
>   are thine."

So profitable is true piety, that it would not
merely be the source of numberless blessings,
but would make all things blessings to you;
pain and sorrow, as well as ease and comfort;
sickness, as well as health; and death, as well as
life. How blessed a state this is to live in, and
much more to die in, you may perceive by the
following considerations.

§ 5. Consider the privileges and spiritual blessings that the disciples of the Lord Jesus Christ
possess. Perhaps, if I mention a few of them in
the language of some, who being dead, yet speak,
I shall present you with a more pleasing enume-
ration of these blessings, than I could offer in

any words of mine.   Hear then how the Christian can describe his wealth :

" 'Tis mine the covenant of his grace,
    And every promise mine;
All sprung from everlasting love,
    And seal'd by blood divine.

On my unworthy favour'd head,
    Its blessings all unite ;
Blessings more numerous than the stars,
    More lasting and more bright.

The great the everlasting God,
    My Father is become ;
Jesus, my guardian, and my friend,
    And heaven my final home.

Jesus, thou art my righteousness,
    For all my sins were thine ;
Thy death hath bought of God my peace,
    Thy life hath made him mine.

For evermore my rest shall be,
    Close to thy bleeding side ;
This all my hope, this all my plea,
    For me the Saviour died.

Thy word, through all the tedious night
    Of life, shall guide my way,
Till I behold the clearer light
    Of an eternal day.

Light are the pains that nature brings,
    How short my sorrows are,
When with eternal, future things,
    The present I compare !

The Lord has promis'd good to me,
    His word my hope secures ;
He will my shield and portion be,
    As long as life endures.

Yes, when this flesh and heart shall fail,
    And mortal life shall cease ;
I shall possess within the veil,
    A life of joy and peace.

The earth shall soon dissolve like snow,
    The sun forbear to shine;
But God who call'd me here below,
    Will be for ever mine.

And O what treasures yet unknown,
    Are lodg'd in worlds to come!
If rich the enjoyments by the way,
    How happy is my home!

Go, worldlings, boast of all your stores,
    And tell how bright they shine;
Your heaps of glitt'ring dust are yours,
    But my Redeemer's mine."

Or hear the Christian addressing the world:

"Ye simple souls, that stray
    Far from the path of peace,
That lonely unfrequented way,
    To life and happiness;
Why will ye folly love,
    And throng the downward road,
And hate the wisdom from above,
    And mock the sons of God?

Madness and misery,
    Ye count our life beneath;
And nothing great or good can see,
    Or glorious in our death:
Yet good unsearchable
    In Jesu's love we know,
And pleasures, springing from the well
    Of life, our souls o'erflow.

The spirit we receive,
    Of wisdom, grace, and power;
And always sorrowful we live,
    Rejoicing evermore.
Angels our servants are,
    And keep in all our ways;
And in their careful hands they bear,
    The sacred heirs of grace.

Unto that heavenly bliss,
    They all our steps attend;

And God himself our Father is,
    And Jesus is our Friend.
The God we worship now,
    Will guide us till we die;
Will be our God while here below,
    And ours above the sky.

Such, my young friend, are the privileges and blessings of the children of God. In fact, they are so great and numerous, that the promises on_ly which are made to them in the scriptures, are sufficient to fill a volume.*

§ 6. Glance at a few of the blessings, as de_scribed in the scriptures, which the real posses_sors of religion enjoy. *There is joy* at their con_version *in the presence of the angels of* God; *joy over one sinner that repenteth.* They are *born of God;* are *new creatures in Christ Jesus;* in them *old things pass away,* and *all things become new.* They are *blessed,* for their *transgression is forgiv_en,* and their *sin is covered.* While *the world li_eth in wickedness,* condemned and perishing, *there is no condemnation for them who are in Christ Je_sus.* They have *passed from death to life.* Though their *sins* were *as scarlet,* they are *white as snow;* and though they were *red like crimson,* they are *as wool.* Their *iniquities* are *cast into the depths of the sea;* are as much hidden and as much forgotten as those things which are buried in the fathomless abysses of the ocean. Jesus is the *propitiation for* their *sins;* they *have redemp_tion through his blood.* They are *redeemed, not with corruptible things, as silver and gold, but with the precious blood of Christ.* They *were as*

* See Clarke's Scripture Promises, an instructive and encouraging book. Luke, xv. 10. John, i. 15. 2 Cor. v. 17. Ps. xxxii. 1. 1 John. v. 19. Rom. viii. 1. John, v. 24. Is. i. 18. Mic. vii. 19. 1 John, ii. 2. Ephesians, i. 1. 1 Peter, i. 18, 19.

sheep going astray, but are returned to the shepherd and bishop of their *souls.*   They are *accepted in the beloved;* and *by the Father* are made *meet for the inheritance of the saints in light;* and have a *hope laid up* for them *in heaven.   Being justified by faith,* they *have peace with God, through the Lord Jesus Christ.*   The Son has made them *free,* and they are *free indeed;* and *being made free from sin,* they *have* their *fruit unto holiness, and the end everlasting life.*   The world is *without Christ, without hope, without God;* but they *are no more strangers and foreigners, but fellow-citizens of the saints, and of the household of God.* Even on earth they belong to heaven, for they *are come unto mount Sion, unto the city of the living God, the heavenly Jerusalem; and to an innumerable company of angels; to the general assembly and church of the first born, which are written in heaven; and to God the Judge of all; and to the spirits of just men made perfect; and to Jesus the mediator of the new covenant.*   God *is not ashamed to be called their God, for he hath prepared for them a city.*   They are even *the children of God, and if children, then heirs, heirs of God, and joint heirs with Christ.   Behold what manner of love the Father hath bestowed* upon them, that they *should be called the sons of God; nor doth it yet appear what* they *shall be; but* they *know, that when he shall appear,* they *shall be like him, for* they *shall see him as he is.   In* their *Father's house are many mansions;* and their Lord is gone to *prepare a place* for them ; and *will come again and take* them to himself, that where he is they *may be also.*

1 Peter, ii. 25.   Ephes. i. 6.   Colos. i. 12.   Colos. i. 5.   Rom. v. 1.
John, viii. 36.   Rom. vi. 22.   Ephes. ii. 12.   Ephes. ii. 19.
Heb. xii. 22, 24.   Heb. xi. 16.   Rom. viii. 16. 17.   1 John, iii. 1, 2.
John, xiv. 2, 3

While such is their hope for hereafter, here they *are led by the spirit of God;* are temples of the Holy Spirit; and *God hath sent forth the Spirit of his Son* into their hearts, *crying, Abba, Father.* They are the objects of the eternal Father's tender care. *The eternal God is* their *refuge.* *The Lord of Hosts is* their *refuge. Like as a Father pitieth his children, so the Lord pitieth them;* and loves them with a love more tender than that of earthly parents; for he is their *Father, though Abraham be ignorant* of them, and *though Isaac acknowledge* them not; and if even *father and mother* forsook them, *the Lord would take* them *up. The Father loveth* them because they believe on Christ; and *hath set them apart* for himself. They may *cast all their care upon him, for he careth* for them. Their *Father knoweth that* they *have need* of earthly mercies; he will *withhold no good thing* from them, but to his other blessings will give them *grace and glory.* He *will never leave* them *nor forsake* them; but *with everlasting kindness will* he *have mercy* on them. He that toucheth them toucheth the *apple of* his *eye. The mountains shall depart, and the hills be removed; but* his *kindness shall not depart from* them, *neither shall the covenant of* his *peace be removed. No weapon formed against them shall prosper. Can a woman forget her sucking child, that she should not have compassion on the fruit of her womb? yea, they may forget, yet will not I forget thee, saith the Lord.* He watches them with a father's tender care; *behold the eye of the Lord is upon the righteous, and his ears are open to their*

Rom. viii. 4.   1 Cor. iii. 16.   Gal. iv. 6.   Deut. xxxiii. 27.
Ps. xlvi. 7.   Ps. x. 3, 13.   Is. lxiii. 9.   Ps. xxvii. 10.   John, xvi. 27.
Ps. iv. 3.   1 Pet. v. 7.   Matt. vi. 32.   Ps. lxxxiv. 11.   Heb. xiii. 5.
Is. liv. 8.   Zec. ii. 8.   Is. liv. 10.   Is. liv. 17.   Is. xlix. 14.   Ps. xxxiv. 15.

cry. He will enable them to overcome their mightiest foes, even *Satan* will *the God of peace bruise under* their *feet shortly. The very hairs of* their *head are all numbered.* They have access to God; he hears their secret prayers, and *will reward them openly.* Their *fellowship is with the Father, and with his Son Jesus Christ.* Their *effectual fervent prayer availeth much.* Jesus is their divine Shepherd. He *the Lord is* their *Shepherd,* they *shall not want. He will feed his flock like a shepherd, he will gather the lambs with his arm, and carry them in his bosom.* His *sheep hear* his *voice,* and he knoweth them, and *they follow* him, and he giveth them *eternal life, and they shall never perish, neither shall any one pluck them out of* his *hand.* They are *branches* of Christ the living vine; are *members of his body;* are clothed with Christ;* are *lights* of the *world; salt* of the *earth;* are dear to Christ as *brother, and sister, and mother,* united. — When Christ describes their character, he pronounces them *blessed, for theirs is the kingdom of heaven; they shall be comforted; they shall inherit the* (promised) *land;†* *shall be filled; shall obtain mercy and see God.* When the world persecutes and reviles them, their *reward is great in heaven.* Their *life is hid with Christ in God; and when Christ, who is* their

---

* Few expressions are more striking than this. It has been observed, that putting on Christ implies, " that to God now looking on them, there appears nothing but Christ; they are, as it were, covered all over with him, as a man is with the clothes he has put on. And hence, it is said, in the next verse, they are all one in Christ Jesus, as if there were but that one person." Vide Doddridge in loc.

† Ten gen. The land — the heavenly land, the better country promised to believers. Vide Campbell in loc.

Rom. xvi. 20.   Matt. x. 30.   Ephes. ii. 18.   Matt. vi. 6. vii. 7, 11.
1 John, i. 13.   James, v. 16.   John, x, 11.   Ps. xxiii. 1.   Is. xl. 11.
John, x. 27, 28.   John, xv. 5.   Ephes. v. 30.   Gal. iii. 27.   Matt. v. 14.
Matt. v. 13.   Matt. xii. 50.   Matt. xiii. 16.   Matt. v. 3—7.
Matt. v. 11, 12.

life, shall appear, they *also shall appear with him in glory.* Jesus calls them his *friends.* The blessed angels of heaven are employed on errands of love on their behalf, and are *ministering spirits to the heirs of salvation.* *The angel of the Lord encampeth round about them;* and those happy spirits have a *charge given them to keep* them. Their *names are written in heaven;* are recorded *in the book of life.* They form a *little flock,* to whom it is the *Father's good pleasure to give the kingdom.* For them *a rest remains;* and *eye hath not seen nor ear heard, neither have entered into the heart of man the things which God hath prepared for them that love him.* *The Father himself loveth* them, and is willing to grant their requests; but they have also a great intercessor in heaven, to add weight to their requests; therefore they may *go boldly to the throne of grace.* Christ *ever liveth to make intercession* for them; he is their *advocate;* and while he pleads above, gives them all needful grace below. He ives them *strength;* and left them *peace;* and the *peace of God, which passeth all understanding,* shall *keep* their *hearts and minds through Christ Jesus.* To them *to live is Christ, and to die is gain.* *The Lord will deliver* them *from every evil work, and preserve* them *to his heavenly kingdom;* and as their souls are committed to his care, *he will keep what* they *committed unto him.* Though they are, at best, but *unprofitable servants,* yet their Lord will own, and infinitely reward their little services; so that *even a cup of cold water,* given to one

Col. iii. 3, 4.   John, xv. 14.   Heb. i. 14.   Ps. xxxiv. 7.   Ps. xci. 11.
Luke, x. 20.   Phil. iv. 3.   Luke, xii. 32.   Heb. iv. 9.   1 Cor. ii. 9.
John, xvi. 26, 27.   Heb. iv. 14, 16.   Heb. vii. 25.   1 John, ii. 1.
2 Cor. xii. 9.   John, xiv. 27.   Phil. iv. 7, 9.   Phil. i. 23
2 Tim. iv. 18.   2 Tim. i. 12.   Luke, xvii. 10.

of his disciples out of love to him *shall in no wise lose its reward.* When they speak often to one another, the *Lord hearkens, and a book of remembrance* is written *before him, for them that* thus *fear him, and think on his name. Blessed are they,* they *do his commandments,* and *have a right to the tree of life, and to enter in through the gates into the* heavenly *city.* Though they must die, yet their *end* is *peace. If this earthly house of* their *tabernacle be dissolved,* they *have a building of God, a house not made with hands, eternal in the heavens.* When *absent from the body,* they *are present with the Lord.* The day they depart they are with him *in Paradise.* There *they shall hunger no more, neither thirst any more;* they dwell *before the throne of God;* and *there* is *no night there The lamb that is in the midst of the throne will feed them, and lead them to living fountains of waters; and God shall wipe away all tears from their eyes, and there shall be no more death, neither sorrow nor crying, neither shall there be any more pain.* At length the Judge will descend; then even that body which was *sown in corruption* shall be *raised in incorruption;* it was *sown in dishonour,* it shall be *raised in glory. This mortal shall put on immortality;* and the worthy Judge eternal will say to his friends, *Come, ye blessed of my Father, inherit the kingdom prepared for you, from the foundation of the world;* and they *shall go away into everlasting life,* and *shall shine as the sun in the kingdom of their Father for ever, and so shall* they *be ever with the Lord.* Thus *all things are* theirs *whether the world, or life, or death, or things present, or things to come,*

Matt. x. 42. Mal. iii. 16. Rev. xxii. 14. Ps. xxxvii. 37. 2 Cor. v. 1.
2 Cor. v. 8. Luke, xxiii. 43. Rev. vii. 14, 17. 1 Cor. xv. 42, 43, 53.
Matt. xxv. 34, 46. Matt. xiii. 43. 1 Thess. 4. 17.

all are theirs, *and* they *are Christ's and Christ is God's. Happy is the people that is in such a case; yea, happy is that people whose God is the Lord.*

§ 7. Does not your heart, my young friend burn within you, when reviewing such a catalogue of blessings? Yet it is an imperfect one and the half is not yet told. Do you not exclaim Let these blessings be mine! They may be yours. Listen to Jesus; commit your soul to him; give him your youth; and they shall be yours. O, what treasures can vie with these! The Christian with all these blessings is rich in every sense; rich for time, but richer for eternity. Crowns soon fall from the heads that wear them; parks and palaces soon vanish from their possessors: but the riches of the believer infinitely surpass them all. What can they want who possess such blessings as have been enumerated? To them, what situation can be destitute of comfort? Does their possessor look upwards? it is to his eternal home. Does he look downward, and see the grave at his feet? the grave, which bounds the hopes and ends the joys of others, is to him but a dark passage to eternal day. He has friends, compared with whose friendship that of all the mightiest monarchs upon earth is as insignificant as that of a creeping worm, his God, his Saviour. The young Christian may say, God is mine; Jesus is mine; angels my future companions; and heaven my home.

"Though riches to others be given,
Their corn and their vintage abound;
Yet if I have treasure in heaven,
Where should my affections be found?
Why stoop for the glittering sands,
Which they are so eager to share,

1 Cor. iii. 21, 23.   Ps. cxliv. 11.

Forgetting those wealthier lands,
That form my inheritance there.

Ye palaces, sceptres, and crowns,
Your pride with disdain I survey;
Your pomps are but shadows and sounds,
And pass in a moment away ;
The crown that my Saviour bestows,
You permanent sun will outshine ;
My joy everlastingly flows,
My God, my Redeemer, is mine."

§ 8. A most inestimable advantage attending early piety is, that its possessors will enjoy the Saviour's everlasting love. "Whosoever," saith he, "shall do the will of my Father, which is in heaven, the same is my brother, and sister, and mother." All such are united with him in as endeared and close a union, and enjoy as much of his affection, as if they could join in one several of the tenderest connexions. In youth and in age the best blessings flow from his love. He guides the inexperienced feet of his friends "to fairer worlds on high." In youth his precepts direct, in age his promises support them. His love is an everlasting love. "Who shall separate us from the love of Christ? Shall tribulation, or distress, or persecution, or famine, or nakedness, or peril, or the sword? Nay, in all these things we are more than conquerors, through him that hath loved us. For I am persuaded, that neither death, nor life, nor angels, nor principalities, nor powers, nor things present, nor things to come, nor height, nor depth, nor any other creature, shall be able to separate us from the love of God, which is in Christ Jesus our Lord :" Rom. viii. 35. The love of Christ to his friends extends to another and eternal world. His unwearied affection, once displayed on earth, shines brightest in that heavenly country whence every evil is for ever banished. The limits of the world are much too narrow for his goodness; and within the contracted bounds of mortal life, he displays but a small portion of that love of which eternity itself will be perpetually making fresh discoveries. Generation after generation dies, and the dearest human ties are quickly broken. Our fathers, where are they? Our children, where shall they shortly be? Mixed in the same dust with those who lived five thousand years before them; but that band which joins the humble disciple to the glorious Saviour, remains unbroken. The seas, the vallies, the rocks, the mountains, may all be thrown into one confused mass of ruin; the stars may cease to glitter in the sky; the moon no longer walk in brightness there; the sun be turned to darkness; and of this fair creation, nothing, or nothing but a wreck remain: this must be; but the love of Jesus will be seen in other heavens when these decay. The real Christian may exclaim, Take wing, my soul; pass beyond these mortal things, "beyond the flaming bounds of time," beyond the "last and loved, though dreadful day." — Take wing, my soul; pass in thy thoughts beyond all these: but O, to what world, to what age wilt thou go where Jesus shall cease to love thee, or cease to bless thee! Nay, thou shalt be for ever with the Lord. He, who for thee was content with the manger for his palace, and thorns for his crown, will never forsake thee. He, whose love to thee shone forth so strongly amidst the clouds of worldly sorrow, will not love thee less, now he is surrounded by the splendours of eternal glory. Nor death, nor life, nor evil angels, principalities,

R

nor powers, nothing within the circle of time, nothing within the expanse of eternity, nothing here, nothing hereafter, shall part his humble, faithful, friends and him. Blessed Saviour, the treasure of eternity shall be thy affection; the boast, the bliss of eternity, shall be thy love. O happy they, who enjoy the love of Jesus Christ, though with the loss of all the world! Happy even they, who died to secure it! happy martyrs, who bled to keep it! Happy they, who sought it in youth, though at the expense of every friend besides, of every comfort, and of life itself! Yes, happy martyrs, happy sufferers, who sought and found his love, when all the world hated them for seeking it! They have it still. Their persecutions are no more. Their friends, from whose bosoms they were torn, and whose hearts bled to see them bleed, have long since gone to the chambers of the dead; but they have not lost the love of Jesus, nor will they through eternal days. God of heaven, teach my youthful reader to count all things dross, compared with this most precious blessing.

§ 9. Connected with the last blessing is the equally inestimable one of the eternal Father's love. If brought, through his dear Son, into his family, you will become the object of his tenderest care. So much is said on this subject, in the sixth section of this chapter, that it is the less needful to enlarge. What can be more touching than to be assured, that the eternal God pitieth his children, as a parent pitieth his infant offspring; that he not merely knoweth their frame, not merely is acquainted with all their weakness, frailty, and sorrow, but remembereth, ever keeps in view, that they are but dust; and that it is a far more possible thing, not merely for one, but for every mother to forget the infant babe she fondles on her bosom, than for that great but blessed God to cease to love his children. What can be more pleasing than to hear, that he, though so infinite in power and majesty, is not ashamed to be called their God; but has prepared for them a residence, where his own hand shall wipe every tear from every eye! and where he will own and love them as his children for ever and ever! When the Danish Missionaries in India appointed some of their Indian converts to translate a catechism, in which it was mentioned, as the privilege of Christians, to become the sons of God; one of the translators, startled at so bold a saying, as he thought it, said, "It is too much; let me rather render it, they shall be permitted to kiss his feet." Too great indeed we might have supposed such privileges, if God himself had not so plainly revealed them. Too vast we might have supposed such love, if God himself had not so clearly manifested in the gift of Christ, that nothing is too vast for love like his. If you remember your Creator in the days of your youth, he will manifest all this love to you; he will guide you safely through a thousand snares, and keep you from those evils which beset your slippery path. Yes, young man, or young woman, many whom the Lord has guided, are already in heaven; and many a thoughtless youth that has refused his guidance, is lifting up his eyes in hell, while you are reading these lines. Make God your guide, and he will guide you safely to his eternal kingdom; and love you with everlasting kindness there. Then may you say, "This God is my God for ever and ever; he will be my guide even unto death; and when my flesh and heart fail, the strength of my heart and my portion for ever."

§ 10. Another advantage of early religion is, that its possessors avoid the evil of an entirely unprofitable life. When Paul sent Onesimus, who had been a dishonest fugitive slave, back to his master Philemon, he spoke of him as one that had been unprofitable, but was now profitable to the apostle himself, and to his former employer. It is, my young friend, an awful fact, that while destitute of early piety, you answer none of the ends of your being. You are unprofitable to God, for you bring him no glory; you are un-profitable to Christ, for you make him no thankful returns for all his dying love. You are unprofitable to the world around you; your associates are not encouraged by your example to follow the ways of peace, but, by your negligence and folly, are hardened in their sin. You are unprofitable to your dearest relatives. If they are the friends of Christ, instead of cheering them by your piety, your irreligion is their grief and sorrow; and if they are unacquainted with the gospel, instead of striving to lead them to a concern for its blessings, you go madly with them to destruction. You are unprofitable to yourself, for, alas! while negligent of God, you are adding sin to sin, and are making the heavy load of your transgressions heavier; are filling up the measure of your iniquities; and thus you are heaping up wrath against the day of wrath. O wretched youth! and would you live but to make your own hell the more dreadful? your own perdition the more awful? Would you live a cumberer of the ground? useless as the mischievous thistle? baneful as the deadly nightshade? and, in the sight of God, more hateful than the poisonous serpent? Were it even certain that God would spare you to repent at some future time, yet, through mere delay, how many barren, and worse than useless years, would you pass! The late convert loses much peace and joy; much holiness and happiness; many opportunities of serving God; and much of that grace, of which even the youngest never obtained enough. Growth in grace is a work of time. An infant does not, in an hour, obtain the strength, the vigour, the comeliness, and stature of manhood. Though an infant has all the parts of the future man, he has them in a weaker state. The new convert, compared with the confirmed Christian, is like an infant. He is in Christ, yet but a little child in Christ. He is possessed of the same dispositions as the more confirmed Christian, but in a weaker state; and by the growth of years his graces are brought nearer to perfection. So universally is this the case, that even the apostle Paul, not long before his martyrdom, after being almost thirty years a Christian and an apostle; still declared, that forgetting the things that were behind, he reached unto those that were before; and asserted that he was not yet perfect. O, how much of divine grace must they lose, whose best years slide away before the work of life is begun! Those years that might be inestimably beneficial to themselves, are but a dismal blank; worse than a blank, are years marked with the stains of black ingratitude, neglect, and sin. Should you delay obeying the gospel, you will lose much grace here, and then may expect to lose much glory hereafter; and even if a pardoned penitent at last, might have to utter such a wish, as the celebrated Earl of Rochester is said to have uttered; he wished that he had been a crawling leper in a ditch, a link boy, or beggar, or had lived in a dungeon, rather than dishonour God as he had done.

§ 11. But, my young friend, reverse this scene. Imagine religion to be your early choice; Jesus chosen betimes, as your Lord, and prized as your salvation; and God adored as your God: and, O, how changed do all things appear! Then would you, in some humble measure, glorify his dear name, who bought you with his blood. Then would you recommend his gospel, and display the influence of his love. Then, though you would ever feel yourself an unprofitable servant, an unworthy creature, yet your five talents, or two, or one, would be employed for the honour of your beloved Lord. One of our poets said of a departed friend,

> " His virtues walked their narrow round,
>   Nor made a pause, nor left a void;
> And sure the eternal Master found
>   His single talent well employ'd !"

If you have no more than one talent, O, that hereafter the same may be truly said of you!

Early religion would cause you to glorify God. His name would be honoured by you; his will done in you; his glory promoted in your life, and advanced by your example. Then too would you be profitable to your dearest friends. Are they pious, how would they rejoice over you, and lay down their heads more calmly in the dust, when leaving a beloved child to fill up their place in the church of Christ below, when they depart to that above. O my young friend, if you have parents whose prayers have long ascended to God in your behalf, gladden their hearts, by choosing their God for yours; let them say over you — "This my son, or this my daughter, was dead, and is alive again; was lost, and is found."

But perhaps you reply, "My parents and friends are altogether unacquainted with religion; they live careless of God, and have taught me to do the same." Alas! if this is the case, it is a lamentable one; yet perhaps youthful piety might render you profitable to them. Do you love them; and can you bear the thoughts of soon losing them for ever, or of meeting them only in that miserable world, where affection never enters? Yet this must be, if you and they make light of Jesus and salvation. Much as you may love each other now, all that love will be forgotten, if you should together be banished to everlasting darkness and despair; and would you not save them from that dreadful ruin! O! if you would remember your Creator in the days of your youth, and perhaps this may lead them to think of those things which belong to their everlasting peace. Mr. Baxter relates, that at Kidderminster, which, under his ministry, became almost "one house of prayer," his first and greatest success was upon the young; and he adds, "when God had touched their hearts with a love of goodness, and delightful obedience to the truth, their parents and grandfathers, who had grown old in an ignorant, worldly state, did many of them fall into liking and love of piety; induced by the love of their children, whom they perceiv ed to be made by it much wiser, and better, and more dutiful to them." Perhaps God might thus bless your early attention to his gospel; and surely if any thing could increase your future blessedness, it would do so to think that those you loved here, had, through your early religion, been led to turn from the way to hell, and to enter that to heaven. At any rate, seek God for your God; if you cannot persuade your friends to follow Jesus with you, yet follow him yourself. That is indeed an unhappy family, in which there is not one heir of heaven; in which all are going contentedly to destruction. Early conversion would surely be profitable to yourself; it would make all the blessings that have been mentioned as the Christian's portion, yours.

Then also would you be profitable to others. The ministers of the gospel might then be gladdened by you; the church of Christ delight in you; the angels of heaven rejoice over you. Perhaps, if spared for future years, you may become a parent; and what a blessing it would be to your family to train them up in the ways of peace. God might reward your exertions by their conversion; they might act the same part to their children; and they again to theirs; and thus religion, beginning in your early conversion, might flow on in your family for ages to come. Think not that this is an improbable case; it has doubtless been often realized.

§ 12. In addition to the blessings I have enumerated, it is the happiness of the real Christian, that all events in life, are designed as blessings to him. All are meant in mercy, and all will end in glory. Even afflictions are blessings, blessings in disguise. "Whom the Lord loveth he chasteneth, and scourgeth every son that he receiveth. All things work together for good to them that love God. Our light affliction, which is but for a moment, worketh for us a far more exceeding and eternal weight of glory." The Christian often finds the path to heaven most secure, when most beset with thorns; and the sea of life safest, when most stormy. Afflictions to the children of God prove the best of mercies. The smiles of this world might allure them to ruin; but its frowns urge them towards heaven. The martyr's flames have often preceded the throne of heavenly joy; the crown of thorns has been the forerunner of a crown of glory; and they have drunk the most bitter dregs of grief's most bitter cup, who shall hereafter rejoice evermore. It has been said, that on board a ship, in the midst of a violent storm, when the mariners were in distress and alarm, one little boy remained composed, and being asked the cause of his composure, answered, " My father's at the helm." So may the Christian say in every trial, " My Father, my Almighty Father is at the helm; and he will steer me safe through every storm; or, when he pleases, say to the tempest, Peace, be still !"

§ 13. One distinguishing advantage of early religion is, that it prepares the soul for every possible event. By committing your all to the Lord Jesus Christ, you would make an early escape from all the dreadful danger, to which you are exposed by sin; and would obtain an early title to glory, honour, and immortality. Possibly it may be the will of God, that you should live to threescore years or more below. An early knowledge of Christ would then secure to you that protection, and that guidance, which would make your life a life of piety and peace : happy would it be for you to live, for you would live to the Lord. But, perhaps, God designs only a few more months for you. If so, though it might be a happy thing for you to live, it would be a happier to die. Possessed of an interest in Christ, you would find the shortest life the shortest path to heaven. Early death would be early blessedness. The world might lament your early, and, in their view, untimely departure ; while you were rejoicing in having gained so speedy a triumph ; in having reached,

> ———"With sails so swift, that peaceful shore,
> Where tempests never beat, nor billows roar."

They who land there before they have passed even the short span of twenty years in this world, will never wish to come back and pass another twenty here.

Let me relate to you a little history, illustrative of this and one or two of the preceding sections. Some years back, in a village in Derbyshire, there lived a young and thoughtless girl : her name was Mary. Like most around her she knew not God. Her days were chiefly employed in a cotton mill ; and if a holiday came it was an opportunity for vanity and sinful pleasure. Soon after she had completed her thirteenth year, the season for the wake of a neighbouring village arrived ; and she proposed to attend that scene of dissipation and folly. A young woman, who had herself chosen the better part, persuaded Mary to accompany her to hear a sermon. She went. The place of preaching was the cottage of a humble, aged Christian, one of the Lord's poor. The preacher's subject was, *The carnal mind is enmity against God.* Mary listened ; the Lord opened her heart ; she felt the power of divine truth, in a way she had never done before ; and left the house with feelings very different from those, which she had on her entrance. She had done with the wake. She felt herself deeply sinful and corrupt ; her mind was harrowed up with distress ; and eternal salvation became the object of her desires. Now farewell to her former vanities and follies ; she forsook them for ever ; and from that evening began to live anew. She sought, and at length found peace in believing ; and in her 17th year was solemnly admitted into the church of Christ. In this sacred connexion she adorned religion by consistent conduct ; she prized her religious privileges ; was affectionately attached to her minister ; and secured the esteem and regard of her Christian friends : abroad, she honoured the gospel, in her narrow sphere ; and at home, was the comfort of her parents. A few months after her admission into the church of Christ, the symptoms of a consumption appeared, and God quickly called her to himself. In her days of languishing and weakness, the Lord was her supporter. She said that she found his promises sweeter and sweeter ; that there are comforts and delights in his word, which none know but those who enjoy them ; and that she never enjoyed so many blessings as during the time of her affliction. Death had lost his threatening sting. She knew in whom she had believed ; professed a wish to depart : I am not, said she, afraid in the least of dying at any time. At different times she expressed her hope and peace ; or called on the friends that surrounded her dying bed, to praise her God. At length she calmly entered into rest, before she had spent 18 years on earth. See, my young friend, how much the grace of God may do for them, who embrace religion in early life, even in a little time. On her thir-teenth birth-day, Mary was a thoughtless girl; and ere her eighteenth could arrive, a saint in light. Within the intervening span of something more than four short years, she was enabled to forsake the world; to find a Saviour; to profess his gospel; to honour that profession; to lan-guish calmly through months of sickness; to conquer death; and doubtless land in heaven. In that little time she found her Lord; finished his will, and went to rest. How blessed was ear-ly piety to her! She might when first awaken-ed, have said, "I am not yet fourteen, surely here-after will be soon enough for me;" and had she reasoned thus, and had she put off, though but for a few years, her inquiry for salvation, God, it seems, by early death, would have put it off for ever. Delay not then to accept that blessing which is the source of every other; your life is as uncertain as was hers.

§ 14. One inestimable advantage attending the blessings which early religion would give you is, that these shall never be taken away from their possessors. *Mary*, said the Lord, *hath chosen that good part, which shall not be taken away from her.* As for the lovers of this world, their *all* is here, and shortly their *all* will be for ever lost to them. Soon may it be said of the young, the vigorous, and the gay, who know not God, Where are they? Gone from the world they loved so well. Where their health, and youthful bloom? Gone! for ever gone! Where their gaiety and delights, their hours of thoughtless merriment, their frivolous amusements, their vain companions? All gone. There is not one earthly treasure, of which its possessors can affirm, that none shall separate them from it. Alas! poor creatures, ye gay, ye wealthy, ye lovers of pleasure, "what vain things are they, that you embrace and cleave to! Whatsoever they be, soon must you part. Can you say of any of these, Who shall separate us? Nay, you may even live to see, and seek your parting. At last you must part, for you must die: then farewell to vanity, merriment, and pleasure; farewell, if you had even sat on thrones, to parks and palaces, gardens and honours, crowns and kingdoms, dearest friends and nearest kindred, all must be parted with, and what have you besides?" If you, my young reader, are a lover of this world, what will you have left soon? But if a possessor of early religion, you may say, "Not thus fleeting are my treasures. *Thou art my portion, O Lord;* others have parks, palaces, and crowns; or wealth, gaiety, and pleasure; this is their portion : but thou, the God of heaven and earth, art mine ; and mine for ever. When the miser shall have lost his wealth, and crowns have fallen from the heads that wear them; when the man of this world shall have left the world he idolized, and all their delights shall have forsaken the young, the pleasure-taking, and the gay — thou wilt still be mine : thou wilt be my support, when rocks crumble into dust, and mountains tremble to their base ; and when the sun shall shine no more ; and when the earth itself shall have vanished like a falling

star, that blazes and expires — thou wilt be mine
still, my God, *and my portion for ever.*"

And now, were it possible to call from the dead
some that have died in youth, O, what a confir-
mation would they give, to all that has been urged upon you here! They who have followed
Jesus while young, might say to you, " Follow
him we followed. We soon embraced his gospel, yet not one hour too soon. Early as we began with religion, we began much too late; and
could we have felt grief in heaven, we should have
grieved, that we did not sooner know, and love,
and serve our Lord. Death cut us down in the
morning of our days, yet we did not die too soon;
for we had bowed betimes at the feet of Jesus;
and had found eternal life in him. He washed
our sins away; he renewed our hearts; and prepared heaven for us, and us for heaven. He
taught us to set our affections on things above.
We saw others engaged with all their hearts, in
the shadowy concerns of time; we pitied them,
and trod the path of life. We smiled in death.
Divine grace made us conquerors over the grave;
and now we rest from all our labours. Heaven
is a long, long, happy home. Follow our Lord,
and he will be your Lord. Receive him, and he
will receive you. Commit your souls to him,
and all will be well with you, for time and for
eternity."

A MEDITATION ON THE SUBJECT OF THE CHAPTER,
CONCLUDED WITH PRAYER.

Come, O my soul, and in serious meditation,
again review these pleasing motives for yielding
thyself, thy all, to God. I am passing through
the world like an eagle through the air. I am

young, but youth and health have vanished from millions, and will soon vanish from me. Could I now gain the throne and become the ruler of this mighty kingdom, yet, in a little while, a throne and a kingdom would be of no importance to me; but I hear of things that will concern me for ever, of blessings that may enrich me for ever. I hear of treasures of eternal worth; treasures, like those which angels enjoy, and which make even angels happy. Thrones and kingdoms upon earth never will be mine, even for a fleeting hour; but these far better riches may be mine "when rolling years shall cease to move;" these may be mine through one eternal day. O, let me glance again at this list of blessings! Forgiveness, how much I need it! Forgiveness so free, and full, and entire, that though my sins are as scarlet they shall be white as snow. — Peace with God; peace even in this troublesome world; peace far above all that earth can impart, and which "nothing earthly gives or can destroy." — The love of Jesus; love, stronger than death, and more lasting than time; love, which was manifested *for* me when he groaned on Calvary; and love, which would be manifested *to* me, infinite years beyond the day, when it shall be said, The judgment is finished, the world, the sun, the stars, are no more. — Adoption into the family of God, and the privilege of becoming a child of the Most High; the dear object of his eternal love. O, precious blessing! what more precious can even an archangel possess! what higher privilege! what nobler honour! Can he go higher than to say, I am a child of God? O my soul, wonder and adore! The highest distinctions of archangels themselves may be thine; and thou mayst have the privilege of saying, Now, even in this dying world, am I a child of God; and it doth not yet appear what I shall be, but I know that when he shall appear, I shall be like him, and see him as he is. — Even here, I may enjoy his kindness and his care; know him as my father, and rejoice in him as my portion; even here, may have an interest in all his exceeding great and precious promises; and in the heights, and depths, and lengths, and breadths, of his immeasurable and everlasting love. Even here I may look to Jesus as my elder brother, my friend, my Saviour, my Shepherd, my forerunner, my guide, my guard, my boast, my bliss, my King, my God. But, beyond all the scenes of time, his word reveals a brighter world. There I may possess an inheritance, incorruptible, undefiled, and that fadeth not away; an inheritance, compared with whose pure delights, the sweetest earthly pleasure is but bitter pain; compared with whose wealth, the treasures of kings are poverty itself; and compared with whose duration, ten thousand times ten thousand years are as the twinkling of an eye. All this, and infinitely more than any tongue can express, or heart can conceive, I may possess. When Jesus invites me to go to him, and take his yoke, he invites me to make all this my own. And canst thou hesitate, O my soul, or canst thou delay? Shall I refuse so kind an invitation? Shall I lose all these eternal treasures, for the things of a moment, that perish in the using? O, let me not act so base, so foolish, so unprofitable a part! I see, indeed, that godliness is profitable for all things; and would be infinitely profitable to me. Without it I had better never have been born.

Without it I must be a mere cumberer of the ground. Then my very being would be a curse to myself; and I should be a curse to my friends, and a curse to the world; but with it, in my humble sphere, I should be enabled to glorify my God; I should live to my blessed Redeemer; and might die leaning, as it were, my languishing head for support upon his Almighty arm.

Great and blessed God, from revolving these things in my mind, to thee would I turn. O, let them not be lost upon me; let these precious blessings all be mine. Deny me other treasures, if thou wilt but give me these. Let me " win Christ," and know him as mine; and know all the blessings which flow from his love, either on earth, or in heaven, as also mine. Give me the comfort of hope; the assurance of faith; and the heaven of holy love; that heaven in the soul, on earth, which is the forerunner and the earnest of an eternal heaven within me, and around me, when time shall be no more. Let me not have merely a wavering hope, but a strong unshaken confidence that thou *art my God;* that thy prom- ises are my charter; thy love my portion; thy kingdom my inheritance. While early religion is thus profitable and honourable, and easy piety, let it be my immediate choice. Let me not, by delay, make repentance more bitter, and conver- sion more difficult; but may I feel true humility and sorrow for having wasted, and worse than wasted, so much of my life; and again, let me entreat thee to give me grace, gladly to yield the rest to thee; or if, O compassionate Father, thou seest that I have been led to this happy choice, then, confirm me in it, and never let sin or the world divide the bands which bind my soul to thee; but may I be blest in Jesus, and humbly and faithfully cleave to him. Grant me but these blessings, and then make whatever pleases thee, welcome to me. Let afflictions be welcome, as the chastisement of thy hand; and pain, as sent to meeten me for the rest, where there shall be no more pain. If thou art pleased to prolong my days, let life be welcome for the sake of living to my Lord. But if thou hast determined otherwise respecting me, if a few weeks or months are to finish my pilgrimage below, let even early death be welcome, as a speedier removal to eternal life; and let those years, which are taken from my mortal course, be added to that eternal day, to which thou hast promised to conduct all the humble followers of thy Son. Great God, thou seest nothing in me, to add weight to these requests; and never wilt thou see such worthiness in a creature so unworthy; but grant them for his sake whose blood was shed to wash away my sins. *Amen.*

CHAPTER XI.

THE PLEASANTNESS OF EARLY PIETY.

"On parent knees, a helpless, new-born child,
Weeping thou sat'st, while all around thee smil'd;
So live, that, sinking in thy last long sleep,
Calm thou mayst smile, when all around thee weep."

§ 1. As another reason for early piety, glance at some of the pleasures which true religion yields. It is the common delusion of the world, that religion is a melancholy thing; unsuitable to the young and sprightly; and of such a nature that it would blast all their pleasures, and render their lives dark and dreary. The word of God, on the other hand, describes true religion as the only source of real comfort. It is the only remains of Paradise below. That holy Book declares, that "the ways of wisdom are ways of pleasantness, and that all her paths are peace." It also tells us of "joy and peace in believing;" of "rejoicing in God;" "rejoicing in the Lord always;" of "rejoicing" in Christ, "with joy unspeakable and full of glory;" of "delighting" in "the Lord." The scriptures represent it as the Christian's portion to possess "a peace which passeth all understanding;" "if sorrowful," to be "always rejoicing;" to "glory even in tribulation;" and even if "the fig-tree should not blossom, and there should be no fruit in the vine," if the "labour of the olive should fail, and the fields should yield no meat," if the "flocks should be cut off from the fold, and there should be no herd in the stall;" if, in short, famine and desolation were ravaging all around, still to "rejoice in the Lord, and joy in the God of his salvation."

§ 2. If, after this, you wish for human testimonies, to the comforts which true piety affords, you may have them in abundance. Not that you should ask the men of the world. This would be as absurd as to request a man born blind, to describe the beauties of a fine prospect. As he, who never saw, cannot tell what pleasures sight affords; as he who never heard, cannot describe the delights which music yields its admirers; no more can they, who never knew religion, tell you

Prov. iii. 17.   Rom. xv. 13.   Rom. v. 2.   Phil. iv. 4.   1 Peter, i. 8
Ps. xxxvii. 4.   Phil. iv. 7.   2 Cor. vi. 10. Rom. v. 3.   Habak. iii. 17, 18

what its pleasures are.   But would you know whether religion is the best source of happiness, ask those who possess it in reality.   How many such would tell you, they never knew what true delight was, till they found it in religion!   How many such would unite their testimony with that of a young person, known to the writer, on the evening after her solemn admission into the church of Christ, "This has been a happy day to me ; I hope I shall be faithful unto death, and then my last will be a happier!"

§ 3. True religion, though it forbids conformity to this world, and directs you to set your affections on the things above, yet forbids no lawful use of the innocent comforts of earth and time.   It is true, it denies you the play-house, that hot-bed of vice, the licentious romance, the silly novel, and those scenes of worldly revelry, which a poor deceived world call happiness ; yet these are not sources of real happiness, even to those who love them so well.   On one occasion, when some of Colonel Gardiner's dissolute companions were congratulating him on his happiness in licentious dissipation, a dog happened to come into the room, and he could not forbear groaning inwardly, and saying to himself, "O that I were that dog!"   Such was his happiness, and such is doubtless that of thousands more. Early piety would give you the best pleasures. Through the knowledge of Jesus you would have peace. Peace within. Conscience, that else must be a troublesome monitor, would become a delightful friend ; while the Holy Spirit would witness with your spirit that you are a child of God. Peace with God is another source of true delight, and this too would be yours; you might look on the Most High as a tender Father, and beloved friend, while to the careless sinner he is a dreadful foe.

§ 4. Early piety would open to you another fountain of real pleasure, by forming your heart for the enjoyment of delights, far, far superior to those of sense. In communion with God, in meditation on divine promises and love, the Christian has those pleasures which he would not exchange for all the pleasures of the world. Even his tears of penitential grief afford him more sincere delight, than they find in all their noisy mirth. The public, as well as the private services of religion, also yield true delight to those, who, partaking of renewing grace, are capable of relishing the sacred pleasure. Hear how one who knew these pleasures, could express his feelings, "How amiable are thy tabernacles, O Lord of Hosts! My soul longeth, yea, even fainteth, for the courts of the Lord; my heart and my flesh cry out for the living God. Blessed are they that dwell in thy house: they will be still praising thee. For a day in thy courts is better than a thousand. I had rather be a door-keeper in the house of my God, than to dwell in the tents of wickedness. O God, thou art my God; early will I seek thee: my soul thirsteth for thee, my flesh longeth for thee in a dry and thirsty land, where no water is; to see thy power and thy glory, so as I have seen thee in the sanctuary. Because thy loving-kindness is better than life, my lips shall praise thee. Thus will I bless thee while I live; I will lift up my hands in thy name."

Ps. lxxxiv. 1, 2, 4, 10. lxiii. 1—4.

§ 5. In various other respects the ways of wisdom are ways of pleasantness. Is it pleasing to think of dangers escaped? early religion would give you this satisfaction. You might, with wonder and delight, reflect that God had snatched you from perdition, and that though once an heir of wrath, the danger were over, and you an heir of heaven. Is it pleasant to think of treasures obtained and friends possessed? This pleasure would be yours. You might read the long catalogue of the Christian's blessings, and say of each, "This is mine. This promise is made to me." You might look upwards to the abodes of bliss, and exclaim, "There dwells the ever-blessed Jehovah, and he is my God. There is the adored Immanuel, and he is my Saviour. Those bright abodes, which lie far beyond the reach of mortal sight, are my future home. The stars that adorn that spangled firmament,

'Are glittering dust beneath the feet
Of those who dwell with God.'"

In health and prosperity you might say, "God gives me much here, but how much more have I hereafter; how much better are my treasures there!" Or in poverty, sickness, and pain, you might smile and say, "My all is not laid here." Sweet is it for a seaman, that has escaped the storm, fixed on a rock, to smile on the waves that are beating beneath; but O, it is far more sweet to smile at all the terrors of time, as vanquished enemies and baffled foes! Who should be so happy as they, who have a humble confidence that eternal happiness is theirs? Who should enjoy such peace as they who can look at death without fear, and view it as the path that leads their souls to God, to Jesus, to heaven; to glory, endless as that of their Creator; and to happiness more real than sorrows are below! Who should possess such solid comforts, as they who can turn their eyes to the grave, and dread not the prospect of lying there; who can raise their thoughts to the starry heavens, and rapturously consider, that they shall outlive these glorious fires, and shine, adorned with brighter glories, when stars and sun shall shine no more! Who should be so happy as they, who can contemplate without dread, that solemn period, when the world shall burn; the trumpet sound; the Judge descend; the dead awake; and happiness or misery inexpressible, unchangeable, and eternal, become the lot of every human being! Go and look into an open grave, try to fancy it opened for you, and see whether you can imagine this with peace and composure. If you cannot, learn that all your delights do not make you happy, for into the dreaded grave you must ere long descend; and thousands possessed of the blessings of humble piety, have trodden that gloomy path with satisfaction; and desired to depart and be with Christ.

Is it pleasant thus to look forward, with sweet anticipation, to future scenes of happiness? This source of pleasure would become yours, if a possessor of early piety. Is it pleasant to have a friend ready to welcome us when a long journey is ended? Jesus is the young Christian's friend, he waits on the distant shore of heaven. In their passage through the river of death he will uphold his humble friends; and welcome them to glory on their arrival there. The Christian too, indulges the pleasing hope of reunion there, with the pious friends he has loved below.

He can contemplate the happy bands above.
Patriarchs and prophets, apostles and martyrs
and numbers to the world unknown, who have
loved the Lord, and won the promised crown;
and among them he perhaps enumerates some,
once dear, still dear to himself, who have finished their pilgrimage, and whom he hopes to meet
again, when he shall finish his.   O happy meeting!   O blissful prospect!   Would not you possess it? and when you reach the close of life,
do not you desire the pleasure of panting for the
skies? the pleasure of being able to appeal to
the Lord, that you have humbly loved him?
Do you not wish to say at last, "Gracious Redeemer, on thee I rest my hopes; my best obedience has been too imperfect; my most faithful
duties stained with too much imperfection; my
love too cold; my thankfulness too weak; yet I
expect eternal life, for it was purchased for me
by thy blood.   I look to heaven; it was secured
for me by thy merits, thy sufferings, and thy
death.   Gracious Lord, thine be the honour
while the infinite advantage is mine.   It yields
me pleasure now to know, that thou seest that I
love thee; and have loved thee, from my early
days.   Thou hast seen me truly thine, imperfect
as I am; and though I have often offended thee,
yet I bless thy name that I have been kept from
dishonouring thee, by those numerous and dark
crimes, which I should have committed if I had
not remembered thee betimes.   Though I have
not done my duty, and am an unprofitable servant, yet I know thou wilt not forget the little services of my youth, and those of my riper years;
but I look forward with joyful hope to the time
when I shall see thee as thou art! and though

my time is almost finished, yet I rejoice in the sweet prospect of passing eternity in thy presence, and there will I cast at thy feet that crown which I have in expectation, and which was bought with thy blood."

§ 6. True piety is pleasant, for it is a source of pleasure even in the midst of pain. Man is born to sorrow as the sparks fly upwards; and though many young persons seem to suppose that that world which has been a storm to others shall be a calm to them, yet experience soon removes the delusion. No situation on earth can give perfect peace. Even the most peaceful and happy dwellings, where love and harmony ever abide, cannot supply that blessing, for into them pain has its avenue, and death its entrance; death, that dissolves the fondest ties, and takes away the life that is dearer than our own. But no affliction can befall the true Christian, under which his Redeemer will not give him suitable support and consolation. A gentleman was invited to visit an indigent man deeply afflicted; and gave the following account of what he witnessed: "On entering the cottage, I found him alone, his wife having gone to procure him milk from a kind neighbour. I was startled at the sight of a pale emaciated man, a living image of death, fastened upright in a chair, by a rude mechanism of cords and belts, hanging from the ceiling. He was totally unable to move either hand or foot, having *more than four years* been entirely deprived of the use of his limbs, yet the whole time suffering extreme anguish from swellings at all his joints. I asked, " Are you left alone, my friend, in this deplorable situation?" " No. Sir," replied he, in a touchingly feeble tone

T

of mild resignation, "*I am not alone, for God is with me.*"   I asked him if he ever felt tempted to repine under the pressure of so long-continued and heavy a calamity? "*Not for the last three years,*" said he, "blessed be God for it!" the eye of faith sparkling, and giving life to his pallid countenance, while he made the declaration; "for I have learned from this book in whom to believe; and though I am aware of my weakness and unworthiness, I am persuaded that he will not leave me nor forsake me.   And so it is, that when my lips are closed with locked-jaw, and I cannot speak to the glory of God, *he enables me to sing his praises in my heart.*"

§ 7. My young friend, are not such hopes, such prospects as have been mentioned, sources of real pleasure?   If you are a follower of the world, what is there in all your vain delights, that can bear any comparison with that holy peace, that pure delight which flow from the love of God, and a hope full of immortality?   If you yourself perceive no charms in these pleasures, ask those who have tried them, what support and delight they yield even in the last awful hours of life.   Go to the sick-bed of the humble believer, say, "Poor sufferer, can you find comfort in the midst of anguish?" "Yes," says one, "I have pain, but I have peace, I have peace."*   "What, can you contemplate death itself with comfort?" "Yes," replies another, "I bless God I can lie down with comfort at night, not being solicitous whether I awake in this world or another."†   But they who made these declarations had reached advanced life.   Go then to the sick-bed of the dying youth; ask him, "Can you feel any plea-

* Baxter.   † Watts.

sure, while sickness blasts all the joyous prospects which the young possess, and threatens
you with an early tomb?" Let one reply who
being dead, yet speaks, "O, that I could but let
you know what I now feel! O, that I could show
you what I see! O, that I could express the thousandth part of that sweetness that I now find in
Christ! you would all then think it well worth
while to make it your business to be religious.
O, my dear friends, you little think what Christ
is worth upon a death-bed. I would not, for a
world, nay, for millions of worlds, be now without Christ and a pardon. I would not for a
world live any longer: the very thought of a pos-
sibility of recovery makes me even tremble.
Come, Lord Jesus, come quickly. Death, do
thy worst. Death hath lost its terribleness.
Death, it is nothing. Death is nothing (through
grace) to me. I can as easily die as shut my
eyes; or turn my head and sleep; I long to be
with Christ; I long to die. O, that you did but
see and feel what I do! Come and behold a dying man more cheerful than ever you saw any
healthful man in the midst of his sweetest enjoyments. O Sirs, worldly pleasures are pitiful,
poor, sorry things, compared with one glimpse
of this glory, which shines so strongly into my
soul! O, why should any of you be so sad, when
I am so glad? This, this is the hour that I have
waited for."* Or now ask the pious young woman, who, while others of her age are flaunting
away in vanity and folly, lies on the bed of pain
and suffering. Say to her, "Is religion pleasant
in your esteem?" "Yes," she might reply, "yes,
I am very happy: I would not change situation

* Janeway.

with any one living.   Do not weep for me: I
have no wish to live; if I might have life by
wishing for it, I should rather choose to die, and
go to my Redeemer."   "I long to go home."
"I am truly happy, and if this be dying, it is a
pleasant thing to die."   "Not for all the world,
not for a thousand worlds would I be restored to
health."*   The purport of these expressions was
actually uttered by two young ladies, neither of
whom completed her sixteenth year.   O happy
they who learn so soon, so well to die!   And
could you follow these to the triumphant family
above, and see that glory which no heart con-
ceives, then might a heavenly voice say to you,
"Hither lead the despised and neglected, but
pleasant paths of early piety."   My young friend,
shall they lead you there?   Can you be truly
happy in any other way?   Can you be happy
too soon in this?   Seek happiness, then at once;
O, seek it in the love of your Redeemer, and the
favour of your God.

A PRAYER, IMPLORING THE PLEASURES OF EARLY RELIGION.

Ever blessed God, thou art thyself infinitely
happy; thy presence gladdens the holy hosts of
heaven; and thy word discovers the way by
which I, a child of dust, may pass from toilsome
life to never-ending rest!   May I, through the
Lord Jesus, receive from thee that grace which
will make me, in these my early years, a partaker
of all the sweet comforts that religion yields.
May I possess that pure delight, that holy joy,
that steadfast peace, which flow from humbly
believing on a crucified Saviour.   May I view

* Eliza Cunningham and Elzia M----.

him as GOD MY SAVIOUR; and may my spirit rejoice in him, *with joy unspeakable and full of glory.* While many of the young around me "grasp seeming happiness, and find it pain;" court pleasure, and win perdition; may I obtain solid peace, and rest, and happiness in thee. Lord, lift thou up the light of thy countenance upon me, and cheer me with thy smile. Give me, O my God, a humble assurance that I am thine: and may I look backward with pleasure on dangers escaped; and praise thee, for bringing me from darkness to light, and from the power of Satan to thyself. Number me with thy saints; and by faith may I see Salem's golden towers, and heaven's eternal mansions; may I behold the blood-bought crowns, the palms of victory, and robes of light, designed for those who follow Jesus, and who are faithful unto death. Let me live, rejoicing in him as my guide, my Saviour, my all; and let me die, by the eye of faith discerning him waiting on the heavenly shore, to welcome me to himself, and to introduce me into thy presence with exceeding joy. And till that solemn moment arrives, when I must exchange time for eternity, O, grant that I may find the ways of early wisdom the ways of true pleasantness, and paths of most solid peace! May my heart be attuned for devotion, my soul be transformed to relish the sacred pleasures, and to delight in the holy exercises of meditation, praise, and prayer. Thus may *I have meat to eat, which the world knows not of;* pleasures of which they cannot partake; and may it be my meat and drink to do my Father's will. Let me find in thy promises, consolations more valuable than a thousand worlds. In serving and loving thee, in communion with thee, and in anticipating thy kingdom, may I taste, even in this world, some humble foretaste of the joy to be possessed hereafter.

Blessed Redeemer, I look to thee. To thee would I come, not merely for life, but for happiness also. May I draw water *with joy, from the wells of salvation.* Give me to drink from that fountain, of which thou hast said, *Whosoever drinketh of the water that I shall give him, shall never thirst; but the water that I shall give him, shall be in him a well of water, springing up into everlasting life.* May I partake of this water, and thirst no more ; but feeling through thy grace, an ever-flowing spring of holy joy in my own soul, may I look with indifference on the boasted delights of a vain world. Whatever happens to me, *let not* my *heart be troubled;* but believing in God, and believing in thee, may I find the *light afflictions, which are but for a moment, working* for me *a far more exceeding and eternal weight of glory.* Grant this, O thou most compassionate Saviour, to me, one of the most unworthy of thy creatures, and thine shall be the praise. *Amen.*

CHAPTER XII.

THE HAPPY CONCLUSION OF A RELIGIOUS LIFE A MOTIVE FOR EARLY PIETY.

"And when the closing scenes prevail,
When wealth, state, pleasure, all shall fail;
All that a foolish world admires,
Or passion craves, or pride inspires;
At that important hour of need,
'JESUS' shall prove a friend indeed:
His hand shall smooth thy dying bed,
His arm sustain thy drooping head;

And when the painful struggle's o'er,
And that vain thing, the world, no more,
He'll bear his youthful friend away,
To rapture and eternal day:
Come then be his in every part,
Nor give him less than all thy heart."

§ 1. IT is, my young friend, the peculiar excellence of religion, that its blessings yield most support, when that support is needed most. The humble Christian does not love a forgetful God. They whose strength and prime are devoted to their Maker's glory, will experience his presence and support, when their flesh and heart fail; and when death is at hand, to remove them to the eternal world. If you remember your Creator, in these your blooming days, he will remember this kindness of your youth through all the scenes of your following life, and when you come to lie down and die. Death is approaching; and when all sublunary objects can yield you no support, God would remember that, in you, he had a child conflicting with the last foe; and you might, with pleasure, think

"Though unseen by human eye,
My Redeemer's hand is nigh;
He has spread salvation's light
Far within the vale of night."

Though death is naturally dreadful to man, yet many of the young disciples of the Lord have passed, with calm composure, or holy joy, through its dark valley to the realms of everlasting day.

§ 2. You are called on to imitate those *who, through faith and patience, are inheriting the promises.* Take then a view of the concluding scene of the life of one, who in his youth became a disciple of the Lord. Think not that in referring you to the apostle Paul's departure, as an

example of holy triumph over death, I refer you
to that of too elevated a character. Like you, he
was but man. Like you, was once a sinner. The
same blood that washed away his sins, may blot
out yours. The Saviour who was his all, is willing
to be yours. The grace he possessed, you may
obtain. The strength, by which he conquered,
you may enjoy. The Spirit, that made a temple of his heart, is willing to make one of yours.
Though not called with a call miraculous as his,
though not employed in labours important as
those in which his life was spent, yet you may
be dear to his Lord; entitled to the same supports and privileges; and an heir of the same
blessings as he.

Long had this blessed apostle been, like his
Lord, a man of sorrows; and his years had been
worn out in labours. At length the end arrived
when he might take a farewell to earth; and he
did so with a calmness worthy the heir of a better
world. His triumphant language was, " I have
fought a good fight; I have finished my course;
I have kept the faith; henceforth there is laid up
for me a crown of righteousness, which the Lord
the righteous Judge shall give me at that day; and
not to me only, but unto all them also that love his
appearing." " I know in whom I have believed;
and am persuaded that he is able to keep that
which I have committed unto him against that
day." The world he was about to quit, concerned
him no longer. He could smile at its hatred, and
pity its happiness. A brighter, a better, and an
eternal scene lay before him. We may imagine
him looking back on past scenes of suffering and
labour; retracing in his thoughts many a weary
step, and many a painful hour; and then raptu-

rously exclaiming — "This is all over now; my course is finished; the victory is won; my dangers are passed; I have kept the faith. In vain would earth or hell attempt to excite one fear, or raise one doubt within my breast. I know in whom I have trusted. I know that Jesus is my Saviour, and an eternal weight of glory mine. I know that God is my portion; heaven my home, and that a few more days will land me safely there."

§ 3. O my young friend, let me tell you, and tell you seriously, that you must die, and unless you obtain the consolations of religion, must know their importance when too late. Think, then, that *thus*, in your case, early piety might disarm death of its terrors, and drive away the cloud of gloom that hangs over the grave. *Thus* might you also leave this world of vanity, assured of an interest in Jesus, and of everlasting rest. O happy, happy they who thus can die! happy they who so peacefully depart in blooming youth, or withering age, from scenes of sorrow, or from scenes of comfort! still happy they, who die blessed in an *unseen* Saviour's love; and soon to be blessed by a *present* Saviour's gracious welcome to the abodes of glory! Happy they, beyond all thought and all expression! beyond the power of mortal tongues to tell, or of narrow time to utter! Let the vain world keep its possessions! let the fashionable and the gay enjoy their short-lived gaiety, and quickly-ending pleasure! Let the wealthy exult in their stores, and the noble in their honours! these are not the happy. The solemn death-bed, where the humble, faithful disciple of Jesus has lain, has often afforded a happier spectacle than the most happy ever beheld in scenes of worldly revelry and pleasure. Many followers of the world may be found *professedly* happy while sporting amidst the gaieties of this life, but where one so when leaving them for ever? Many cheerful in the world, but where one so when going out of it? They may be cheerful living, but the Christian can be so when dying too.

Perhaps you look on death as dreadful; but many as young as you have met it without a fear; and without a wish to stay longer here, have passed through that important hour to life, to happiness, to Jesus, heaven, and God. What causes the difference between them and you? Is it not this? They knew in whom they had believed, and, knowing this, knew also that heaven was their home. O my young friend, embrace that gospel, whose blessings formed their support! Then if life, that most uncertain of all uncertain things, should end long before you expect its conclusion, it will not end before you are found ready for a better.

§ 4. It is not merely apostles and martyrs that have passed triumphantly into eternity. Many of the young disciples of the Lord have died with as much composure, and as much holy joy as they. In 1808, died H. S. Golding, in the 24th year of his age. When he felt the approach of death, he is stated to have uttered these rapturous expressions: "I find now it is no delusion! My hopes are well founded! Eye hath not seen, nor ear heard, neither hath it entered into the heart of man to conceive the glory I shall shortly partake of! Read your Bible! I shall read mine no more—no more need it!" When his brother said to him, "You seem to enjoy foretastes of heaven," " O," replied he, "this is no longer foretaste — this is heaven! I not only feel the climate, but breathe the air of heaven, and soon shall enjoy the company! Can this be dying? This body seems no longer to belong to the soul! it appears only as a curtain that covers it; and soon I shall drop this curtain, and be set at liberty!" Then putting his hand to his breast, he exclaimed, "I rejoice to feel these bones give way, as it tells me I shall be with my God in glory!"

The last words that he was heard to utter, were, "glory, glory, glory!"

In July, 1827, died, at an early age, a young disciple of the Saviour, related to the late eminent missionary, Mr. Ward : her name was Jane. When about fifteen, she embraced religion, and sought peace in a Saviour's love, encouraged by the gracious promise, " Come unto me, all ye that labour and are heavy laden, and I will give you rest." The happy influence of true piety upon her heart, was displayed in her conduct; and is pleasingly expressed in a letter written about two years after her admission into the church of Christ. The heart that dictated, and the hand that wrote, now moulder in the dust of death, but some expressions written by that now mouldering hand, may teach the young the worth of early piety. " I am in perfect health, but not knowing how soon death may come. I am hastening to the grave, but not with sorrow; for I know in whom I have believed, and that he is able to keep what I have committed unto him. I must soon part with all below; and with you, my dear minister, but not for ever; for I hope we shall soon meet in Christ, and part no more.

It is my desire to press forward. O that I could glorify my Redeemer more than I do! Behold, God is my salvation. Blessed be the Lord that he hath enabled me to say this! If I had a thousand hearts and a thousand tongues, they all should be employed in praising and adoring the great Redeemer. O that I could leave the world and all its sins! When my mind is taken up with the thoughts of eternity, then I want to be gone to that world, where neither sin nor sorrow shall wound.

> Where they who meet shall never part,
> Where grace achieves its plan;
> And God, uniting ev'ry heart,
> Dwells face to face with man.

I want more grace to subdue all the evils within, and bring them into sweet and humble subjection to the will of God. I would be his entirely, and his for ever; his in life; his in death; and his to all eternity; and then I know he will be mine for ever. Life is uncertain, but death is welcome; death is no more the king of dread to me, through Jesus Christ. I long to be with him. I am young, but not too young to die; not too young to glorify my Redeemer; who hath bought me with his precious blood. The Lord has been my refuge in time of trouble. Praise him for me, for I do not, I cannot, half enough. His boundless love to me is unsearchable. Remember me in the prayers you offer to God. Prayer will not be wanted long. Praise will soon begin in brightest strains."

My dear young reader, these sentiments were not expressed by a Christian worn out with age, and ripened for heaven, by a long course of piety; but they were those of an amiable girl of seventeen, nine years before the important summons to eternity came. Have you her comforts? is her Saviour yours? The peace thus imparted by a knowledge of the Saviour, Jane enjoyed, when the solemnities of eternity drew near. Her last illness was long and painful. Many hours of severe distress did she pass in her sick chamber, or on her bed of death, but all was peace within.

She said, "I have enjoyed for some years more comfort than I can express; then why should I repine!—When I am not torn with pain, I have always felt peace and pleasure—I wish to be in heaven with my Saviour—I trust I am waiting for his coming; I feel extreme pain at times, but I do not *feel one pain in my mind.*" At times she expected recovery, but could say, "When I began to get better, I was not anxious to recover—I am now very willing to suffer, if the Lord will give me grace and strength—If I knew I were not to recover I should be happy;—I can say with the Psalmist, O God, my heart is fixed;—I know he is mine; I know that I am his;—I have not a wish to recover."—Often did she express her confidence in her Saviour, which at times rose to the full assurance of faith. "My mind is very happy—in a very happy frame, and a thankful frame—I have not exultation, but I know that if all the world were lost I should be saved."—She anticipated with comfort an entrance on her heavenly Father's home. With all this gladdening confidence, was mingled deep humility; "I am," she said, "an unworthy sinner, and have done nothing for my salvation." In her latest hours, when the power of speech was almost gone, she faintly whisper-

U

ed, "Happy, happy," and seemed in prayer to say, "Come, my dear Saviour!"— Shall you die thus? Can you die thus unless you seek the Saviour as yours? and yield, like Jane, your youth to him?

Anne Bailey in early youth sought her God; but found no settled peace for several years. Thus tried, she felt tempted to give up hope; but still persevered, and at length obtained the peace she sought. Enriched with that blessing, she desired admission into a Christian church; and when about eighteen made the solemn profession of religion.

Her subsequent course was one of consistent and honourable piety. She was, in various ways, the subject of affliction. Under one trial, she thus expressed her feelings: "By the grace and assistance of my God, none of these things shall move me from my steadfastness in the Lord. Many, many, my dear M—, are the trials I am called to encounter daily; but that time is not far distant, at the longest, when I shall have done with trials; and then I shall be for ever at rest. Though every earthly friend should forsake me, I have a friend in Christ, that will not: and there is still a way of access to the throne of grace. I hope we shall meet in that world, where our employment will be praise to him who hath washed us from our sins in his own blood."

A few months after the date of this letter, she was attacked with an illness from which she never recovered; and which, with a few intervals of less severe suffering, confined her principally to her bed, for upwards of six successive years During this long period of affliction, her patience, resignation, and peace were exemplary. Instead of repining at what she suffered, she often expressed her gratitude for what she enjoyed; and her comfort from what she anticipated. Many cheering expressions of the peace that filled her soul dropped from her lips during these wearisome years. Her resignation appeared entire. "It is enough for me," she observed, " to know that I am suffering the will of God." Her countenance frequently beamed with benignity and sacred composure. The Saviour she loved was her hope: and, as eternal scenes drew near, her hope retained all its cheering power. A friend observed to her, that her hope was worth the world. "More than the world to me, Sir," was the expressive reply. When her last day approached apace, nothing like a wish to stay longer was visible. Not "one longing, lingering look" did she seem to cast behind on the world she was about to leave. She said, "I desire to depart and be with Christ: I long to be with my Saviour." She observed, that she would not change places with any of her Christian friends, who were in health around her; and spoke in her last hours of being "very happy." Her desires at length were accomplished: and her Lord took her to her endless home.

My young friend, learn from this short narrative, that early religion is indeed a precious blessing. Here you see it cheering a young disciple through successive years of illness. While the young around her were exulting in the sprightliness and bloom of youth, the bed of pain was her inheritance, the chamber of affliction her dwelling; yet the Saviour's love rendered her, in that sick chamber, happier than those who know not God are in the midst of youth, and gaiety, and health. The Saviour's love shed the comforts of heavenly tranquillity around her bed of pain; brightened with immortal hopes her chamber of suffering; and when the last solemn scene drew nigh, rendered death, usually the king of terrors, more desirable than life with all its attractions. If you are a disciple of the Saviour, but tried with doubts and almost overwhelmed with sadness, let this young Christian's experience encourage you; learn from her history, that years of distress, while seeking salvation, may be followed by years of settled peace — of peace so rich, and so firm, that long affliction shall not weaken its power, nor death disturb its holy calm.

Another young disciple of the Saviour, in his last illness, observed to the writer, that the thoughts of eternity were most pleasant to him. He spoke of himself as lying at the Saviour's feet, willing to receive ease or pain; and said, " Death is never once a terror. I am not afraid to die; it rather seems lovely. Christ is every thing.—He is all.—I see more beauties in him."————

Such cheering instances of the power of divine grace have been almost numberless. One of the last expressions of a dying saint whose piety began in youth, was, " Welcome joy."* Another,† who sought God when but thirteen, feeling her pulse while death was stealing on her, said, " Well, it will be but a little while before my work in this world will be finished. Then I shall have done with prayer. My whole employment in heaven will be praise and love. Here I love God faintly, yet I hope sincerely,

* Elliott.   † Mrs. Housman.

but there it will be perfectly. I shall behold his face in righteousness, for I am thy servant, Lord, bought with blood, with precious blood; Christ died to purchase the life of my soul. A little while and I shall be singing that sweet song, ' Blessing and honour, and glory, and pow er, be unto him that sitteth upon the throne, and to the Lamb for ever and ever.' " With smiles she often said, " Come, Lord Jesus, come quickly O blessed convoy, come and fetch my soul to dwell with God, and Christ, and perfect spirits for ever and ever! O the glory, the glory that shall be set on the head of faith and love!" Soon after she said, " Farewell, sin! farewell, pains;" and then in holy peace expired.

Many brought from all the abasements of idol atry and heathenism have felt in their dying hours the sacred peace imparted by the Almigh ty Saviour. A converted Hindoo,‡ said in his last illness, " God is my only hope. Life is good — death is good; but to be wholly eman- cipated is better. He is my God, and I am his child. He never leaves me; he is always pre- sent." And alluding to the expressions, Grace be to you, and peace from God our Father and the Lord Jesus Christ, he said, " Peace, peace, I now find in my own heart that peace." An- other converted Hindoo,§ when dying, said, " My Saviour hath sent his messenger for me, and I long to go to him." A dying chief in one of the Sandwich Islands, referring to his Sa- viour, observed, "During the day I think of Him; during the night I think of Him; in pain I think of Him; in ease I think of Him; I do not forget him, and I trust he will not forget me."

‡ Petumber. § Krishna

My young friend, shall such comforts be yours? While you see them found even by those who once were heathens, will you neglect the Giver of them? If you have not committed your soul to Jesus, will you still hesitate to do so? Perhaps your time for doing so is almost gone. Perhaps your days of health and vigour are almost fled. Perhaps you now see your last summer or your last winter; the winter of the grave may be your next. Is any thing so important that it should lead you, for a single hour, to neglect that Saviour, whose favour will concern you for ever? O how gladly would millions, who were once the great, the noble, the wealthy, the young, the sprightly, and the gay; who once shone in the ball-room, and glittered in the theatre, welcome another day of grace, like that you now enjoy! O how gladly would millions, who were such but twenty or thirty years ago, now flee from the wrath to come! but, ah! they cannot; their day is past; but you may, and let me hope you do embrace the gospel; and let me, as it were, take you by the hand, and lead you forward to future scenes.

§ 5. You must die; yet if possessed of a humble assurance that Jesus is your Saviour, you may die in peace; and when that hour comes which has been passed with comfort by thousands who were safe in Jesus, and with terror by millions who were not; you undismayed may meet that solemn hour. Then, when languishing in your last sickness, you may wish for nothing less, and fear nothing more, than recovery and longer life. O! when this scene of vanity is ending; when all your ornaments must be changed for a shroud, and all the amusements of youth, or the cares of riper years, for the solemnities of the eternal world; then indeed will early piety appear a blessing past expression. Then all that you are eager for now will have vanished like a dream; the pleasures and the griefs, the cares and the hopes of youth, and life, will be no more; but the blessings of religion will not have fled away.   Then, when the last sands of life are running out, you may gladly say, These solemn, painful days will quickly hasten me over the tempestuous sea of life; and land me "On the peaceful shore of blest eternity."

And when you reach the very borders of that awful and amazing state, as with an angel's eye, you might survey a vanishing world, and take a last adieu of earth and time. — "Farewell, ye scenes of imperfection! Farewell, folly, sin, and vanity!   Farewell, all that once I knew — the spots I trod — the places where I dwelt — the scenes endeared by friendly converse — the retreats made sacred by youthful devotion — all farewell! I go where joy for ever reigns.   I go where sickness never comes.   I go where death is never known.   I go where perfection and purity, happiness and endless life, shall be my long, long portion.   I go from mortal to immortal things; from dying men to the living God; from fickle mortals to the steadfast Saviour; from sinful creatures to joyful saints and holy angels. Adieu, vain world of cares, and doubts, and fears; yet, sacred world, where heaven was made my portion!   Adieu, thou weary seat of troubles and imperfections; yet, endeared region, where the Saviour's love dawned upon my soul; and glory, honour, and immortality, became my inheritance! Adieu! for ever, departing world, adieu!

But O! welcome, ye blessed spirits, that come to convey me to my God! Welcome, my Saviour's gracious call to his abode! Welcome, ye blissful scenes of peace, and love, and joy, and praise! Welcome, heaven! Welcome, everlasting life!

§ 6. At length your last conflict ends — your pulse stops — to beat no more for ever — your last hour comes — and goes — and you have done with the world for ever. Your tongue is silent — your eyes are closed — the silver cord is loosed, and the golden bowl is broken — surrounding friends look not on you, but on your lifeless clay — the soul is gone — gone to other scenes — to an unchanging, eternal world. O my young friend! dark and dismal as this hour appears to the eye of sense, if you are found in Jesus it will not be so to you; but when your last painful struggle is over, in a happier world will your departed spirit find that the blessed Jesus did not forget the kindness of your youth. Then will your triumphs begin. Others may hear your parting groan, your expiring sigh, while you triumphantly pass into your Redeemer's presence. O blessed change, when mortals weep because a friend is dead, but angels exult because a friend has entered real life! Those who loved you may complain, "Alas! our beloved friend is dead to-day!" But could we hear the words of angels, we might hear — " Another heir of glory has now begun to live — another child of sorrow has left all sorrows for eternal joys — the sad chamber of sickness for these blessed mansions of heaven — weeping mortal friends, for Jesus and for God; and now is this happy spirit with the Lord of Glory, who, a few hours ago, was a prisoner in a feeble, diseased, and dying body!"

§ 7. O my youthful reader, if all the other advantages of early piety were to vanish in a moment, surely these should be sufficient to lead you to make humble religion your lasting, only choice. A few hasty years, at longest, must lay you in the dust; but O! think of such an entrance into glory, and of an eternal dwelling there! Think of the joy with which, after a life of humble religion, your spirit would ascend into the presence of your Saviour, even before your forsaken body was committed to the grave, even before your lifeless limbs were stiffened with the cold of death! Think of the congratulations of the holy saints and martyrs that fled to heaven before you, and of their warm welcome on your arrival there! Think of the approving smile of your Redeemer and your God! that smile which would repay in one hour, the labours of ten thousand years. Think of the delightful words, "Come, thou blessed!" Think of the joy with which you would behold the God you loved, and the Saviour you trusted! And O! think of that great day when the divine Redeemer, before an assembled world, would give you the crown of glory, that fadeth not away! Then you, a shining inhabitant of heaven, would see, without concern, the sun turned into darkness, and the moon cease to shine; the stars fall from heaven, and the heavens vanish away; and when the last trumpet shall have proclaimed, that time shall be no more, you might rejoice, that though time had ended, eternity will never end; that though earthly pleasures proved a dream, heavenly delight will endure for ever and ever; and O! you might add, "This eternity, this heaven is mine!"

And now

who read these pages be unmoved by motives so powerful, that they should soften even hearts of stone, but by thy spirit make them successful; for without him even these will be urged in vain. Pity the young, that may be careless of these solemn truths; lead them to the Saviour. Then shall they find him their friend in life, in death, and at judgment, and for ever; and Thee their God through endless days. For Jesus's sake, thus bless them, O thou compassionate Lord of all.

CHAPTER XIII.

THE FUTURE HAPPINESS OF THE YOUNG CHRISTIAN A MOTIVE FOR EARLY PIETY.

§ 1. HAVING, my young friend, endeavoured to persuade you to embrace early religion, by a view of the scenes through which you must pass on this side the grave, let me now beseech you to contemplate the infinitely important scenes beyond that solemn bound of earthly things.

The word of God reveals an awful judgment; but long before its solemn scenes take place; long before the resurrection day, your soul will pass into an endless world. The scripture doctrine is, that immediately after death the spirit passes to a state of glory or wretchedness. Thus Jesus said to the penitent malefactor, " *To-day shalt thou be with me in Paradise;*" the apostle spoke of being " *absent from the body, and present with the Lord;*" and Lazarus is represented by the Lord as conducted to heaven; and Dives as

Luke, xxiii. 43.   2 Cor. v. 8.

waking in hell, even while his brethren were living upon earth. But the scriptures also teach us, that neither the happiness of the blest, nor the misery of the lost, will be complete till the day of general judgment. Then the body will rise in a new and immortal form, to partake of the happiness or wretchedness of the soul. Then will the doom of each individual be solemnly and publicly pronounced, and the happiness of the saints perfected, and the misery of the ungodly awfully increased.

§ 2. In the state of intermediate happiness many now rest from their labours. Some of these once wandered in sheep skins and goat skins, being destitute, afflicted, tormented. Others were sawn asunder, or torn in pieces by wild beasts, or lingered for days in slow fires, or passed through fiercer flames to heaven. Could you ask these, whether what they now enjoy is worth the pains they underwent; " Ah !" they might reply, " ten thousand times more. What we possess, would amply recompense the labours of ten thousand lives, the sufferings of ten thousand ages." If you find an interest in the Lamb of God, you will soon be summoned to join these spirits of the just made perfect; and, when the last conflict is over, with inexpressible delight may you spring upward to eternal rest ! How great the change ! What new scenes and prospects will that hour present ! what new joys inspire ! what new treasures unfold ! what raptures overwhelm the soul, just landed on that peaceful shore ! " Is this heaven !" may the newly arrived pilgrim exclaim : "how grovelling were my highest thoughts to this ! Are

Luke, xvi. 22. John. v. 29. Tim. iv. 14. Rev. xx. 12, 2 Thes. i. 6

these the spirits of the just ! these the holy angels of light ! these my companions for ever ! O how despicable was all I ever imagined compared with this ! Are these they whose robes were washed in Jesus's blood ! Is this their abode for ever, and is this mine ! O had I conceived this below, how should I have sighed to leave that dark dungeon, earth ! Is this my Saviour, and is this my God ! O insufferable, yet transporting glory ! How mean, how worthless is the world I left ! yet there are millions grovelling in its dust; and, but for heavenly grace, I might have done so too !" O blessed, inconceivably blessed change for the holy soul, that thus passes from the dismal chamber of sickness to the bright and healthful regions of heaven ; from dying pains to boundless bliss; from the converse of sinful mortals to the presence of the infinitely gracious and glorious God; from a contentious, tumultuous world, to endless peace, and rest, and love!

§ 3. Now, for a few moments, turn your thoughts to the day of general judgment; "that day for which all other days were made." That day, while it covers the wicked with confusion, will realize the young Christian's fondest hopes. You must behold all its solemnities. Then God "shall bring every work into judgment, with every secret thing, whether it be good, or whether it be evil." "We must all appear before the judgment seat of Christ, that every one may receive the things done in the body, according to that he hath done, whether it be good or bad." "I saw a great white throne, and him that sat on it, from whose face the earth and the heaven fled away.

Eccles. xii. 14.   2 Cor. v. 10, 11.

And I saw the dead, small and great, stand before God: and the books were opened: and another book was opened, which is the book of life: and the dead were judged out of those things which were written in the books, according to their works. When the Son of Man shall come in his glory, and all the holy angels with him, then shall he sit upon the throne of his glory; and before him shall be gathered all nations; and he shall separate them one from another, as a shepherd divideth his sheep from the goats: and he shall set the sheep on his right-hand, but the goats on the left. Then shall the King say unto them on the right-hand, Come, ye blessed of my Father, inherit the kingdom prepared for you from the foundation of the world. Then shall he say unto them on the left hand, Depart from me, ye cursed, into everlasting fire, prepared for the devil and his angels. And these shall go away into everlasting punishment; but the righteous into life eternal." How solemn is this representation — how infinitely so will be the reality! Here is an assembled world—all generations are met at once —around are countless angels, spectators of the great event—there is the Lord of heaven, enthroned as the Judge eternal. With the same ease as a shepherd distinguishes and parts his sheep and goats, does the Judge divide this mighty multitude; and then pronounces that doom which will make heaven's eternal mansions ring with praise, or hell's tremendous dungeons yell with horror.

§ 4. Before that judgment throne you and I must meet; there must I account for the motives that have influenced me in writing these pages, and you for the improvement that you have made of them. How happily will you meet that day, if now you listen to your God, and choose the path of early piety and peace! If you now remember your Creator and your Saviour, he will remember you in infinite mercy then; for, O boundless grace! the eternal Judge will then delight to honour those who honoured him betimes below. Could you now behold the Lord in that glory, what trifles compared with his favour, would all that life can give appear! Small would seem the value of the universe, in comparison of hearing from his lips, " *Come, thou blessed!*" Riches, pleasures, joys, splendour, would be vanity itself; the passing shadow not so empty, nor the flying feather half so light. Even crowns and kingdoms, and all for which the soul is neglected, would appear so worthless, that you would not raise a finger to gain them all. If you partake of his grace here, you will see him there as your beloved Saviour and your kindest friend. Infinitely welcome will be those solemn and decisive words of his, that will fix your happiness for ever: " *Come, ye blessed of my Father, inherit the kingdom prepared for you from the foundation of the world.*" What rapturous meditations will fill their souls who hear this sentence! what sweet immortal praises flow from their lips! Early piety will then appear true wisdom; and probably the far greater part of that glorious company will be seen to have sought their God in youth. " It is passed," may each of these exalted conquerors exclaim! " It is passed: the scene at which I trembled, and yet rejoiced, in mortal life, is passed; and O!

the prize for which I prayed, the blessedness for which I looked to Jesus, through the few years of mortal life, is all my own! It is finished! my conflicts are finished, and my glory completed. I have heard the sentence of my Judge; and listened while an assembled world heard theirs. I have seen the Lord Jesus, that Divine sufferer, who was all my salvation; whom on earth I loved and trusted, and whom I followed, though with steps much too unequal; and now it is complete, my victory is complete — my fears are vanished quite away — my hopes are changed to certainty — but never did my highest hope reach this triumphant scene. Blessing and honour, and glory and power, be for ever and ever to him that sitteth on the throne, and to the Lamb that washed me from my sins in his own blood."

If you, my young friend, give yourself to the Lord, even the prospect of that day may yield you pleasure. A young Christian once observed "If I were sure the day of judgment were to begin within an hour, I should be glad with all my heart. The thought of its certainty and nearness is more refreshing to me than the comforts of the whole world."

§ 5. Happy will they be who reach that heavenly country. Its glories cannot be decribed "Eye hath not seen, nor ear heard, neither have entered into the heart of man, the things which God hath prepared for them that love him." "I beheld, and lo, a great multitude, which no man could number, of all nations, and kindreds, and people, and tongues, stood before the throne, and before the Lamb clothed with white robes, and

1 Cor. ii. 9

palms in their hands; and cried," our "salvation" be ascribed "to our God and to the Lamb." "These are they which came out of great tribulation, and have washed their robes, and made them white in the blood of the Lamb. Therefore are they before the throne of God, and serve him in his temple. They shall hunger no more, neither thirst any more; neither shall the sun light on them, nor any heat. For the Lamb, which is in the midst of the throne, shall feed them, and shall lead them unto living fountains of waters; and God shall wipe away all tears from their eyes. And he will dwell with them, and they shall be his people, and God himself shall be with them, and be their God. And there shall be no more death, neither sorrow, nor crying; neither shall there be any more pain; for the former things are passed away." How pleasing are these descriptions! yet the most remains untold. In that peaceful rest, no languor or weariness oppresses the active spirit; no disease or death shortens the endless life. No feeble infancy or withering age; no aching head, nor painful limb, nor troubled heart is there. No blasts of grief there blight the joy; no clouds of distress darken the eternal day; but there are spotless purity, peace, never disturbed, and happiness, for ever unalloyed. There they whose names are written in the Lamb's book of life possess mansions not made with hands; and crowns of glory that shall never fade away. The "righteous will shine as the sun in the kingdom of their Father;" and there, "in his presence is fulness of joy, and at his right-hand are pleasures for evermore." There glorified

Rev. vii. 9. 14—17.   Rev. xxi. 3, 4.   Matt. xiii. 43.   Ps. xvi. 11.

saints and holy angels form one blessed family
in the presence of God and the Lamb. O happy day! when all who have followed Jesus
here, shall dwell with Jesus there. O nappy
world, where all are happy! Could the Christian gain a glimpse of that, how would he pass
the rest of his time below, as an exile longing
for his home! O my young friend! flee at once
to that Saviour who would give this heaven to
you; then soon will his welcome voice prove to
you, that early piety is a blessed choice indeed.

§ 6. Think of the state of those who in past
ages sought or slighted this boundless blessedness; and O! let their condition now quicken
your desires for eternal life. Paul once stood a
prisoner at the bar of Festus, and Agrippa said
to him, *"Almost thou persuadest me to be a Christian;"* but, alas! it was but almost. Of how little value now are all those things which once de-
terred him from seeking eternal life, by embracing a despised gospel! Seventeen hundred years
have rolled away since Agrippa departed from
this world, and all his pleasures and all his splendour are no more. The crown he wore exists no
longer — the pomps of life have for many ages
forsaken him. What are they now to his immortal soul! All for which he neglected eternity is gone. Paul stood in bonds before him,
but his bonds are vanished; he no more endures
the pain of these; but the blessed effects of his
knowing a Saviour's love endure. The lustre of
his crown outshines Agrippa's perishing diadem,
and never will it lose one ray of its glory. The
streams of his happiness are undiminished, and
will continue so for evermore. Altogether a
Christian then, and altogether a bright inhabitant

X 3

of heaven now.   Above seventeen hundred years has Agrippa lost his fleeting honours, pomps, and pleasures.   Above seventeen hundred years has Paul forsaken prisons, stripes, and bonds; has taken possession of his unfading inheritance; and lives and reigns in the kingdom of his God.   And let these years be repeated ten thousand times over, they would form but a little span of that eternity, which is now the only measure of his happiness, his splendour, and his triumph. Which, my young friend, chose the better part? you cannot surely hesitate to say.   O choose the same!   By all the blessedness of a happy eternity, be persuaded, with Paul, to *count all things loss* that you *may win Christ and be found in him, not having* your *own righteousness* as your trust, *but that which is by faith in Christ.*   Be wise for eternity.   Devote your youth to God.   Remember him now, and he will remember you in mercy for ever.   He will be your God here, and your God in that bright world, millions of years beyond the day when sun, moon, and stars shall be blotted from the firmament.   And the time shall come when, if it should be asked, "How long has that glorious spirit been an inhabitant of heaven?   How long has it been enjoying God and itself in that state of perfection?   The answer would be such, that a line reaching even to the remotest star, would not be able to contain the number of ages, nor would millions of years be sufficient to number them down."   O! then, remember eternity.   It is said that a pious man once had this question put to him: "Why do you spend so much time in reading, meditation, and prayer?"   He, in reply, lifted up his hands and eyes to heaven, and solemnly said — "*For ever — For ever — For ever.*"

§ 7. O for ever! for ever! for ever! Think of this; and think that early acquaintance with the Lord Jesus Christ leads to all this eternal blessedness! Eternity is the brightest jewel in the triumphant believer's crown. Eternity makes heaven a heaven indeed. If the Christian's life here, instead of being crowned with numerous blessings, were but one scene of distress, yet with eternal life as his portion, how short would be the sorrow! how long, how lasting the joy! how hasty the pain! how endless the delight! how few the moments of grief and conflict! how many the ages of triumph and bliss! Earth you cannot have long, but heaven you may have for ever. Here you can not long enjoy even the poor fading pleasur s of time, but there you may possess a wh le eternity of blessedness. What sweet words m ast "*for ever and ever*" be to those happy spirits that have entered heavenly rest. "This paradise for ever. This mansion of our God for ever. This blessed society for ever. This tranquil rest and calm repose, this peace and love for ever. This pure unbounded happiness. This world of bliss, and light, and joy for ever!" Infinite ages shall roll away; vast eternity still glide along; but not one sorrow will they know; not one sigh will escape their hearts; not one tear drop from their eyes; not one joy will they lose; not one passing cloud will bedim their day. In Immanuel's land will they ever dwell; still will they enjoy the blessings of their Father's love, and of their Redeemer's favour, in the highest perfection, nor ever fear the loss of what they have; and O it will be so great, that they will never wish for more! For ever and ever is the measure of their bliss; and O what is the *for ever* of heaven! None on earth can describe it; none comprehend eternity. Were the house you inhabit to be filled with the finest sand, and then emptied so slowly that but the smallest grain should be taken out once in ten thousand years, how many millions of ages would pass away before the last grain were removed! yet compared with eternity, these countless years would be like the twinkling of an eye. Were the mighty seas, which dash their waves upon so many shores, to be suddenly changed into one mass of ink, and then to be employed in numbering down figures, and the least figure to signify a million of years, what countless ages would be numbered down before the seas were emptied; yet he who wrote the last figure might say, "These ages are not eternity; they are nothingness itself, compared with that: — less than one drop to all the sea; less than one moment to all these infinite years: they are like a tale that is told, or a sigh that is forgotten." Were this vast world one mass of sand, and were the Most High, by his infinite power, to create as many worlds as there might be grains of sand in this, and were he then to commission a ministering angel to destroy them all, by removing grain after grain, yet so slowly that he should remove but one grain in a million of years, what millions, and millions, and millions of years, beyond all thought and conception, would pass away before one world were thus destroyed! and O what before all these numbers were! What an eternity would be here! An eternity! no, not a moment compared with it. Sand after sand would be removed, though at so infinitely slow a rate; world after world would be destroyed; and the angel would finish his task; but finish not eternity. Eternity would be eternity still. One grain of sand would bear some proportion to these numberless worlds; one moment to these countless millions of ages; but all these would bear none to eternity;—when they were past, it would still be " beginning— rather beginning to begin." And had we lived through these inconceivably countless years, when we had seen them pass, and even pass a thousand times over, we might still say, " But a moment of eternity is passed." Beyond ages that we might almost deem an eternity, other eternities would rise in endless succession. Such is the *for ever* in heaven. Eternity is yours, and it is mine. In a short time, the hand that has written these pages, and the eye that reads them must be turned to dust; but in eternity we must live for ever and ever, the companions of angels or of devils.

A PRAYER, IMPLORING A PARTICIPATION IN THE BLESS- INGS ENUMERATED IN THIS AND THE PRECEDING CHAPTER.

Great and gracious God, in thy hand is the breath of every living thing, and the life of all mankind. From thee I have derived that exis- tence which thou hast determined to make as lasting as thy own. But though immortality must be my portion in the future world, yet I know that in this it is appointed unto all men once to die; and I am hastening to that hour, which will more than realize all my hopes or all my fears. Behold me supplicating mercy at thy footstool; and in, and through thy Son, make me a partaker of that grace, which shall issue in everlasting glory.

How solemn, great God, is the prospect of appearing in thy presence! How shall I endure that awful, that amazing change, which will then take place in my condition! How shall I meet thee! Wilt thou welcome me to thy presence, or bid me depart for ever! O let this doubt be resolved before I die! Blessed, for ever blessed be thy name! that, in thy glorious gospel, thou hast shown how a sinner like me may become just before thee; and O let the grace there displayed prepare me for the solemnities of death and eternity. May I view life as a moment, and esteem it my chief concern, in this world, to glorify thee, and reach everlasting rest. May the blessed Jesus blot out my sins in his own blood, and thus prepare me to appear with comfort in thy sight. May my youth, my strength, my health, my heart, my soul, my life, my all, be henceforth consecrated to thee. Number me with thy children, and give to me the disposition of a child; with filial love, with patient submission, with holy delight, may I look up to thee; and may the language of my soul be, Abba, Father. May I enjoy such assurance of acceptance in the beloved, as will enable me to "read my title clear to mansions in the skies." May I know that he has *loved ME and given himself for ME.* Only bless me, O Lord, with this assurance, and death itself shall be welcome to me! Unite with me, in faith and hope, every friend I fondly love; and may they, too, go to Jesus, bearing his reproach; and thus prepare us all to join in those triumphant stra. s — O death, where is thy sting! O grave, where is thy victory! Thanks be to God, who giveth us the victory through our Lord Jesus Christ.

At length, O most merciful Father! the solemn hour will come, and I must die. O in that hour, when my flesh and heart fail, be thou the strength of my heart; may thy rod and thy staff comfort me! O in that hour, when all the tenderness of sorrowing friends will avail me not, be thou more to me than all the world! Disperse, by thy presence, the gloom that shades the grave; and brighten that otherwise dark valley with the sweet dawnings of immortal day! Cheer my departing spirit with the consolations of thy love; and may thine everlasting arms be my support! In the last hours of dissolving nature, enable me to testify the value of thy love, and may those, who witness my dying moments, see me favoured with such blessings as shall make them feel that early piety is real wisdom. Gladly may I take my farewell of earth, and leave friends and kindred without regret, assured of going to dearer, better friends above. Then may He, who suffered for me, be the foundation of all my hope; and leaning my languishing and dying head upon his compassionate arm, may I breathe my last, and sleep in Jesus.

And when, O Lord, I am numbered with the dead, when my last hour is finished, and all the joys or sorrows of life concluded for ever, O then may those ministering angels, that watch thy children's steps, become my convoy to the abodes of bliss! And may my joyful spirit, though bereft of the sweet converse of those it held most dear below, yet find that it shall for ever hold much sweeter converse with angelic friends,

Then may *an abundant entrance be administered unto* me *into the everlasting kingdom of* my *Lord and Saviour Jesus Christ.* May he introduce me into thy presence; there, with all thy saints of ancient days, in glorious happiness to wait the still fuller accomplishment of thy promises when time itself shall finish. There, O my God, may I exult in thy presence, even while those I left behind attend this feeble body to its last long home. While they, with affectionate tears, commit " earth to earth, ashes to ashes, dust to dust, O may I be rejoicing in having reached that land where a sigh was never uttered, nor a tear ever shed. And, merciful Father, if friends or relatives should survive me that know thee not, O may my death be their life! and may they go from my grave to prepare for their own!

And when the period for that state of intermediate glory, which thy word reveals, shall have past, may my sleeping dust arise to the resurrection of life; enraptured may I view the Judge eternal on his great white throne; with gladness may I hear the last trumpet sound, and the last thunders roll; with pleasure see the last lightnings play, and the stormy scenes of time conclude. And O from the kind hand of Jesus, may even I receive that *crown of life, which fadeth not away;* the crown, *which the Lord, the righteous Judge, will give, at that day, to all that love his appearing.*

Then, O my most gracious God, fixed in eternal rest, then, blessed with all the bliss of heaven, may I with all thy ransomed family unite in rendering thee praises for those infinite wonders of redeeming love, for which eternity itself will never praise thee enough. Then may I and millions more unite in that sweet song, "Worthy is the Lamb that was slain to receive power, and riches, and wisdom, and strength, and honour, and glory, and blessing. Blessing, and honour, and glory, and power, be to him that sitteth upon the throne, and unto the Lamb for ever and ever." *Amen.*

CHAPTER XIV.

NO REAL GOOD POSSESSED BY THOSE WHO ARE DESTITUTE OF RELIGION.

§ 1. THOSE considerations from which I have hitherto endeavoured to show the infinite importance of early piety, have been mostly of a pleasing kind; but if you be one on whom all these have been urged in vain, permit me now more briefly to display the value of religion, by presenting to your view some of the dreadful evils to which the want of it will expose you.

Consider the words of the Lord Jesus to an amiable youth, " *One thing thou lackest.*" He wanted that one thing, which is of infinitely more importance than every thing united besides. Humble religion is the best of blessings, and the want of it

"Is worse than hunger, poverty, and pain,
And all the transitory ills below."

Religion is so truly the one important blessing, that it would, in the end, make up for the want of every thing, while all earthly blessings united can never supply its want. Were the whole world your own, it could not give you real peace in life : it could not quiet the stings of conscience ;

Y

it could not ease you in the hour of pain, nor support you on the bed of death; nor obtain for you a place in heaven. If you possess friends, the most faithful, endeared, and affectionate, yet they cannot supply the want of his friendship, whose favour is better than life. They cannot drive sickness, pain, or death away; nor cheer your trembling soul when going to meet an injured God; or when standing at his awful bar. Helpless comforters would they then be; nor could their prayers, or tears, or agonies, arrest the dreadful sentence, " *Depart from me, ye cursed.*" Neither in God's sight will any personal, any mental, or even any moral recommendations stand in the stead of humble piety. " *You must be born again,*" or never enter heaven. Without that divine change, God will look upon you as an object of abhorrence; and all that is most pleasing in human esteem, will no more recommend you to him, than dressing a putrid corpse in fine apparel would do to recommend it to man. The richest dress could not make such a melancholy object pleasing; but if life, and the bloom of health and youth were restored to it, then it would be so, though in the meanest garb. While destitute of religion, you, in the divine sight, are only a disgusting mass of corruption and iniquity; nor can the bloom of health and youth, or the charms of beauty, nor the attractions of all the pleasing endowments imaginable, hide from the eye of God the loathsomeness of ruling sin. He is declared to *hate all workers of iniquity*. (Ps. v. 6.) Even to be satisfied with being almost a Christian, is to continue destitute of all real good; you would then be like a *whited sepulchre,* fair without, but within full of uncleanness. In this way you would go to hell, as it were, by the gate of heaven. But if your nature were renewed, and the divine image formed on your soul, then though you were on earth most despised, yet God would approve and love you.

§ 2. The want of religion is a want which deprives you of a thousand benefits and comforts. You live, without true wisdom, for *the fear of the Lord is the beginning of wisdom, and the knowledge of the Holy is understanding.* They must be strangers to wisdom who are strangers to Christ, the wisdom and the power of God.—You want the forgiveness of sins ; all your crimes are upon you, and the least of them is heavy enough to sink you to hell. Forgiveness is the portion of those who have come to Jesus for it. — You want composure of mind and inward peace. The peace which passeth all understanding cannot be yours. — You may be asleep in sin. — Your conscience may be seared as with a hot iron ; or you may be indulging dreams of future happiness, which never will be realized ; but the true peace of a humble and pious mind cannot be yours till you are Christ's. He left the blessed legacy of Peace, not to the world but to his own. — You want peace with God. *There is no peace, saith my God, to the wicked.* You are naturally alienated from God by sin, and till reconciled to him, God must be to you an awful Judge, and you a rebel, deserving his severe displeasure ; and boundless as his love is to those that return to him by Christ, yet to others he is a consuming fire. — You want his fatherly care. In the hour of distress you have no God to go to that you can justly call your friend and Father. His children may ap-

Prov. ix. 10. Isa. lvii. 21. Heb. xii. 29.

proach him as their own; the language they are
taught is, *Abba Father;* but you are destitute of
this sweet interest in him. — You want all interest in the love of Christ; how tender is his affection to his people! but you have no part nor
lot in this matter. It is a treasure in which you
have no share. Unhappy youth! to be without
a Saviour's love. Wretched creature! to have
no part in that treasure, compared with which
the treasures of a thousand worlds would be as
dross and dust. You live without a part in any
of the blessings Christ bestows. He is no Saviour of yours, though you may insult him with
the title of Saviour. He is no shepherd of yours,
for you refuse to submit to his gentle yoke, and
are not one of his flock. If you call the blessings
of his gospel, grace and glory yours, you are deluding your own soul, for they will never belong
to you till you belong to him. It is to his sheep
only that he gives eternal life; but *you will not
come* to him *that you may have life.* Calling him
Lord, Lord, will avail you not, for he has solemnly declared, " Not every one that saith unto me
Lord, Lord, shall enter into the kingdom of heaven; but he that doeth the will of my Father
which is in heaven. Many will say to me in
that day, Lord, Lord, have we not prophesied
in thy name; and in thy name have cast out devils? and in thy name done many wonderful
works? And then I will profess unto them, I
never knew you : depart from me, ye that work
iniquity." Thus you have no Saviour to take
your sins away; no intercessor to plead for you
before the eternal Father's throne; no shepherd
to guide you through the wilderness of life.

Gal. iv. 6.   John, v. 46.   Matt. vii. 21.

Bright, indeed, are the hopes of those who are truly the young disciples of the Lord ; but none of those hopes are yours. O, the blest eternal mansions of purity and joy ! the sweet immortal morning of never-ending day ! O, the kingdom of God ! the smile of his countenance ! the tokens of his love ! O, the welcome of a Saviour ! and the crowns of glory that he purchased, when wearing a crown of thorns ! O, the blessed society above ! the bright natives of that higher world, or revered saints from this ! These are the hopes, that the dwelling, those the friends, that the humble Christian shall shortly possess. But, alas ! for you no glorious mansions are prepared ; no Saviour smiles ; no heaven blooms ; no immortal day shines for you. No crown of life awaits you ; and none are ready to welcome your entrance on eternity but those infernal beings, who with hellish joy may exclaim, *Art thou become like unto us?*

You want also those blessings that should comfort you in death. All the false supports and deluding pleasures of the world will then be vanity of vanities, and what have you besides? — You want a title to the bliss of heaven. — You have no reason for supposing that your name is " written in the book of life ;" for " he that believeth not shall be damned," and " except you be converted you shall not enter into the kingdom of heaven." Heaven is no home of yours. The friends of Christ and the children of God are the heirs of it ; for they are " begotten again to a lively hope of an inheritance incorruptible, and undefiled, that fadeth not away, reserved in heaven for them ;" but the followers of the world are

Mark, xvi. 16.   Matt. xviii. 3.   1 Peter, i. 4.

the children of Satan, and have no part there; they are "the children of wrath, without Christ and without hope." (Ephes. ii. 3. 12.) Unhappy young man, or young woman! this is too surely your sad condition. O wretched creature! how poor are you in the midst of all you may possess! how truly miserable, in the midst of all your gaieties and pleasures! Poor trifler, you have not one cheering promise in the book of God. If you turn to God, you will have many, but now you have not one. Not one promise that you shall be kept out of hell, even for one month; but many awful threats, that if you die as you are, you shall be turned into that flaming prison. Poor, indeed, are you, all you have will leave you soon. Your hasty pleasures will soon depart, and you must lie down in the dust of death; and leave for ever the world you love so well; while a dreadful and neglected eternity will appear before your trembling soul.

§ 3. The want of religion not merely deprives you of numberless blessings, but exposes you to numberless evils. While without this one thing needful, sin in one form or another, will reign over you. You will be the easy prey of temptations; companions in folly will lead you astray, and Satan guide you in the way to destruction. Dreadful are the evils that sin occasions. An old writer has truly said, "It brings upon us infinite sorrows, plagues, miseries, and the most fearful judgments, blindness of mind, hardness of heart, horrors of conscience, vexation and anguish of soul, bondage under Satan, the prince of darkness, and banishment from God, the fountain of all bliss; and mischiefs more than either tongue can tell, or heart can think. It kills an immortal soul eternally, which is more than all the bloody men on earth or all the desperate devils in hell can do. It will bring upon it in the world to come sorrows without end, and past imagination." How sad an end is this to a few short years of sinful delight!

§ 4. The want of religion is a want which spoils all other blessings. The longer the humble Christian lives, the more he may advance in grace, and ripen for a crown of brighter glory; but if you live without religion, life will be no blessing to you. The longer you live the worse will be your guilt, the more numerous your sins, and the greater your future condemnation. For you in vain the Saviour died. His gospel is to you the *savour of death unto death*. For you in vain apostles preached, and martyrs bled, to hand a gracious religion down. For you in vain the followers of Jesus pray. The sun shines on you in vain, for it shines to light you to destruction. The years roll on in vain, for every added year increases your load of guilt. Health blesses you in vain, for your soul is sickening to eternal death. All the mercies of this world, and all that respect the next, are spoiled or lost to you, and are, "but like a talent of gold, to a man sinking in the sea, which only serves to plunge him deeper in ruin." So that, harsh as it may sound, it would really have been better for you to have been cut off in your sins, and been sent to hell years ago, than to live here adding to the number of your sins, and then sink to endless wretchedness. Yes, unhappy youth, if you continue careless of religion, every added year will prove a curse instead of a blessing. The longer you live in this world, the deeper will be your misery in the next. The more mercies you enjoy, the more guilt you contract. The more blessings you receive from God, the baser is your ingratitude and sin in refusing to give him your youth. A dying profligate once said, " I have been too strong for Omnipotence. I have plucked down ruin." Thus, by carelessness and neglect, you change God's blessings into curses. Oh, what would you think of a sick man, who, by some fatal power, should change all the remedies, by which a kind physician would restore his health, into a subtle poison, which should occasion him years of misery, and torture him to death! Distracted wretch! you might exclaim, all are kind to him but himself! how happy might he be, if he felt half the pity for himself, that others feel for him! Do you slight your God? You act this part; rather a far worse than this; you change his healing medicines into poison; his blessings into curses. You heap up wrath against the day of wrath. By the very mercies of God, you are preparing matter for your own torment; not merely through a few fleeting years, but through a dreadful eternity. Distracted youth! did you feel half that pity for your own soul, that others feel for you, how happy would you become! how many are kind to you! how cruel are you to yourself! O, cease thus to run in the path of destruction, you may yet find that one thing, the want of which is so dreadful. O, seek it now, for they that seek the Lord early, shall find him.

" While Jesus speaks, his voice regard,
And seize the tender hour;
Humbly implore the promised grace,
And God will give the pow'r "

CHAPTER XV.

THE YOUNG SINNER'S INGRATITUDE TO GOD, AND CRUELTY TO HIS OWN SOUL, URGED AS REASONS FOR EMBRACING RELIGION IN YOUTH.

§ 1. I HAVE already, my young friend, shown you, that by the piety of youth you may testify the most gratitude for divine love; and that God would remember this kindness of your youth, to your infinite advantage: but perhaps you still remain undecided. I beseech you then, spend a few moments in meditating on the unkindness of a youth of sin to God, and on its cruelty to your-self. Indulge those thoughts that may now be useful; but which will otherwise fill your last hours with horror, and plant your dying bed with thorns.

While you continue careless of religion, you lead a life of base ingratitude to the God that gave you being. Ingratitude has been pronounced

"Of vices first, most infamous, and most accurs'd."

It is indescribably base when manifested to a friend or parent, in this world; but baser still is ingratitude to God. Has not he given you life, and crowned that life with comfort? Whence flows the ease of health? or whence the cheerful vigour of youth but from his kindness to you? Whence the friends, the parents, the comforts that you have enjoyed? All are the gifts of God. He has blessed you here, and in the gift of Jesus, provided for your blessedness hereafter; and does all this goodness merit no thankful return? Shall God be thus kind to you, and you unkind to him? Do you remember a fable, which perhaps you may have read in your child-hood? A compassionate countryman found a serpent, chilled with frost; he pitied it; he put it in his bosom. The vital warmth restored it to life and activity; but what was its first action? It would fain have destroyed its benefactor. Apply this fable to the present subject. Has not God done more for you than words can express? Are not you indebted to him for life, breath, being, and all things? Through his fostering care, you have reached the vigour and bloom of youth; and what are your first actions? Neglect of God and religion; and thus base ingratitude and sin. O, is not this imitating the serpent? It is true, your abused benefactor is beyond the reach of real injury; but your ingratitude is the same, as if he could receive the greatest injury from you. You deny him your favoured youth. The time in which you are most favoured by God, the blooming season which he values most, that very time, that very bloom, you give to Satan, the world and sin. O! while you act this part, little as you may suspect it, the venom of the *old serpent* is rankling in your heart.

Perhaps you delude yourself by imagining that you shall present him the latter part of life; but does not his goodness claim all your days? Besides, what can the aged convert offer? " His riches? but he can use them no more : his pleasures? but he can enjoy them no longer : his honour? but it has withered on his brow : his authority? but it has dropped from his feeble hand. He leaves his sins, when they will no longer bear him company."

§ 2. In neglecting early piety, you are ungrateful to the Son of God. He humbled himself to earth, he hungered and thirsted, groaned and wept, endured the thorns, the scourge, the cross, and even bled and died in pity to your soul; and he demands no return, but what is for your good as well as his glory. He demands your heart, and you refuse to give it. Were not they basely cruel and ungrateful to him, who cried, " *Not this man but Barabbas* ;" who thus preferred a murderer to the Lord of life; but you act as guilty a part while you prefer the world, that delusive destroyer, to a dying Saviour, and a gracious God! Rather you do worse than the murderers of the Lord of glory did. Many of them knew not what they did, when they preferred the murderer Barabbas to the blessed Jesus. You are more ungrateful to Christ than they; while you profess to view him as the Son of God, and Saviour of men, and yet, in reality, prefer to him, not Barabbas, but sin and Satan. Perhaps you say, " Surely I do not act this horrid part;" but O! deceive not your own heart, for in God's esteem you do, while you refuse to yield your youth to Christ. Though you may merely neglect his grace, yet according to the Scriptures, *grace neglected is grace refused ;* and though you may be merely careless of the Lord Jesus, through thoughtlessness or love to the world, yet it is most certain, that *a Saviour slighted is a Saviour rejected;* and O dreadful! rejected for what? for vanity, folly, and pleasure; or, in plainer words, for the service of the world, and the devil. And O! rejected by whom? by one to whom Christ has an everlasting right. He has such a right to you, and in denying your heart to him you are not merely guilty of the most base ingratitude, but of the vilest injustice. You rob him of his right. You rob not man, but God; you rob God of his honour, and the divine Saviour of what is most justly his; God said of old to Israel, "Will a man rob God? yet ye have robbed me." The language of his word is, "Ye are not your own, but bought with a price, therefore glorify God in your body, and in your spirit, which are God's." What would you think of a man, that might rob an affectionate parent, to give what he stole from his best friend, to a most detestable and cruel enemy of that parent and of himself? Oh, folly, madness, wickedness, ingratitude! My young friend, is not this the part you act, if you deny Jesus what is his due? and give what his love claims to his greatest enemy and yours! If you refuse him your youth and prime, to which he has an endless right, and give that youth and prime to Satan? Love so amazing, so divine as his, demands "your life, your soul, your all;" and shall it have no grateful return? When you owe God every thing, will you be so base as to give him nothing?

§ 3. In refusing your youth to God, you are guilty of the greatest cruelty to yourself. Better far had it been for you never to have been born, than to come into the world to spend a few sinful years, and then to go and make your sad abode with devils and the damned; where the worm never dieth, and the fire never shall be quenched. You would think any one dreadfully cruel to himself, who might cut and mangle his own body, who might tear off his own flesh, who might thrust his own limbs into the fire, and keep them there, in misery till they were consumed.   But which is worst, to mangle a *mortal* body, or undo an *immortal* soul? to thrust a limb into the fire, or to throw the soul into hell?   If you beheld one, that, by a fall from his horse, or from a house-roof, had his limbs broken, and lay writhing in agony on the ground, would you not declare him cruel to himself, if a friend stood by ready and able to cure him, and he were to refuse the needful help?   But which is worst, to linger down to death in agony, through slighting a surgeon's aid ; or linger a few years, a depraved, condemned, and ruined creature, and then sink to endless wretchedness, through neglecting a divine Saviour's help?   If your body were in such melancholy circumstances, you would welcome friendly aid, and while your soul is in a state far more melancholy, I beseech you, neglect not that of the Lord Jesus Christ. You would not be so cruel to yourself, as to thrust a foot, or a hand, or even the point of a finger into the fire ; O, be not so cruel to your own soul, as to undo it with a sure and everlasting destruction!   Every moment that you delay to turn to God, is a moment of cruelty to your soul, your own, your immortal soul.   What would you think of a husbandman, who, in spring, might sow his fields with poisonous weeds, and say, "I'll pluck them up in winter!"   Distracted man!   Where would be his harvest?   In winter, he should be enjoying the harvest, of which the seed was sown in spring, and not then, in want and misery, be tearing up the weeds that had ruined his land.   And will you, by neglecting early piety, sow the seeds of sin in youth, hoping to pluck up the poisonous weeds in age? Perhaps that age may never come.   With all

z

your soul-destroying sins in their full vigour, you may be snatched away to receive the judgment of an insulted and injured God. But if that age should come, it may almost be a hopeless task, then to mortify those corruptions which have been gaining strength through all the years of life; and which have brought forth much fruit unto eternal death. Cruel as the distracted husbandman would be to himself, more cruel will you be, if you spend the prime of life in storing up causes for bitter repentance hereafter, and thus make what should be your best years, your guiltiest and your worst. Alas! how dreadfully baneful to your best interests, is carelessness and irreligion on the edge of an eternal world! A drowning man will catch at a reed; a poor wretch sinking into an unfathomable abyss grasp a twig; but ah, miserable madness of unhappy men! though about to plunge into vast eternity, they slight that helping hand which offers sure deliverance. Still they go on, careless whither, till death, that forceful preacher, discovers all they would not learn, but which they must by sad experience know. O then for a reed of hope! then for a Saviour's helping hand! then for one day of offered mercy more! Misers would give their idolized wealth, monarchs their kingdoms, worldlings their pleasures, for such a blessing once again. Oh, miserable folly! to set no value now on those things, for which they would, ere long, think the wealth of worlds a trifling price. On this side the grave, to let eternal salvation be almost the only thing they neglect, while on the other, it will be the only thing that is worthy of their desire.

§ 4. In neglecting early piety, you are un-

kind to all that wish you well. To that blessed
Spirit, who strives with you; to those holy angels, who would fain rejoice over you; to those
ministers of the gospel, that labour and pray for
your conversion; to those friends, if you have
such, that are the friends of Christ, and that wish
to see you such also. How much comfort you
deny them! What pleasure your conversion
might give them! but you refuse them this pleasure. While thus basely ungrateful to your God,
to the Lord Jesus, and to the Holy Spirit;
while thus cruel to yourself; while thus unkind to angels, to ministers, to Christian friends;
whom, O young sinner! do you please? Only
those malignant spirits, who seek your ruin; only the devil and his angels. They look on you
as their own. Only hell can rejoice over you,
while the church of Jesus mourns; and while if
angels could weep, they would weep for you.
Oh! will you please your hellish foes, sooner than
your compassionate God and Saviour! Oh! will
you do that at Satan's secret bidding, which you
will not do at Christ's open command! Will
you comply with the devil's call, and yield your
youth to him, while you neglect the call of God,
and return him nothing but neglect and sin?
Oh, could you see that hateful foe, would you
then act this wicked part? yet, if you will not
prepare to meet your God, remember you will
soon be given up by him into the hands of Satan; then you will find that you were infinitely
cruel to yourself, as well as basely ungrateful to
God, while pleasing hell instead of heaven.

O, my young friend, would you lead a life so
basely wicked? Would you have to reproach
yourself hereafter with choosing destruction, in

spite of what God and man do to make you happy? Would you have, at last, to lament that you have rushed headlong into hell, in spite of all that was done to turn your feet into the way of heaven? Prevent such sad reflections I beseech you. As ever you would find mercy at the bar of God, fly to the God of mercy now. Seek Jesus in these the fair days of your youth. I know with many young persons, it is now an easy thing to slight the friendly warning that bids them follow the Saviour, and to avoid, or deride the friend that gives it; but it will be dreadfully hard at last, to remember slighted warnings — abused privileges — a gracious God forsaken — a kind Saviour neglected — a wasted youth — a heaven lost — a hell incurred — and a devil pleased instead of God. One way only remains for you to escape all these evils, it is, to go to Christ for life. May God lead you to him.

CHAPTER XVI.

THE VANITY OF YOUTH, AND THE UNCERTAINTY OF LIFE, REASONS FOR THE IMMEDIATE CHOICE OF EARLY PIETY.

§ 1. A DIVINE writer, when urging on the young attention to eternal things, employs this solemn argument: "Childhood and youth are vanity:" Eccles. xi. 10. And is it not so? " Perhaps even now, while you hesitate, you die. Perhaps the shuttle has passed the loom, that wove your winding sheet. Perhaps in yonder shop, lies rolled up, and ready to be severed off, that piece of cloth, destined to be your shroud." The admonition of the Lord is, "Boast not thyself of to-morrow; for thou knowest not what a day may bring forth:" Prov. xxvii. 1. What is there so firm in youth, in health, or strength, that on their continuance, you should venture the salvation of an immortal soul? On no morning of the year can you positively say, that you shall see the evening; on no evening can you be certain of beholding the approaching morning. They who promise fair for most years in this world, may be the very first to enter the next. Possibly even by to-morrow, you may have forsaken this world for ever.

§ 2. Consider what others were a few seasons ago, that are now fixed in the eternal world. They were as young, and perhaps, alas! as thoughtless and as gay as you. When you pass through a burying ground, look at its graves; read the inscriptions there; and see how many, in the bloom of life, have been cut off and called to meet their God. There lie the young, the healthy, and the strong. There lie many whom the world once charmed, and who for it slighted their immortal souls. And what is the world to them now! Perhaps before twelve months more depart, your now youthful and healthful body may be like theirs; your active limbs may be mouldering into dust; your eyes closed upon the world; and all its pleasures, will neither pain nor please you in the grave. Where are they now, and where must you shortly be? They a few years back, were as gay as you can be, but O! all earthly things are for ever past with them. You are young now, so were they then; but

youth and vigour have forsaken them. You are
healthy now, so then were they; though since
numbered with the dead. The world then seemed as enchanting to them, as it can do to you;
they were as much set upon its dying pleasures,
but, they are gone; and O, what is it to their
poor breathless dust! What will it soon be to
yours! They are mouldered back to dust.
Their very coffins are decayed. Their gaiety is
over. Their joys are past. They are gone into
the world of spirits. They have met their God.
O, what new scenes have opened upon them!
With what terror have they, who refused God's
grace in this world, been dragged by hellish
fiends, to everlasting burnings! Could some of
these unhappy creatures now address you, did
not the malignity of their nature prevent them,
they might say, "Avoid our folly. Shun our
misery. Sin and the world have undone us;
heart-rending thought; undone us for ever. A
little while back, pleasure, health, and youth,
were ours! Then we were as eager in the pursuit of fancied happiness, as you can possibly
be. The world appeared drest in as gay colours
to us, as it now does to you. We trusted in our
youth, and looked on future years as our own,
which, alas! we never lived to see. Vanity and
pride filled our hearts; pleasure was our idol;
and the world our delight. Alas! we lived as
if it were our home, and forgot that we were but
travellers through it, to eternal scenes. We
quenched the warnings of conscience; we scorned the admonitions of pious friends; and
thought those strangely impertinent, that reminded us of death and the grave, though, alas!
we were so near to both. We deemed religion

a melancholy thing; and scorned those blessings, for which we should now think a thousand worlds a little price. We ridiculed the folly of professing to be strangers and pilgrims upon earth; and looked down with contemptuous pity on those, whose chief concern on earth, was safely to reach heaven. We thought our folly wisdom, and their true wisdom folly. We heard the tolling bell, but forgot that it would soon toll for us. We saw the opened grave, unmindful that that land of silence would quickly be our long home. Trifling as you, we stopped not to consider what we were, and what we soon must be. But youth failed us, death arrived, and the lying vanities of life fled at its touch. Then we discovered our misery. Then we saw our want; but, Oh! too late. Woe is us! Our day of grace is gone. The tidings of mercy are now unheard by us. The blood of Jesus can never cleanse us; nor the compassion of God reach us now. For the vain pleasures of a moment, we have ruined a whole eternity."

§ 3. O my young friend! would the tale of horror, that such unhappy creatures, if permitted, could relate, make you feel how vain is youth? remember, I beseech you, that it is as vain, as if you could hear their doleful lamentations. Millions of the young die every year. More than half mankind die before they have reached their twentieth year; and what is there in you, to shield you from so common a lot? are you stronger, or healthier, or more sure of life than others? Perhaps,

"The young disease, that must subdue at length,
Has 'Grown with your growth, and strengthen'd with your
    strength.' "

Or how easily may a fever seize upon you, and in a few days reduce you from the highest health, to feebleness and death! How quickly may any sudden change from heat to cold, or many other causes, inflame your lungs, or some other vital part, and in a few days, lodge you — where? In the eternal world. How soon may a cold turn to a consumption, and before you think yourself seriously ill, you may be incurably so! How soon may numerous other diseases, at God's bidding, accomplish their awful errand! You perhaps now look forward to future years, which probably will never be yours; but if they should how soon the years now to come, will be years departed! Others ere long will tread upon your grave, as thoughtlessly as you do on theirs, who went before you. You live in a dying world, in a land of graves. On some spot of earth or other, fresh graves are ever opening. No minute passes in which some do not die. While you breathe some breathe their last. While you think of eternity, others as young as you, are passing thither, enraptured or dismayed. Ah, hapless state of an unhappy world! Some dying in youth, and others fooling their precious youth away. Some going to give up their sad account, and others swelling the black list on theirs. Some neglecting early piety, and others, too late, mourning their folly in doing so. Some trifling with a Saviour, and others trembling before him as their Judge. How soon, if you belong to the former of these classes, will time number you with the latter! You are on the verge of eternity, and some younger than you are daily dying, and entering on its amazing scenes. O, remember that youth is vanity, and life itself no better. And should you continue careless of the Lord Jesus Christ, how bitter ere long will be the remembrance of your wasted youth! This one short and vain life is the only season, in which you may obtain peace with God, and receive the gift of life eternal; and would you still throw this one away? Alas, unhappy youth! who are so truly wretched as they, who do this, excepting they who have done it! Would the starving beggar that has but one penny, toss that away! or the sailor that has but one way of escaping shipwreck, neglect that one! or the traveller who sees but one path from a tremendous precipice, slight that one! and will you waste in sinful delays, the flower and prime of that one vain life, in which eternal life may be sought in Christ and surely found? O! rather unite in the Psalmist's prayer, "So teach us to number our days that we may apply our hearts unto wisdom."

§ 4. Often indulge such reflections as these on the passing scenes around you.

That sun is setting, and has once less to set on me; in time I may soon behold its rise, but enter eternity before it set. This year is closing, and will never more close on me; it is finished; and has brought me so much nearer to the hour when time itself shall end with me.

Do I see a leaf in summer torn from the bough, on which it grew? such is my life. We all do fade as a leaf. Like the leaf, when age the winter of time comes on, it must fade; but as a summer storm may tear the leaf from the tree, and cast it to the ground, so disease may attack my health, and lay my body among the clods of the valley, and send my spirit to God who gave it. O, may I flourish in faith and love, that thus being found waiting, I may welcome the coming of my Lord, though at the most unexpected hour.

Am I taking a journey, in a carriage going rapidly along? the trees, the hedges, the fields, the houses, seem all hastily passing by me; and would lead me to think, that I am sitting still to observe them glide away. But, ah! it is I who move, and they are still! Thus fast am I hastening to the end of my little journey of life, though I mark not its progress, or be thoughtless of its close.

Do I observe a sportsman aiming at a flying bird? it has left no trace behind, and probably his shot may bring it to the ground, and prevent its passing through the expanse before. My past years are gone as the years before the flood; and the years that are before me I may never enter Death, that surest of marksmen, may have already received his dread commission, to number me with the dead. O, may faith and love prepare me for eternity before I feel the awful stroke of death! Seek then, my soul; O, seek without delay, these precious blessings! My stay here is all uncertain. My youth is vanity. My days are swifter than a shuttle; but what will become of thee, if these fleeting days should end, and thou shouldst then be found in thy present state? O, let me seek in Christ deliverance from my sins. Then grace shall make even the vanity of youth a blessing rather than an evil.

> "Be wise, my soul, be timely wise,
> Flee to the atoning sacrifice;
> The gospel promises embrace,
> And trust thy all to Jesus' grace."

CHAPTER XVII.

THE SORROWS AND DANGERS THAT ATTEND THE WAY OF TRANSGRESSORS, A REASON FOR THE CHOICE OF EARLY RELIGION.

§ 1. WHILE the various blessings, which attend a knowledge of the gospel, combine to form a motive for embracing early piety, motives of an opposite but most weighty kind, arise from the disappointments and the miseries, that attend the path of transgressors. "The way of transgressors is hard." "There is no peace to the wicked;" God to them "distributeth sorrows in his anger."

Were we unacquainted with any actual miseries attendant on irreligion, yet there would be enough in the divine word, to convince you that it is ruinous and destructive. Depravity and corruption have led you into the ways of sin; and it is blindness that keeps you contented there. "The understanding of men is darkened, being alienated from the life of God, through the ignorance that is in them, because of the blindness of their heart." "The natural man receiveth not the things of the spirit of God, for they are foolishness unto him." "The god of this world," (or Satan,) "hath blinded the minds of them which believe not, lest the light of the glorious gospel of Christ, who is the image of God, should shine into them." While in this state, you resemble a blind man in the midst of treacherous enemies; he does not see them, and so he does not fear them. Thus, on the edge of destruction, you are unconcerned, because blind to your state;

Prov. xiii. 15.   Is. lvii. 21.   Job, xxi. 17.   Eph. iv. 13.   1 Cor. ii 14.
2 Cor. iv. 4.

for did you see your real state, while uninterested in the Saviour, you might perceive yourself to be, as it were, hanging by a single thread over the mouth of hell; devils waiting to receive you; the eternal Judge frowning upon you; and nothing wanting to seal you up under endless despair, but the command of God to snap the brittle thread of life asunder. You are blinded by Satan, and led captive at his will. Is not this a state of wretchedness? yet this is yours; though spiritual blindness prevents your perception of it.

§ 2. But perhaps though such is your truly dismal condition, you have not felt its danger, nor been alarmed at its horrors. You have thought, and still think, the ways of iniquity pleasing. Yes, unhappy youth, in the flush of health, in the moment of unbridled passion, while the future is forgotten, and death and judgment out of sight, the young sinner may find in them a transitory though brutish pleasure. The profligate, the drunken, and the lewd may be gratified for a few moments with their base delights. The civiler and more moralized, in the giddy ball room, or licentious theatre, or when wasting invaluable time over a novel or romance, may think themselves happy; but,

" Short is the course of every lawless pleasure,
Grief, like a shade, on all its footsteps waits;
Scarce visible in joy's meridian height,
But downwards as the blaze declining spreads,
The dwarfish shadow to a giant grows."

Though sometimes the ways of irreligion may yield a short though guilty pleasure, yet often worldly delights are bitterness, in the pursuit as well as in the end. They are unsatisfying. The sinner pursues them for happiness! and yet is not happy. The lover of pleasure follows his pleasures, yet finds little or no pleasure in them. Have you never known this? Have you never by a smiling countenance, tried to hide the un-easiness of your heart? Have you never seem-ed happy, in the view of others, when full of in-ward misery? In the vain round of amuse-ments, conscience, like a still small voice with-in, often tells the sinner, that the end of these things is death. Conscience, with an unwelcome voice, sometimes warns the deluded followers of the world, that while the one thing needful is neglected, they are poor in the midst of riches, and on the verge of eternal misery, even in the midst of worldly pleasure. Has not this sacred monitor thus at times followed you, and made you uneasy even in spite of yourself? Has it not even at the playhouse, the card table, or the dance, told you that death, judgment, and hell, were at hand? The careless sinner, who seems so cheerful, who laughs so loud, who appears so merry, through these inward stings, often feels, in the midst of all his delight, a load of remorse and wretchedness. The anecdote of Colonel Gardiner, mentioned Page 204, is a well known illustration of this remark.

A young friend of the writer, who had long tri-fled with religion, thus to a near relative express-ed her feelings: "The wicked are like a troubled sea, they cannot rest; and do I not daily experi-ence the truth of this assertion? If my present course yielded me any real pleasure, then my folly might be in some measure excusable, but it yields none; for the threatenings of God's word, the affectionate warnings of my parents, and the stings of my own conscience, continually conspire to blunt the edge of worldly enjoyment, and leave me indeed a miserable creature. Reflection I cannot bear. Oh, no! for then indeed I feel the agonies of a guilty and accusing conscience. I know, I feel that I shall never have a peaceful mind, never taste real bliss, till I from the heart give up the world, till I from the heart embrace real religion. I have drunk of the cup of worldly pleasure, and for its amusements slighted my Saviour and neglected my own soul. And what have I gained? Nothing — but I have drawn sighs from the hearts, and tears from the eyes, of those whom it ought to be my study to render happy; offended God; done despite to the Spirit of his grace; trampled on the blood of the Saviour; and undone my soul! — And with a consciousness of this, can I ever be happy? No — I know by experience that the way of transgressors is hard." My youthful reader, have not you felt something of what is here described? Perhaps you have felt it all.

Were no more wretchedness than this to attend the way of transgressors, if you have any pity on your own soul, your language should be, " Let me devote myself to God, and seek in him those true delights, which the ungodly never knew!" But what has been mentioned forms only a small part of the sorrows, attendant on a life of sin. Not merely does sin bring destruction in the next world, but its frequent fruits are wretchedness and ruin in this.

Behold the prodigal: (Luke, 15.) He thinks himself happy. In jollity and merriment he squanders his possessions away; but see him soon, he is sunk in the lowest depths of wretchedness. Where are his pleasures? his companions? his gay-spent days and festive nights?

They are gone.   He feeds the swine, and longs
to satisfy his hunger, even with the husks on
which they live.   How many have been reduced
to misery as great as this, who but for a youth of
sins, might have passed through life in comfort!
  Sabbath-breaking has been mentioned as one
of the most common sins of youth, and how sad
are its fruits!   It often takes the lead in a legion
of crimes.   The sabbath-breaker is not long
merely a sabbath-breaker.   The writer of these
pages once attended a criminal, who suffered
death for murder, and he spoke of sabbath-breaking as a sin that led him to others! perhaps few
criminals have reached the gallows, who had not
to ascribe their destruction in a great measure to
this crime.   Many have expressly mentioned
this as the source of their guilt and misery.   In
1816 five men suffered on the gallows, at the
same time, in the Isle of Ely, one or two of
whom had been in a decent situation, and who
all bore this sad testimony to the effects of sabbath-breaking. "We most sincerely warn you all
to avoid those sins, which have been the means of
bringing us here.   By all means avoid irreligion
and vice of all kinds; particularly swearing,
drunkenness, and sabbath-breaking."   One of
them declared that drunkenness, whoredom, and
sabbath-breaking, had brought them all to their
untimely end.   The awful judgments of God
on sabbath-breakers, have also proved their way
a way of sorrows.   Many have gone out in the
morning, on sabbath-breaking parties of pleasure, who, ere the evening came, were cut off by
a sudden and unexpected doom; and sent all
unprepared into the eternal world.   Not long
back two parties containing eleven or twelve per-

sons perished during one sabbath-day, in the river Thames.   Could some of these unhappy creatures now address you, they might say, " Forsake your destructive pleasures ; cease your sabbath-breaking parties, lest our doom be shortly yours. Alas ! our broken sabbaths, are our misery now.   Had we improved them, how different had our state now been. Learn wisdom from our folly. Your sabbaths are not all gone, but ours are, and we would give the world to have spent them in the ways of God.   Alas ! we profaned them ; and God was angry with us, and snatched us from the world where mercy may be found, and fixed us in that sad abode, where no sabbath ever shines."

Drunkenness leads to temporal and eternal destruction ; it entails disease on the body ; beggary on the estate ; and damnation on the soul. " Who hath woe ? who hath sorrow ? who hath contentions ? who hath wounds without cause ? who hath redness of eyes ?   They that tarry long at the wine.   Look not thou upon the wine when it is red, when it giveth its colour in the cup. At the last it biteth like a serpent, and stingeth like an adder.   Woe unto them that rise up early in the morning, that they may follow strong drink ; that continue until night, till wine inflame them !   Woe unto them that are mighty to drink wine, and men of strength to mingle strong drink !   Drunkards shall not inherit the kingdom of God."

The guilty indulgence of loose and wanton desires, though so awfully prevalent, entails on multitudes of young transgressors, years of misery and early death.   " There is a chaste affec-

Prov. xxiii. 29 — 32.   Isa. v. 11, &c.   1 Cor. vi. 10.

tion, which fixing on a single object, and operating under the guidance of discretion, produces the most generous sentiments in the heart, and the most tender endearments in domestic life. Such a passion, by forming an attachment at once the most faithful, delicate, and lasting, has often a happy influence over the whole course of our following years. But lust is an unhallowed fire, which burns only to destroy health, honour, and peace."* "For the lips of a strange woman drop as an honeycomb, and her mouth is smoother than oil : But her end is bitter as wormwood, sharp as a two-edged sword. Her feet go down to death ; her steps take hold on hell. I beheld among the simple ones, a young man void of understanding, and he went the way to her house ; in the twilight, in the evening, in the black and dark night : And, behold there met him a woman, with the attire of an harlot, and subtle of heart. With much fair speech she caused him to yield. But he knoweth not that the dead are there ; and that her guests are in the depths of hell. He goeth after her straightway, as a bird hasteth to the snare, and knoweth not that it is for his life. Remove thy way from her, and come not nigh the door of her house ; lest thou give thine honour unto others, and thy years unto the cruel : And thou mourn at the last, when thy flesh and thy body are consumed. Let not thine heart decline to her ways, go not astray in her paths ; For many strong men have been slain by her. Her house is the way to hell." Picture to yourself a young man, the slave of this destructive sin. He might have enjoyed health and vigour ; have been a comfort to others, and a bless-

* Thornton. Prov. v. 3. vii. 7. ix. 18. vii. 22. v. 8, &c.

ing to himself: but his crimes have ruined his health; disease sends him to an early tomb; and his murdered soul goes hence, laden with the guilt of that crime, of which the Most High has solemnly said, "They that do such things shall not inherit the kingdom of God. For this ye know, that no whoremonger, nor unclean person, nor covetous man, who is an idolator, hath any inheritance in the kingdom of Christ and of God. Let no man deceive you with vain words: for because of these things cometh the wrath of God upon the children of disobedience."

Does a young woman give way to the seducer, alas! she finds the way of transgressors hard indeed. Reproaches of conscience, loss of character, with the other bitter fruits of this crime, become her sad portion. Perhaps she goes onward in sin, and ends in prostitution; then has she peace? Ah no! she has become in reality, the off-'scouring of all things. How different is such a one from what she might have been! and from what others are, who have made God the guide of their youth. They the ornaments and comforts of the families to which they belong; but she, ah! what is she? "An abandoned prosti tute! lost to all sense of shame, and to every right feeling! she lives only to propogate disease, and wickedness. and misery, and death, and damnation, to all who come within the reach of her pestilential breath! She becomes one of the grand agents of hell, in the accomplishment of these infernal works."* How deep is now her wretchedness! A minister* who was called by his situation to address some hundreds of these poor creatures in a year, for several years

Ephes. v. 5.　　* Scott's Sermon on Licentiousness, p. 21, 22.

together, made this statement. "Let them be hardened and callous to what other subject they may, there is one on which they all feel, and feel acutely. Speak to them of the *extreme misery to which they have reduced themselves,* and you touch a string which vibrates from heart to heart through the whole company : they are all melted into tears."

Connected with these crimes, dishonesty often takes its dreadful place. Parents are robbed by ungodly children. Masters are plundered by those they employ. But bitter are the fruits of this disgraceful sin ! bitter for time, as well as eternity. Fear of detection, distrust, discredit, and in the end, the prison, transportation, or the gallows, are the frequent termination of those dishonest courses, to which profligacy and lewdness lead.

O, could those who have tried to the utmost, what delights transgression yields, address you, they would assure you, that the ways of irreligion are full of sorrows. Behold in your imagination, the sabbath-breaker, that went out on a party of pleasure, brought home, as hundreds have been, a ghastly corpse See the drunken and the lewd, wallowing for a few short years, in the mire of sensuality ; then view them putrefying with disease ; then see the close of all ; view them expiring, filled with consternation and horror, perhaps blaspheming God and dying : dying miserably as that wretched atheist, who, when told that nothing could be done for him, and that he must die ! clenched his fists, gnashed his teeth, and said with the utmost fury, " God, God, I won't die !" and immediately expired. See this, and then say, Are these the ways of pleasantness? Is this the path of peace? No, not unless damnation is pleasant, and hell the abode of peace. All who have tried the paths of sin have found them hard. Even devils could assure you of this. When was it that they knew happiness? It was before they sinned.

§ 4. Neglect of religion is an inexpressibly dangerous evil. Perhaps you look with horror on some of the sins already mentioned, yet you cannot, while you live without God, say, Thus far will I go in sin, and no further. You cannot, when you please, calm the tempest of unruly passions, by saying, Peace, be still. Few are hardened in iniquity, and sealed for perdition at once. The way of sin is a progressive way. Little did Hazael think, when he conversed with Elisha, that he should afterwards murder his master, and become the monster he became. Little did David, when he first turned his eyes on Bathsheba, suppose that he should soon plunge deep in base adultery, and atrocious murder. Little did Peter think, when he first denied his Lord, that to that falsehood, perjury and profaneness would so quickly be added. Little did the youth, who dies the victim of youthful lusts, imagine, that the first wanton thought he indulged, was the forerunner of all his guilt and misery. Little did the thoughtless girl, who ends her life a prostitute, think, that when indulging a vain pride in dress and show, she was paving the way for all her future guilt and wretchedness; but, ' The way of the wicked seduceth them."

§ 5. Perhaps you are clear of all these open crimes; perhaps you may continue so; you may be amiable and moral, but still **you are a sinner;**

Prov. xii. 26.

and it is inexpressibly dreadful to delay turning to God. Little did thousands, once like you, imagine where the ways of irreligion end. It is dangerous to trifle with God. The Spirit has begun to strive with you, but you know not how soon he may have done. You may quench grace, but cannot kindle it. These three kinds of persons are seldom brought to heaven. Those who long persist in sin ; those who long enjoy the means of grace in vain; and those who fall from God. Perhaps because you imagine there is nothing flagrant in your pleasures you think them innocent delights. But are they such in the sight of God ? Are they such, while they steal your heart from him ? Are they such as will give you pleasure at last?

Not merely are the ways of irreligion inexpressibly dangerous, but all their delights so transient, that it is distraction to neglect eternal life for them. They pass away like an arrow, and end in the most bitter despair. O, leave the world, before the world leaves you ! O look to Jesus, before he says, " I never knew you, depart from me !"

§ 6. " A death-bed, is a detector of the heart ;" it proves that the ways of sin are ways of sorrow. What are worldly pleasures then ? What comfort can they give ? It is said that Mr. Hervey, was once travelling with a lady, who expatiated largely on the pleasures of the play-house. She mentioned the pleasure of thinking beforehand of the play, the pleasure of seeing it, and the pleasure of recollecting it afterwards. Mr. H. mildly observed, that there was one pleasure which she had not mentioned. She inquired what that was ; and he replied, the pleasure of recollecting it upon her death-bed. She felt the remark, and is said to have sought better pleasures. The miseries that await those who are strangers to humble piety have been awfully displayed in the dying hours of multitudes who had slighted that one thing needful.

The author of the "Night Thoughts," describing the last hours of one who was once esteemed a man of pleasure, states,

"Refusing to hear any thing from me, he lay silent, as far as sudden darts of pain would permit, til the clock struck. Then with vehemence exclaimed, 'O time, time! it is fit thou shouldst thus strike thy murderer to the heart. How art thou fled for ever!— A month! O for a single week! I ask not for years; though an age were too little for the much I have to do.'

"On my saying, we could not do too much: that heaven was a blessed place —'So much the worse. 'Tis lost! 'tis lost — Heaven is to me the severest part of hell!' Soon after I proposed prayer. 'Pray you that can. I never prayed. I cannot pray — nor need I. Is not heaven on my side already? It closes with my conscience. Its severest strokes but second my own.' To a friend he said,

"'Remorse for the past, throws my thoughts on the future. Worse dread of the future strikes them back on the past. I turn, and turn, and find no ray. Didst thou feel half the mountain that is on me, thou wouldst struggle with the martyr for his stake, and bless heaven for the flames; — that is not an everlasting flame; that is not an unquenchable fire.' He afterwards exclaimed, 'O! thou blasphemed yet most indulgent Lord God! Hell itself is a refuge, if it hides me from thy frown.'"

It is related that the honourable Francis Newport, was favoured with a religious education, afterwards became altogether careless of religion, and died in the following awful manner.

At one time, looking towards the fire, he said, "Oh! that I were to lie and broil upon that fire for a hundred thousand years, to purchase the favour of God, and be reconciled to him again! But it is a fruitless vain wish; millions of millions of years will bring me no nearer the end of my tortures, than one poor hour. O eternity! eternity! who can properly paraphrase upon the words — *for ever and ever!*"

"In this kind of strain he went on, till his dissolution approached; when with a groan so dreadful and loud, as if it had not been human, he cried out, "Oh! the insufferable pangs of death and damnation!" and so died; death settling the visage of his face in such a form, as if the body, though dead, was sensible of the extremity of torments."

Another person, who was a gay and thoughtless lover of the world, uttered the following, among other expressions, in his dying hours.

"O! that I had been wise, that I had known this, that I had considered my latter end. Death is knocking at my doors: in a few hours more I shall draw my last gasp; and then judgment, the tremendous judgment! How shall I appear, unprepared as I am, before the all-knowing and omnipotent God! How shall I endure the day of his coming! O! that holiness is the only thing I now long for. I would gladly part with all my estate large as it is, or a world to obtain it.

Now my benighted eyes are enlightened. **What** is there in the place whither I am going but God? Or what is there to be desired on earth but religion? The day in which I should have worked is over and gone, and I see a sad horrible night approaching, bringing with it the blackness of darkness for ever. Heretofore, woe is me! when God called, I refused; when he invited, I was one of them that made excuse. Now, I receive the reward of my deeds; fearfulness and trembling are come upon me; and yet this is but the beginning of sorrows! It doth not yet appear what I shall be; but sure I shall be ruined, undone, and destroyed with an everlasting destruction!"

A young woman who had lived negligent of the great salvation, not long before she died, burst into tears, and said, "O, that I had repented, when the Spirit of God was striving with me! but now I am undone." She afterwards exclaimed, "O, how have I been deceived! When I was in health, I delayed repentance from time to time. O, that I had my time to live over again! O, that I had obeyed the gospel! but now I must burn in hell for ever. Oh! I cannot bear it. I cannot bear it." Not long before she died, she said, "Eternity, Eternity. Oh, to burn throughout eternity!"

Perhaps you think such cases, though dreadful, not frequent; but, it is to be feared, they are by no means rare. Within a few days, several awful instances, of the danger and misery of an irreligious state have been mentioned to the writer. One unhappy creature in his dying hours, among a number of dismal expressions, used such as the following: "Oh, that hell! Why must I leave this earth! O, that hell!" A farmer, filled with enmity against real religion, went from his house into an adjacent field, uttering a wish that he might never enter the kingdom of heaven, if he did not ruin a pious neighbour whom he disliked; and scarcely had he reached the bottom of the field, before he dropped, and died. Another, who was a Socinian in principle, and in practice profane and worldly, had, by an apoplectic fit, been warned to prepare for meeting his God; but he would not listen to the warning; his health returned; he loved the world; he put far off the thoughts of death, and often talked of living to his hundredth year. One afternoon, it was stated he expressed his expectation of this to a person, in a neighbouring village: Ah, sad presumption on to-morrow! that very evening, he was seized by another fit, and hurried all unprepared, as it is to be feared he was, to the bar of his Judge.

A young woman who had occasionally attended the writer's ministry, though, alas! in vain, was laid upon the bed of death. In that solemn situation, her lamentations and bitter grief, were most affecting. She confessed that she had neglected the great salvation. "Oh!" she exclaimed, "Oh, my hard heart! I find no softness in it. It will not relent. Is there no forgiveness for me? Am I not to be saved, Lord?" Her most frequent cry was, "Lord, break my hard heart!" In a few hours after this, she died.

A sick man whom the writer visited, who once had pious impressions, but did not yield to them, observed, "I would give ten thousand worlds to be pardoned." The language of another sufferer, often seen by the writer, was deeply affecting. "I know I am not forgiven. Oh! it is dreadful to die! Oh, millions and millions of years — it is dreadful! O that I could live till I am forgiven! It is too late now! It is all over! O that I had come to Christ sincerely!" When spoken to of the Saviour's mercy, she answered, "That is what makes it so bad, to sin against so great a Saviour." Alarmed with the prospect of eternal ruin, she said, "Nothing in this world is to be compared with it. The *Lord will not be played with* too often."

Another young woman who had attended the writer's ministry, but who continued a careless worldly girl, was hurried, by a sudden disease, into the eternal world. It was stated that not many hours before her death, she warned her sister, not to walk in the ways in which she had walked, declaring that they led to hell, and that she was going thither.

Is such the conclusion of a life of sin? Are such the consequences of making light of Christ? O, then, as you would avoid the awful end of transgressors, forsake their destructive path! If you continue in it, your own departure from the world, may hereafter resemble theirs, whose unhappy end has been now described. Bitter would it then be for you, to think of those sins, and of that neglect by which the soul is undone. Alas! what madness is it to choose damnation, if you may but go, what is to corrupt nature, a pleasant way to hell.

Listen not to the voice of seducers who would lead you to ruin. They promise you liberty, but are themselves the slaves of sin. Their artifices to lead you into sin or to keep you in your present state, are stratagems of Satan to ingulf you in eternal misery. When the insidious but smiling seducer would tempt you astray, think with yourself, "Can I bear my Creator's anger? Can I endure my Judge's frown? Can I dwell with everlasting burnings? Shall I neglect eternal life, and choose eternal death, for things that perish in the using?" — May God forbid. *Amen.*

CHAPTER XVIII.

THE TERRORS, AND FEARFUL CONSEQUENCES OF DEATH AND JUDGMENT, TO THE UNCONVERTED, A REASON FOR EARLY PIETY.

§ 1. HAS what I have already urged on your attention produced, under God, the desired effect? or has all been urged in vain? if it have, let me, before I leave you for ever, entreat you to consider those awful scenes, to which you are hastening so fast.

Should you love the world ever so well, should you enjoy it ever so much, and even live in it through the longest term allowed to man, yet short is the longest, and when past, a nothing. You must die. How thoughtless soever you may be of death and eternity, they are nearer to you every hour, and you, even you must die. If you continue to live without God, you must die without him. Imagine yourself leaving the world in that awful state. You *must* leave it *thus,* unless you repent and remember your Creator. Imagine your last day arrived. This scene of vanity is ending. The world you loved is leaving you for ever. Behind you is a wasted and sin-spent life. Before you is the grave, judg-

ment, and eternity. Your day of grace is finished. Your soul, loaded with innumerable sins,
is going to meet that God, to whom all your secret guilt has been revealed. Where can you
look for refuge? Man cannot help you, and you
have every reason to believe that God will not.
Now sins forgotten come to mind again. Now
guilty pleasures stare you in the face; but all
their charms are gone. Now fears and terrors
crowd upon your soul; and devils seem to beck-
on you away. All is darkness and misery before; all guilt and folly behind. O fearful state!
O fearful end of an ungodly life! You must
plunge into eternity; and justly dread the awful change. No friend can go with you; you
must die alone, and go alone to meet your God.
All else is forsaking you; and he who would never have forsaken you, he who would have been
your friend for ever, even he will refuse to receive you. How you would dread to be carried
to sea alone on a single plank; or to be tossed
alone upon some unknown shore, where you knew
none, and none knew you! But what is this to
passing into another world, where all is strange
and new; a world so different from this poor
transient state, that all is awful, and all eternal
there! Yet thither you must go. The hour, the
dreadful hour arrives. Your last moment comes,
you die; and ah! the agonies of death are succeeded by the fiercer torments of damnation and
despair. No kind angels welcome your departing spirit. No gentle messengers appear to convey it to eternal rest. O doleful state! if this
were the worst; but far worse than this remains
untold. Your sweet season of mercy is gone;
and in vain you wish for mercy and for time

that you felt the power of divine truth, and yet went on to sin again. The sermons of ministers, the admonitions of friends, and the warnings of the Bible, will all be remembered in judgment, and produced, to show how much greater is your guilt, than theirs, who lived in heathen lands, and heard no tidings of salvation. Then too it will be known what poor trifles, what base delights, you preferred to the love of God and the joys of heaven. O, think not to escape! God will bring *thee* into judgment. Though thou shouldst be hardened in life, and even deluded in death, yet when thou hast had thy day of sin, God will have his day of vengeance; and when thou hast had the pleasure, thou must have the pain. Think not that you have done with the sinful pleasures and follies of past years. You have not done with them yet; the delight is gone, but the sad account remains behind. You perhaps call your youthful sins, frolics, or innocent sports, or foibles at the worst, but if you are thus deceived, God is not. Your slights of religion; — your neglect of his service, and his ways; — your broken sabbaths; — your wasted days; — your pride; — your vanity; must all be answered for on that tremendous day.

§ 5. Know, O young man, if you are a follower of the world, you must then receive the reward of all your sinful actions; your riotings and revellings, your drunkenness and debaucheries, your hardening others in sin, your wanton songs, your profane words, shall all come to light, and insure your damnation. Though you may be a wanton profligate, or even a scoffing infidel, yet God will bring you into judgment; and infidel as you may be, will make you tremble be-py saints and angels, that might have been their companions for ever, but now not one friend among them.   To see what they might have enjoyed, and what their sin and neglect of Christ have lost. And Oh, though heaven is shut against them, hell is open to receive them; that is the region, which they must take instead of heaven; that seat of horrors; that mournful gloom; that outer darkness; that wretched abode of everlasting fire, and ever-tormenting fiends. Oh, dreadful hour, when they enter that flaming prison, yet there they must await eternal judgment.

§ 3. Ah my young friend, remember that the hour, the now forgotten, but, if you live in your sins, the terrible hour of eternal judgment will arrive. You may forget it now, but will be unable to forget it then. You possibly laugh at the expectation of it, but will then find it dreadfully serious, to see and feel its terrors. *You*, even you, *must* hear the archangel's trumpet. *You* must behold the descending Judge, and the burning world. Willing or unwilling, ready or unready, there you must appear. There will be no shrinking from trial; no escaping the notice of the Judge; no lingering longer in the grave. Appear you must, for, " the Lord Jesus shall be revealed from heaven with his mighty angels, in flaming fire, taking vengeance on them that know not God, and that obey not the gospel of our Lord Jesus Christ : Who shall be punished with everlasting destruction from the presence of the Lord, and from the glory of his power. God will render unto every man according to his deeds. Unto them that are contentious, and do not obey the truth, but obey unrighteousness, in-

2 Thess. i. 7 — 9.

dignation and wrath, tribulation and anguish, upon every soul of man that doeth evil. Rejoice, O young man, in thy youth, and let thy heart cheer thee in the days of thy youth, and walk in the ways of thy heart, and in the sight of thine eyes; but know thou, that for all these things God will bring thee into judgment. And whosoever was not found written in the book of life was cast into the lake of fire." Do you believe that such a day will come, and can you forget it? forget that day, that joyful, or that dreadful day, which will come as surely as the sun shines in the heavens; forget that awful day, when you, without any fear or hope of change, must become like the angels of heaven, or the fiends of hell. O, will you forget it? If you were going on trial for your life, before an earthly judge, how anxious would you be to procure an acquittal; and when you have to go before an infinitely higher Judge, whose decision will be life or death eternal, will you be so distracted as to remain unconcerned?

§ 4. There you must account for the deeds done in the body. Then your actions must be tried; your words examined; then the black aggravations of your crimes will fully appear. O sinner, then it will be known, how you broke through the checks of conscience; and the restraints of religion; how you were warned of your danger, and exhorted to repent, but still, obstinately impenitent, went forward to destruction. Or if your heart has, at times, been seriously impressed, and yet in vain, it will then be seen, as one of the aggravations of your sins,

Rom. ii. 6. 8. 9. Eccles. xi. 9. Rev. xx. 15. Rom. xiv. 12. 2 Cor v. 10. Matt. xii. 36.

that you felt the power of divine truth, and yet went on to sin again. The sermons of ministers, the admonitions of friends, and the warnings of the Bible, will all be remembered in judgment, and produced, to show how much greater is your guilt, than theirs, who lived in heathen lands, and heard no tidings of salvation. Then too it will be known what poor trifles, what base delights, you preferred to the love of God and the joys of heaven. O, think not to escape! God will bring *thee* into judgment. Though thou shouldst be hardened in life, and even deluded in death, yet when thou hast had thy day of sin, God will have his day of vengeance; and when thou hast had the pleasure, thou must have the pain. Think not that you have done with the sinful pleasures and follies of past years. You have not done with them yet; the delight is gone, but the sad account remains behind. You perhaps call your youthful sins, frolics, or innocent sports, or foibles at the worst, but if you are thus deceived, God is not. Your slights of religion; — your neglect of his service, and his ways; — your broken sabbaths; — your wasted days; — your pride; — your vanity; must all be answered for on that tremendous day.

§ 5. Know, O young man, if you are a follower of the world, you must then receive the reward of all your sinful actions; your riotings and revellings, your drunkenness and debaucheries, your hardening others in sin, your wanton songs, your profane words, shall all come to light, and insure your damnation. Though you may be a wanton profligate, or even a scoffing infidel, yet God will bring you into judgment; and infidel as you may be, will make you tremble be, fore that bar, which is the object of your contempt and ridicule now. Or if you are all that is moral and amiable in the sight of men, yet if destitute of saving grace, God will see in you ten thousand unforgiven sins, for which he will condemn you then. Know, O young woman! that God will then bring you also into judgment. Your sabbaths wasted in indolence or trifling merriment — your time squandered on poisonous novels — your heart wrapped up in dress and gaiety, while God and religion are shut out of it — your glass consulted, while the Redeemer is neglected — your fondness for worldly delights — your forgetfulness of your poor immortal soul — all these sins and many more, are crying to heaven against you, and not one, in that awful day, will be forgotten. Perhaps all who wish you well for ever, strive in vain to impress your heart; but God will make you listen, God will bring you into judgment. Vain will be the pleas and excuses that now deceive yourself and others. The Judge will pronounce the dreadful sentence; he will say, " Depart from me, ye cursed, into everlasting fire, prepared for the devil and his angels," and depart you must. Oh, dreadful sentence! to *depart from Christ,* the only source of happiness — to depart from him *ac cursed,* laden with the heavy curse and wrath of God, never to be removed — to depart from him, accursed, *into everlasting fire,* and that the fire, which was *prepared for the devil and his angels!*

§ 6. O stop, my young reader! while this sentence sounds in your ears; stop, and consider your ways. Can you bear to have it, with all its horrors, pronounced upon you? If not, O, turn to God. Consider, that if you harden your heart against this friendly call, that time is coming when you must remember it. *In the latter days,* says God, *ye shall consider it perfectly.* God will then remember the sins and ingratitude of your youth. At that last day you may call for mercy, and God refuse to listen, as he now calls on you to turn to Christ, and you refuse to hearken. His word says, "Because I have called, and ye refused; I have stretched out mine hand, and no man regarded; but ye have set at nought all my counsel, and would none of my reproof; I also will laugh at your calamity, I will mock when your fear cometh. Then shall they call upon me, but I will not answer; they shall seek me early, but they shall not find me. They would none of my counsel; they despised all my reproof; Therefore shall they eat of the fruit of their own way, and be filled with their own devices." Then, when all his terrors are set in array against you, how will you answer him? You cannot say you were not called to serve him, for the lines you are reading would witness against you. You cannot say you were too young, and expected longer time, for he has taught you that the youngest are not too young to die, and that those who seek him early shall find him. Alas, what will you then think of this warning! how tremble before your Maker for the sins of your youth. The Lord Jesus Christ will remember your ingratitude and wickedness; and when they who sought and found him betimes, have entered his eternal rest, while he crowns them with his everlasting love, you, a poor trembling, unforgiven creature, may knock at the door of mercy, then for ever shut. You may join your voice with

Jer. **xxiii.** 20. Prov. i. 24—31.

that of foolish millions, in the dismal cry, *"Lord, Lord, open unto us!* Leave us not in endless woe, and infinite despair. Leave us not the prey of devils, and the scorn of hell. Leave us not without one glimmering beam of hope, through a dreadful eternity." Alas, vain cry, the Judge will say, *I never knew you, depart from me!* O, be wise! and guard, by early piety, against the terrors of that day. The eternal Judge will not be thus inexorable, unless, by your choice of sin, you make him so. Give him now your heart, and he will then give you a crown of life which fadeth not away.

§ 7. But if you will not regard this advice, you will then know your cruelty to your own soul. Then you may sadly exclaim, " God was kind to me; he sought my happiness, and had I listened to his voice, I should have been for ever happy. The Son of God was gracious to me. O, how numberless were his compassions; had I regarded them, how blessed should I now have been. The Spirit of God was kind to me; though grieved and resisted, how long he strove with me. O, had I yielded to his gentle influence, no creature surely had been more blessed than I. The servants of God were kind to me. Pious friends warned me, and prayed for me, and wept for me. Faithful ministers taught me, and laboured for my good, and wished for no reward, but my salvation. But I, alas! was unkind to all these, and cruel to myself. I denied them all they sought — my happiness; — all they prayed for — to see me snatched from hell. O, had I had but half that compassion for myself, which others had for me, how blessed had I been

Matt. vii. 23.

now!　O, had I let my God, my Redeemer, my Christian friends, or ministers, have their desire, I should now have been rising to eternal glory; but ungrateful to God, and cruel to myself, I have undone my own soul with an everlasting destruction.　Wretch that I was, to have no pity on myself, while so many pitied me.　Wretch that I was, to rush so madly to eternal flames, while so many strove to keep me out; and alas, so obstinately to refuse such blessings, while so many sought to make me a partaker of them."

CHAPTER XIX.

THE ETERNAL RUIN OF THE UNGODLY A MOTIVE FOR THE EARLY CHOICE OF RELIGION.

§ 1. THERE exists, in many minds, a strong dislike to a faithful representation of those horrors, to which the ungodly are exposed in the eternal world; yet the divine Saviour and his apostles, by denunciations of the terrors of a wretched eternity, warn the sinful to flee from the wrath to come.　Far, my youthful reader, am I from loving to dwell on so painful, so dreadful a subject.　Fain would I have you sweetly constrained by the love of Christ to follow him; but perhaps I address some hardened, or some thoughtless son or daughter of folly, on whom that love has made no impression.　O! then let me make one effort more for your salvation; and though it is a dreadful reason, let me urge one reason more for your accepting the grace of God. And O, eternal God!　now assist me, and by thy terrors alarm that thoughtless soul, which thy love has not affected nor thy promises allured.

§ 2. Dreadful are the representations which the Scriptures give of the punishment of the ungodly. Hell is described as " a lake of fire ;" of fire prepared to punish the "devil and his angels." "At the end of the world, the angels shall sever the wicked from among the just, and shall cast them into the furnace of fire." The Judge shall say, " Depart from me, ye cursed, into everlasting fire, prepared for the devil and his angels. And these shall go away into everlasting punishment." " He will burn up the chaff with unquenchable fire." "The fearful, and unbelieving, and the abominable, and murderers, and whoremongers, and sorcerers, and idolaters, and all liars, shall have their part in the lake which burneth with fire and brimstone ; which is the second death." "And the smoke of their torment ascendeth up for ever and ever; and they have no rest day nor night." "It is better for thee to enter into life maimed, than having two hands to go into hell, into the fire that never shall be quenched, where their worm dieth not, and the fire is not quenched." "The wicked shall be turned into hell, and all the nations that forget God." The Lord Jesus himself tells of one who lived in wealth and pleasure, but he died, and "in hell he lifted up his eyes, being in torments, and seeth Abraham afar off, and Lazarus in his bosom ; and he cried and said, Father Abraham, have mercy on me, and send Lazarus, that he may dip the tip of his finger in water, and cool my tongue ; for I am tormented in this flame. But Abraham said, Son, remember that thou in thy life time receivedst thy good

Matt. xiii. 40, 50.   Matt. xxv. 41, 46.   Matt. iii. 12.   Rev. xxi. 8.
Rev. xiv. 3.   Mark, ix. 43.   Ps. ix. 17.   Luke, xvi. 23.

things, and likewise Lazarus evil things; but now he is comforted, and thou art tormented And besides all this, between us and you there is a great gulf fixed; so that they which would pass from hence to you cannot; neither can they pass to us that would come from thence."

§ 3. What bitter misery must they endure, who feel the wretchedness here described! What outward torment! what inward anguish! How dire will be the horrors of the hellish prison! The place, the company, the state, will all unite to make hell a hell indeed. Figure to yourself a prisoner, in the most dismal dungeon of the most dismal prison. No light ever shines there. The poor sufferer has wept away a score of years in darkness. Black bread is his only food, water his drink. No human tongue ever utters one kind word to him. He hears no sound but the harsh grating of rusty doors, and the rattling of chains. In vain for him the sun shines, he sees it not. Others are happy, but he is wretched. Others have friends, but he has none. Others have homes, a dungeon is his home. Others have clothes, chains are almost his only covering. Others have comfort, no comfort is ever his.— This is a prisoner in the dungeon of some earthly tyrant; but time is flying, a greater than man will soon set him at liberty. Ah! for what would you be in such a situation? Would the whole world bribe you to pass twenty years in such a dungeon? Twenty years thus spent would seem longer than twenty ages. Yet, ah! to those who have sunk to hell, what a heaven would the prisoner's dungeon seem! Compared with the miseries of damnation, his miseries would be blessedness.

§ 4. All the delights of lost souls are gone for ever. Their pleasures, which they loved instead God. are for ever departed. Their laughter is ended; their mirth is finished. They have done with play-houses, and card-tables, and taverns, and romances, and novels. They sing their wanton songs no more; but groan beneath the sting of every guilty pleasure. All their delusive hopes are fled; they no longer dream of heaven; but hope has left them to be tormented by black despair. All their false peace is passed away; and they learn by bitter experience, that there is no peace to the wicked. Once they deluded themselves with presumptuous expectations, and hoped for heaven, while they slighted the only way, that can lead a sinner thither; but now they are dreadfully undeceived. Once they could scorn religion as unnecessary strictness; but, now, too late they know that it was the only real wisdom. With all their pleasures, and delusive hopes, every other mercy forsakes them. No sabbath shines on them. No season of mercy cheers them with its light; their day is ended, and a horrible night of eternal darkness has begun. Once they might have prayed; but then they would not, and in hell they cannot. God calls on them no more; but has forgotten to be gracious. Jesus pities them no more; nor can his blood ever wash away one of their sins, though once it might have cleansed them from all. The Spirit strives with them no more. Once they would not turn; and now they cannot. No one will ever more pray for them: No friendly voice will ever say to them, "Sinner, turn, there is mercy for you." The sermons of ministers shall no longer weary them; for they shall hear of gospel grace no more: the admonitions of pious friends shall no longer trouble them; for in hell they are fixed beyond the reach of hope, or prayer, or admonition, or mercy.

All the blessings of the eternal world, will be for ever lost to them, God will never cheer them with his smile. Never will they pass a single hour, where saints and angels enjoy a whole eternity. They are shut out of the heavenly city. Their eyes will never behold its glories; their ears never be enraptured with its melodies; their hearts never be gladdened with its delights. No crown of glory will ever be theirs. Their tongues shall never join the heavenly anthems of praise, for victory and salvation. God will never wipe one tear from their eyes; or remove one pain from their hearts; but will pour out upon them all the fierceness of his wrath. Jesus will never lead them to fountains of heavenly pleasure; not for one moment, manifest to them the smallest portion of that love, which in full perfection, he will manifest to his friends, through one eternal day.

§ 5. In hell too, every detestable evil, every abominable passion, will reign and triumph. The unhappy creature that sinks into that dreadful prison, will have no companions but tormenting devils, and the spirits of the damned. They, whose lives were the blackest, and whose dispositions the most horrid, will meet there. Nero and Herod, and cruel persecutors; Alexander, and bloody conquerors; the guilty crew of Sodom and Gomorrah; Paine and Voltaire, Hume and hardened infidels; profane blasphemers, ferocious murderers, swearers, adulterers, drunkards, with Satan and his angels, will compose the dreadful society of hell. Among all these there will not be one mild disposition, or one circumstance to soften the rage of the infernal passions they feel within. There, alas! must they dwell, hateful, and hating one another; ever tormenting, and ever tormented; with every hellish passion, and every devilish disposition, augmented by the madness of despair. There not one soft word will be ever spoken; not one mild look ever seen; but rage and fury be vented in curses and blasphemy. O, could you endure in this world, such company for *a single day!* how dreadful is their lot, who must dwell with devils and the damned *for ever!*

§ 6. To all this misery is added, that of the fire that never shall be quenched. And Oh, who can dwell with devouring fire? who can endure everlasting burnings? All the torments which martyrs have suffered, would be almost easy, compared with the torments of damnation. Many of those faithful servants of God have yielded up their lives, in the midst of dreadful burnings; but these were not an everlasting fire. An old writer says, "I have read of the horrid execution of a traitor: being naked, he was chained fast to a chair of brass or some other metal, that would burn most furiously, being filled with fiery heat; about which was made a mighty fire, that by little and little caused the chair to be red and raging hot, so that the miserable man roared hideously many hours for extremest anguish, and so expired. But what an horrible thing had it been to have lain in that dreadful torment eternally." If merely a finger be burnt, or one limb be scorched, how tormenting is the pain! yet what is this compared with sinking in the flaming waves of hell, tormented in every part, and nothing to give a momentary relief! yet this must be the careless sinner's dreadful portion. The Son of God himself has declared the awful truth; and it is hideous cruelty to an immortal soul, to undo it, through a delusive hope, that God's threatenings will not be fulfilled. Can you then, O young sinner! *dwell with everlasting burnings?* you must, if you do not repent If your hand were thrust into a flaming furnace, the torment would be great, but more supportable, if you were assured that in a minute, it should be taken out again: but if your hand were capable of lasting so long, and you were assured that it should continue burning for life, how intolerable would your misery seem! how would you wish for death to end it, yet it would be a nothing, compared with what the spirits of the lost must feel in hell. There *all* the soul, and, after the resurrection, *all* the immortal body, must endure indescribable misery, and no easy part within or without. How dreadful is the state of those, who, dying in their sins, are dragged down by devils, to infinite despair! Oh, what a change, when they are snatched away from the world they loved, to that where there is nothing but malignant spirits to torment them! no sound of a Saviour's love; but horrid lamentations and despair. What fearful horrors stare them in the face on every side! How would they shrink back from the mouth of the infernal dungeon, but Oh! they cannot, for the wrath of an incensed God drives them in. And when once they have entered it, it is for eternity. Alas! how infernal the society, how doleful the abode! Oh the dreadful torments of eternal fire! Oh the horrid company of hellish fiends! Where can they turn their affrighted eyes? Alas! it is every where the same sad spectacle, blackness, and darkness, and devils, and flame. O could they die again, but die they cannot. Roll on, ye everlasting ages, but why roll on? ye will never be nearer to an end.

> "Tempests of angry fire shall roll
> To blast the rebel worm,
> And beat upon his naked soul,
> In one eternal storm."

How dreadful a change is this for the careless sinner! Here he has many comforts, and what he esteems pleasures; there, not one. Here tender friends are his companions by day; but there are no kind companions there. By night an easy bed refreshes his weary limbs; and in calm sleep even his sorrows are forgotten; but there he will sleep no more to forget his misery; but writhe and toss his wretched form for ever on the lake of fire. Here even the most distressed have something remaining to lessen their wretchedness; but there, human kindness cannot enter; and devils cannot love. There is nothing to give, even once in ten thousand years, a momentary pleasure. No ease to mingle with a sea of misery. Not one gleam of hope to brighten an eternal night. Not one drop of water, to cool for a moment the wretched tongue tormented in that everlasting flame. Misery will reign in every heart; despair will scowl on every face; rage, anguish, and remorse, distract every soul.

§ 7. Ah it will be so. To the fire that never shall be quenched, is added the worm that will never die. The lost sinner will feel a hell within, as well as hell without. Infernal passions, like so many ravenous vultures, will tear his wretched soul. Little, young sinner, do you imagine, what misery will spring from this one source. Some unhappy creatures even in this world, have seemed to be lively images of what lost souls must be for ever. A statement to the following effect appeared in 1797, in the New York Theological Magazine. "A young man who had had some serious impressions, but who hardened himself in sin, declared, that after that time when God seems to have forsaken him, his heart became as hard as adamant — his enmity against God increased to a great degree. He did not feel one desire to ask or receive mercy, or the least favour from God. He never reflected on the divine character, but his heart rose in the most violent opposition. 'Whenever,' said he, 'I reflect that God is Almighty, just and holy, — that I am dependant on him — that he can and will do with me what he pleases, my heart burns with rage and fury, and had I power I would execute vengeance upon the Almighty.' He then said to a number under religious impressions, I have heard you relate the feelings of your hearts, and you appear to have some sense of your wickedness; but if enmity of heart against God is wickedness, and that it is I am fully convinced, though I wish to believe the contrary, your present sense is nothing compared with the fountain of iniquity within. I know if all men's hearts are alike you would dethrone the Almighty if you had power. Had I an omnipotent arm, heaven would soon be stormed, and God be cast headlong from his throne.' 'I have no peace,' said he, 'day or night, my torment is as great seemingly as I can endure.

God is constantly in my view, and my heart is constantly burning with rage and fury.' His eyes, his countenance, his air expressed the same feelings with his words. Nothing said availed any thing unless to increase his rage and enmity. "He had," says the writer, "as it appeared to me, the most clear and lively sense of the wickedness of the human heart — of the divine character — of the creature's dependence — and the nature of future torments, of any person with whom I was ever acquainted. His distress was sometimes so great, that he would lie down and roll upon the floor; groan like a man exercised with excruciating pain; and cry, 'O! that I could banish from my mind, all thoughts of God for ever and ever!' At one time he travelled barefoot in the night, twelve miles in a deep snow; and gave as a reason for his conduct, that bodily pain was the only means, by which he could divert his mind from those objects which gave him greater distress; he therefore did it to mitigate his distress." Oh doleful condition! Oh miserable end of a life of sin, if this were all its misery! but as the happiness of saints is never perfected on earth, so there is no reason for believing, that even this dreadful wretchedness is at all to be compared with the miseries of the lost. Words cannot describe, nor imagination ever conceive, what will be the remorse of such a soul. Then will the sinner discern for what he lost the fair inheritance of heaven; and for what poor trifles he sunk his soul to hell. Then will he know what base pleasures of a moment, he preferred to eternal life and eternal glory. Oh how will it wound his soul, to think of grace refused, and Christ neglected! Oh, while he blasphemes his

God, how will he curse his own self-destroying folly, in choosing the way to hell instead of that to heaven, and sin instead of religion! Oh how bitter now will be the remembrance of sabbaths wasted! of mercy rejected! of the calls to which he would not hearken, and the admonitions he would not regard! "Is this the hell," may the unhappy creature say, "that I was choosing when I turned a deaf ear to the advice of God! Is this the fruit of my fancied wisdom! and this eternal flame, the end of all my pleasures! Is even this damnation my own choice? Ah! why have some whom I once knew risen to glory! They were not born the heirs of heaven any more than I. Like me they *were* the children of wrath. Why are they admitted and I shut out! Why are they happy and I miserable! They in heaven and I in hell! Ah! they listened to the Saviour's voice, and I hearkened not. They turned to God, and I refused to turn. They were wise, and I distracted; now they are blest, and I undone. Wretched creature! and have I sold my soul for a moment's base delight? Have I valued eternal glories at so little a price? Have I preferred the world and the devil to a compassionate Saviour and a gracious God? Alas! I have. Woe is me! All is lost! My soul is lost! and damnation with all its horrors, must be mine to all eternity."

§ 8. Eternity Eternity! this completes the sinner's misery O young sinner, if once you sink to hell it will make even hell itself more horrid, to think that you must be for ever there. "The intolerableness," says one, "of your pain and torment, will make every day seem an age, and every year as long as eternity; and yet you must lie there an eternity of these long years." Had a lost soul in hell but the faintest hope of deliverance, though at the end of as many millions of ages as there are drops in the sea, hell would lose half its horrors. But now, alas! eternity, which might have been the measure of their joys, will be the only measure of their torments. There the fire never shall be quenched. Could a lost soul shed but one tear, once in ten thousand years, and do this till a sea as vast, as all the seas on earth together, were filled with tears, all its sufferings, in that long, long period, would be but the beginning of eternal misery. All those millions of years of wretchedness, would bring the unhappy soul no nearer to an end of its torments, than one poor fleeting hour. Oh infinitely miserable creatures! that when millions of years of sorrow are past, can only say, "These flames again, these tortures again;" and when millions more have flown, will still find their miseries beginning; and for ever see an eternity of misery still before them. Were these sorrows to be borne, only for the most numerous course of ages, they would be more supportable; every hour of misery would then bring on an end of all misery; and of the most deeply undone sinner it might be said, that the time would come, when devils should cease from tormenting, and the unhappy should be at rest. Yet, O eternity! that joyful or dreadful word forbids the hope. Oh pitiable folly of unhappy men, wretched madness of miserable sinners! so wilfully to refuse a Saviour's grace, and so obstinately to plunge into perdition. And, O my young friend! is not this yours? If it is, these sorrows will soon be yours. You may forget how fast eternity comes, but will never forget how slow it goes. Do you not pity those, who by one wrong step in youth, entail on themselves misfortune and sorrow for life? but oh, how are you to be pitied who in this short life are ruining an endless one. In this little inch of time, you are bringing a heavy and immoveable curse on a whole eternity. You are doing the worst mischief to your own soul that hell can wish; and worse than a united hell could do. Satan may tempt you to slight salvation; but he cannot make you do it. Oh will you make light of Jesus still? and still refuse your heart to him? Oh if you do; alas for you, that ever you were born! for when your future wretchedness has lasted as many millions of miserable years as there are sands on the sea-shore, it will be but beginning; and when it has continued as many more it will be no nearer ending. A head-ache, or a tooth-ache, or a burning fever, for one night is painful; but what is this to a painful eternity! How slowly go your hours when kept sleepless with pain! how long they seem, while you count hour after hour, in sad succession, and wish the morning to appear! but there is no easy morning to follow the night of hell. How slowly will go a sad eternity there, when no hope of an end appears! What life of sinful pleasure and neglect of Christ can ever make amends for this! How short is the trifling, and how long the sorrow! How short the pleasure, and how long the pain! How short the momentary satisfaction, and how long the dreadful punishment! The Christian, when he looks around, may mourn to think what will be their lot in eternity, whom he sees so careless of eternity now. "These poor creatures," he may often have to say, "unless they repent of their sins, will be lamenting the sinful delights of to-day, ten thousand ages hence; for eternity is theirs." O my young friend, could you now look into that flaming prison, whose terrors no tongue can express; could you see the livid flame, the darkness visible; could you behold those who were once angels changed into devils; and the immortal spirits, that might have reached heaven, now weltering in the lake of fire; could you see this, you would behold what you, even you, must see ere long, unless you seek that grace which leads to glory. Could you see this, it might then be said to you, "Hither tend the paths of transgression. Hither a youth, spent in folly and vanity, has conducted many; here end the pleasures of sin." O, flee from destruction; flee from the tempter; flee from all that would charm you to neglect your God, for such charms allure to hell.

CHAPTER XX.

THE YOUNG READER ENTREATED TO MAKE HIS LASTING CHOICE.

§ 1. It was the blessed resolution of Joshua, that whatever others did, he would *serve the Lord;* a resolution made more than three thousand years ago, but which doubtless yields him satisfaction even to the present hour. And now you have read thus far in this little volume, what is your decision? I have endeavoured to set before you some of the pleasing, and some of the dreadful motives which urge you to embrace the

D d

gospel of the Lord. Yet think not that the half, or even the thousandth part has been told. Faint is the representation here attempted of the love of Christ; the worth of the soul; the joys of heaven; or the terrors of hell. Those awful realities, in solemnity and importance, more exceed the account here given of them, than a thunderclap exceeds the faintest whisper; or than the noon-day sun outshines one glimmering spark. What then is your decision? Have you chosen? or will you choose the way of life? Perhaps you know that you have not; or perhaps you scarcely know whether you are in the way of life or not. If this be the case, examine yourself by a few plain scriptural marks; and try your state, before it be tried by the Eternal Judge.

§ 2.—1. They who are the willing slaves of their sins, are most certainly in the way to destruction. "Know ye not, that to whom ye yield yourselves servants to obey, his servants ye are to whom ye obey; whether of sin unto death, or of obedience unto righteousness?" "The works of the flesh are manifest; which are these: Adultery, fornication, uncleanness, lasciviousness, idolatry, witchcraft, hatred, variance, emulations, wrath, strife, seditions, heresies, envyings, murders, drunkenness, revellings, and such like; they which do such things shall not inherit the kingdom of God." "Let no man deceive you with vain words; for because of these things cometh the wrath of God upon the children of disobedience." "He that committeth sin, is of the devil."

2. They who indulge envy, hatred, malice, or any malevolent passion, are most surely in the way to hell. "If ye forgive not men their tres-

Rom. vi. 16. Gal. v. 19, 21. Ephes. v. 6. 1 John, iii 8.

passes, neither will your Father forgive your trespasses." He that loveth not his brother abideth in death. Whosoever hateth his brother is a murderer; and ye know that no murderer hath eternal life abiding in him." "If a man say, I love God, and hateth his brother, he is a liar."

3. They whose lives may be moral, but who indulge a careless unconcern about salvation, who are thoughtful about this world, but thoughtless about the next, are most certainly hastening to hell. "How shall we escape, if we neglect so great salvation." "See that ye refuse not him that speaketh. For if they escaped not who refused him that spake on earth, much more shall not we escape, if we turn away from him that speaketh from heaven." "A certain man made a great supper, and bade many; and sent his servant at supper time to say to them that were bidden, Come, for all things are now ready. But they made light of it, and went their ways, one to his farm, and another to his merchandise: And they all with one consent, began to make excuse. I say unto you, that none of those that were bidden shall taste of my supper. For many are called, but few are chosen."

4. They who are in the way to heaven, have been brought to see and feel the evil and sinfulness of sin, and have been brought to true repentance; without which no one can be saved. "Except ye repent, ye shall all likewise perish." "Thus saith the high and lofty One, that inhabiteth eternity, whose name is Holy; I dwell in the high and holy place, with him also that is of a contrite and humble spirit, to revive the spirit

Matt. vi. 15. 1 John, iii. 14, 15. iv. 20. Heb. ii. 1—3. xii. 25. Luke, xiv. 16, &c. Matt. xxii. 5, &c. Luke, xiii. 3.

of the humble, and to revive the heart of the contrite ones." "The sacrifices of God are a broken
spirit; a broken and contrite heart, O God, thou
wilt not despise." "Come unto me, all ye that
labour and are heavy laden, and I will give you
rest."

5. They who are in the way to heaven, have
been led to the Lord Jesus Christ for salvation.
"A man is not justified by the works of the law,
but by the faith of Jesus Christ." "Blessed be
the God and Father of our Lord Jesus Christ,
who hath blessed us with all spiritual blessings
in heavenly places in Christ; He hath made us
accepted in the Beloved." "Who his own self
bare our sins in his own body on the tree, that
we, being dead to sins, should live unto righteousness; by whose stripes ye were healed. For
ye were as sheep going astray; but are now returned unto the Shepherd and Bishop of your
souls."

6. They who are in the way to heaven have
such a value for the Lord Jesus, that they prefer
him to the whole world; and they who would not
part with every thing, and even life itself, for
Christ's sake, cannot be his disciples. This truth
is most certainly taught in Scripture, and is so
decisive a mark of our real state, that I beg your
particular attention to it. "What things were
gain to me, those I counted loss for Christ. I
have suffered the loss of all things, and do count
them but dung that I may win Christ." "Unto
you therefore which believe he is precious."
"Lord, thou knowest all things, thou knowest
that I love thee." "Whom having not seen ye

Is. lvii. 15.   Ps. li. 17.   Matt. xi. 28.   Gal. ii. 16.   Ephes. i. 3,
1 Pet. ii. 24.   Phil. iii. 7.   1 Pet. ii. 7.   John, xxi. 17.   1 Pet. i. 1.

love." "He that loveth father or mother more than me is not worthy of me; and he that loveth son or daughter more than me, is not worthy of me. And he that taketh not his cross, and followeth after me, is not worthy of me. Whosoever doth not bear his cross, and come after me, cannot be my disciple." "Whosoever he be of you that forsaketh not all that he hath, he cannot be my disciple." "If any man love not the Lord Jesus Christ, let him be Anathema Maranatha."

7. They who are in the way to heaven set their affections on things above; and they, whose affections are not fixed on heavenly things, whatever their profession may be, have no true religion. "Lay not up for yourselves treasures upon earth: But lay up for yourselves treasures in heaven; For where your treasure is, there will your heart be also." "If ye then be risen with Christ, seek those things which are above." Set your affections on things above, and not on things on the earth." "Here have we no continuing city, but we seek one to come." "We walk by faith, not by sight." "We look not at the things which are seen, but at the things which are not seen; for the things which are seen are temporal; but the things which are not seen are eternal." "Many walk, of whom I have told you often, and now tell you even weeping, that they are the enemies of the cross of Christ, whose end is destruction — who mind earthly things. Our conversation is in heaven; from whence also we look for the Saviour, the Lord Jesus Christ."

8. They who are in the way to heaven, manifest their faith in Christ, by lives of holiness.

Matt. x. 37. Luke, xiv. 27. 1 Cor. xvi. 22. Matt. vi. 19. Col. iii. 1, 2. Heb. xiii. 14. 2 Cor. v. 7. iv. 18. Phil. iii. 18, &c.

They resist sin; they watch and pray; they study and endeavour to be like their Lord; and they who are careless of leading holy lives are perishing in sin. "In Jesus Christ neither circumcision availeth any thing, nor uncircumcision; but faith which worketh by love." "Faith, if it hath not works, is dead, being alone." "Follow peace with all men, and holiness, without which no man shall see the Lord." "Being made free from sin, and become servants to God, ye have your fruit unto holiness; and the end, everlasting life." "In this the children of God are manifest, and the children of the devil; whosoever doeth not righteousness, is not of God, neither he that loveth not his brother." "Mortify therefore your members which are upon the earth." "Take ye heed, watch and pray. I say unto all, watch." "Christ suffered for us, leaving us an example that we should follow his steps." "If ye live after the flesh, ye shall die; but if ye through the Spirit do mortify the deeds of the body, ye shall live." "Hereby we do know that we know him, if we keep his commandments. He that saith, I know him, and keepeth not his commandments, is a liar, and the truth is not in him."

§ 3. Do any of the former of these few plain marks show you to be yet in your sins? or do the latter appear in you and mark you as a child of God? Have you been humbled before God for your sins? Have you fled to Christ for righteousness and life? Have you learned to esteem Jesus and salvation above all earthly good? Would you sooner die for him, than live

Gal. v. 6.　Jam. ii. 17.　Heb. xii. 14.　Rom. vi. 22.　1 John, iii. 10.
Col. iii. 5.　Mark, xiii. 33.　1 Pet. ii. 21.　Rom. viii. 13.　1 John, ii. 3.

without him ? Do you choose heavenly things
in preference to earthly? and is it the chief desire of your heart, and the main concern of your
life, to live as you would wish to die? Multitudes go much further in piety, than all this, but
if these marks of your possessing religion be
wanting, be assured, on God's authority, that
you are no more than almost a Christian at the
best; and far from happiness and heaven. Can
you, when you look back on life, if unable to tell
the time when you were first awakened, yet say,
*One thing I know, that whereas I was blind, now I
see!* Can you see that you have, from your
heart, devoted yourself to God? that you have
seriously and deliberately, chosen him as your
God, and Christ as your Saviour? If you discern nothing of this kind, depend upon it, the
reason is that you are as yet perishing in your
sins. Transactions between God and the soul,
of so much importance as these, cannot possibly
have taken place without your notice and remembrance. When any one has been brought out of
darkness into light, does he not know it? When
a servant has changed masters, is he not aware
of the change? and if he forgets the day, yet he
remembers that such a change has taken place;
and if you had changed the service of the world
and sin, for that of God and Christ, would you
not know that you had done so? Alas you cannot have a plainer proof, that you are in your
sins, than having no knowledge of any alteration
of this kind in your views and feelings. But
should I leave you thus? God forbid! I beseech you to be reconciled to God. I beseech
you to choose the way of life.

§ 4. Youth is your choosing time, The years

between fifteen and twenty-five are an awfully important season. What you are at the end of that period, you will probably be for ever. That laborious and useful minister, Doddridge, not many years before his death, observed, that by far the greater part of those who had been admitted to communion in the church under his care, were, as he apprehended, under twenty-four years of age ; and that of those who had been admitted later, several were brought to religion in their much earlier years. Another minister, who laboured for nearly forty years, and under whose ministry it has been supposed, a thousand persons were converted, is stated to have observed, that he never knew one person, who sat under the preaching of the gospel till his thirtieth year without embracing religion, that ever embraced it afterwards. So true is it, my young friend, that youth is your choosing time. Now therefore decide, whose you will be in this world, and whose you will be for ever. Behold life and death are before you. For eternity you have to make your choice. You have to decide whether you will be a child of God, or a slave of the devil; an inhabitant of heaven, or an out-cast in hell. Your early days are days for beginning to be happy; for securing happiness that will last for ever; and can you do this too soon? If you would possess heaven, seek it now.

§ 5. By the infinite worth of religion, I beseech you make your choice. More than a thousand lives depend upon it, even a whole eternity. All that is deemed most great, and most important, all about which the wise debate, and the noble contend, all for which nations war, and armies die, is as worthless as a feather, compared with the blessings of the gospel.

By all the joys and glories of heaven, I beseech you, embrace early religion. If you wish ever to enter those blessed abodes; if you would ever obtain a crown of life eternal; make this your choice. You *may* obtain everlasting glories; you *may* enter heavenly rest; and when this poor vain life shall have passed, dwell in the presence of God and the Lamb; you may do this, and will you not? Are you bent on shutting your own soul out of happiness? The crown of glory, peace and blessedness, joy and triumph, the sweet society of angels, and the love of God, all may be yours; and will you refuse them all? By these and ten thousand heavenly blessings, I entreat you, seek God as your God. Then welcome death! welcome eternity! welcome all the scenes beyond the grave! welcome the great judgment! welcome heaven!

By the care and kindness of others for you, I beseech you to turn to religion. Shall God entreat you in vain to be reconciled to him? Shall Jesus sue in vain? Shall the Spirit strive in vain? Shall all who labour for your good, labour in vain? O, forbid it, and be wise for eternity.

By all the solemnities of death, I beseech you choose the way of life. Think of your dying hour, of your physician saying, There is no hope; of your friends bidding you a last farewell, of your pulse stopping, your voice failing, your eyes closing, and your soul taking its everlasting flight. And will you for the pleasures of a moment undo that immortal soul? Think of yourself stretched lifeless in a coffin; of your grave opened; of your funeral over; of your body the prey of worms and corruption; and in a little while of nothing remaining of you in this world but a heap of dust; O think of these things, and by these be persuaded, to make that choice now, which will yield you satisfaction when you die.

By the vanity of this world, I beseech you to choose that Saviour, who would guide you to a better. When you see the remains of skeletons, and of mouldered coffins, thrown up in a grave-yard to make room for another who is going to the same long home, think what is the value of this world to them, that lay in those coffins once. Its worth to them is its worth to you. You must die though they are dead. You must need a coffin soon, though they have done needing one. How small is the difference! They have met their God; and you will shortly meet him! They are in heaven or hell; and you upon the edge of one or the other. In this situation, for so vain a world slight not, I entreat you, your im-mortal soul.

By all the eternal Father's kindness, I beseech you yield your heart to him. By his goodness in giving you life; by his kindness in crowning your days with comforts; by his patience in bearing with you when he might justly have spurned you to hell; by his pity in offering you salvation; by his love in giving his beloved Son to death for your transgressions, and frowning on him that he might for ever smile on you; by all this, and by all that goodness of the Lord's, which, if you had ten thousand hearts, would claim them all; I beseech you give him that one poor heart you have. As you would not be base-ly ungrateful, and infernally wicked to your best friend, I entreat you no longer yield to vanity, sin, and Satan, that health and youth which God demands.

By all the compassion and love of the Son of God, I beseech you make his service your sincere and lasting choice. By his deep humiliation and poverty; by his poor manger and his life of sorrows; by his tears and sighs for wretched men; by his bloody agony, and his thorny crown; by his bitter cross, and all his sufferings there; I entreat you give him yourself. Love like his demands your all for ever. By his enduring all this, to save you from the dreadful pains of eternal death, I entreat you defeat not his gracious designs. As you would ever have an interest in his love, as you would have him receive you to his eternal abode, O receive him now as your Saviour, your Lord, your all.

By every feeling of pity for yourself, and compassion for your own soul, I beseech you embrace early religion. Will you not have pity on your own soul, that deathless soul, which at another day, you will want God and Christ to pity? You love your body, would you hate your soul? You love to adorn and preserve the feeble building of clay; would you damn the immortal spirit that dwells within it? You love ease, O, pity yourself, and rush not forward to eternal pain! You love happiness, O, be wise, and choose eternal happiness! As you would not have all your hopes end in despair; as you would not have all your pleasures end in sorrow; as ever you would find pity at the bar of God, and mercy at his hands, pity yourself, and make his love your portion.

If you would not abuse the grace of God to your own destruction; if you would not be the wilful murderer of your own soul; I beseech you embrace the gospel. How hard you would think it, if God had decreed your everlasting misery, and irrevocably shut you out of heaven; and now, when he offers you life and salvation, would you shut out yourself? Would you be so cruel a self-murderer as to expose your own soul to the death that never never dies? for that is the destruction which the soul incurs. You will, you must do this, if you do not turn to the Lord. Could some hardened creature ask you to sign a declaration, that you hated religion; that you determined to have nothing to do with God or the Redeemer; that as for heaven they were welcome to it, who thought it worth their care; and as for hell you cared nought for it;— Could you be asked to sign such a declaration, would not you start back with horror at the proposal of doing so? Or had some one the power of offering you the whole world, and of saying, "I will give you all the happiness of this world, all its wealth and all its honours, if you will give up all hope of heaven, and engage when you die to dwell with the devil and his angels through all eternity:" would you not tremble at the very thought of accepting such an offer? and of being your own wilful destroyer? O, then do not do in reality, what you would not do by such an agreement. Most persons lose their souls as completely as if they bargained for the loss. He who lives careless of religion, says by his conduct, "I choose hell for my portion, and Satan for my master." It comes to the same at last, whether you profess that you hate religion, or live careless of the blessed Son of God. To despise serious religion would sink you to hell, and thus make you the murderer of your own soul; and to live without embracing humble piety, and obeying the gospel, will do the same: and where in the end, is the difference?

By all the sorrows of the ungodly, be persuaded to make your instant choice. By all the misery of dying in despair; "By all the terrors of the tomb; by death and hell;" I entreat you yield your youth to Christ. By the fire that never shall be quenched; by the worm that never dieth; by the utter darkness, which shall never be cheered with one gleam of light; by the misery that shall never know one moment's ease; by all the horrors of an eternity in hell, I beseech you flee from the wrath to come!

By the eternal difference between those who love the Lord, and those who love him not, I entreat you embrace the gospel. All other distinctions will shortly vanish for ever. Youth and age, strength and weakness, will be soon on a level in the grave. My young friend, when you see a person oppressed with poverty and gloom; covered with rags; and worn out with the burden of four score years, while you feel vigorous and gay young and healthy, you perhaps think with pleasure, how different is your lot from his. A little time, and that difference will be over. It will be all over when you meet your God: health, and youth, and vigour, will have fled away; nothing but an interest in Jesus will then avail you. No distinction will remain but that which springs from true religion; and that will last for ever. Here the difference between those who love Christ, and those who slight him, is not most perceptible: but it will be most fully seen in the eternal world. Here the religious and the irreligious meet together. They dwell in the same houses; they

engage in the same business. In the house of
God they sit in the same seats, and hear the same
truths; but hereafter they will be parted far asunder. The last great separating day is hastening
on; and then shall they mingle together no more.
No more shall they occupy the same seats; nor
dwell in the same houses; nor pursue the same
employments. All this will be for ever done
with; and a distance wide indeed, will part them
for eternity. O! as you would then have the distinction of belonging to Jesus, embrace his gospel now! As ever you would share the happiness of those who meet in glory, I beseech you
by coming to Christ, secure it now! How happily will they meet there, who have trodden the
same path of humble religion here! How happily
will the pious child meet his parents! the faithful pastor his flock! relations join relations
again! and friends unite with friends!

And now, my young friend, life and death are
set before you. " I call heaven and earth to record against you, that I have set before you life
and death, blessing and cursing; therefore choose
life." The only alternative presented to you, is,
Religion and heaven; or, *Want of Religion and
hell.* Which, O, which is your choice? Now
is your choosing time. You must be a saint or
a brute here, and an angel or a devil hereafter.
Perhaps you may never again be invited to make
this important choice; and your decision this
day, may be that by which your eternal state will
be fixed. Choose then, I entreat you, the way of
life, if you have not already chosen it. Peace
attends it, and happiness is at its end; happiness
inconceivable, unutterable, and eternal. And
will you choose? or have you chosen humble re-

ligion? If you have, let me take you by the hand, and lead you into yonder fair and spacious world. May I imagine that I see you arrived there? or are you determined never to go thither? May I imagine that I see you before the throne of the Eternal, adorned with the splendours, and blessed in the raptures of heaven? Ah! is it but deception? do you still slight the way that leads a sinner to glory and to God? May I imagine, or is that too happy a supposition, that you ascribe your early choice of the way of life, to the blessing of the Most High on this little volume? O, if in any instance this be the case, blessed be God, who gave the disposition to write it! and blessed be the day that saw it begun! May I imagine, that you look on this as the happy choosing day that led you to Jesus; and thus fix-ed your joy for an eternity, where days, and years, and ages are no more? O my brother, my sister, may I fancy that I meet you there, with your great interests and mine secured for ever? Blessed hour! blessed scene! O, in the prospect of it, let me urge you to make religion your earliest, only choice. It is the best that you can make. Were you prevailed on this day to obey the gospel, and begin a life of early piety, how happy a day would this be to you! The best and happiest day of your life. The day that you might look back upon with most pleasure, even from a death-bed, and from the eternal world. Will you then, in God's strength, determine to make early religion your first concern? and never more to refuse the Saviour's grace? If you will, seek help from God in fervent prayer; commit your soul to Jesus; and then how happily will you ere long enter endless blessedness, when

this vain and inconstant world, this deceitful and
fleeting life, have passed away for ever. Then how
happy will you be a hundred years hence, when
others are as busy about this world, and you are
quite forgotten ; and your very tombstone hardly to be read by passing travellers.   Then, in
what inconceivable blessedness will your happy
spirit dwell, long after not " one wretched trace"
remains of the hand that has written, or the eye
that reads.— Choose but religion. Give yourself
to Christ, and life or death will be equally a privilege.   Your last sigh will then be a forerunner
of eternal praise; your last pang of eternal raptures; and the paleness of death will be seen on
your countenance, but a moment before the glories of eternal life.   Yet a few years, and you,
if you know the Saviour's grace, shall experience
a far more transporting change than any heart
can conceive.   O, could we see what thirty or
forty years will discover, it might then be seen
what are the effects upon your heart, of this little
book.   It might then be known who chose the
happy, who the wretched part.   Young as you
may be, yet a few years and this will be known.
O, flee to Jesus.   Choose religion.   Then will
your life be blessed ; your death happy ; your
eternity glorious.   Remember that this is the
most important choice you can ever be called to
make.   On this it depends whether life shall be
a blessing or a curse ;—yourself an angel or a
devil — God a friend or an enemy ;—Jesus a
kind Saviour, or a dreadful Judge ;— heaven
your home, or hell your prison ;—praise your
sweet delight, or cursings and blasphemy your
dreadful employment;—angels and glorified
saints your beloved associates, or devils and the

damned your horrid companions; — Satan a vanquished enemy, or a horrid tormentor. May the God of heaven lead you to seek your happiness in the Lord Jesus and himself! If you have made early religion your choice, may he lead you forward to the promised crown; and if you are not a partaker of that best of blessings, even now may he soften your heart to penitence, and direct you to his crucified Son; and thus, at length, bring you to that blessed world, where hope shall be exchanged for happiness; faith for sight; grief for gladness; danger for safety; death for life; and where, to complete all, saints will be for ever with the Lord.

CHAPTER XXI.

TWENTY OBJECTIONS TO EARLY PIETY BRIEFLY STATED AND ANSWERED.

PERHAPS, my young friend, you feel that religion is important; but would be excused from attending to it at present. Perhaps you strengthen this disinclination, by some of those objections to early religion which abound in this corrupt world. Permit me to enumerate a few of these, and to give them a plain though serious answer.

Objection 1. I am but young; I have time enough yet; I do not mean to put religion off for ever; but why should I begin with it so soon?

Answer. Young as you are, you are not too young to die; nor if you die in sin, are you too young to be lost for ever. Young as you are, were you to die with only one of your youthful sins upon you, that one would sink you to destruction. Young as you are, you are not too young to be called to meet your God, to stand at his judgment-bar, and to be fixed in heaven or hell for ever. In this Island alone, it is computed, that nearly seven thousand persons die every week; numbers of these are the young; and while so many graves are opening every day, may not one soon be opened for you? Why should you promise yourself that you shall see old age, when so few comparatively reach it? But if you should, "he that in his youth reckons it too early to be converted, in his old age may find it too late to be saved." Few, repent in age. Who are the irreligious crowds that throng our towns and country, but those who neglect God while young? It is a dreadful fact, that few turn to God in age; enough to guard the aged from despair; but so few as to warn the young, not to expect to be made partakers of grace and glory, unless brought to Christ in youth.

Obj. 2. I see many, older than myself, following the world; why should not I do so too?

Ans. Because if they choose destruction, you should not choose it with them. If they abuse the mercies of God, and heap up wrath against the day of wrath, you should not do the same. If you saw some aged neighbours taking the way that would lead them to prison and the gallows, you would not say, "They ought to know better than I, why should I not follow them?" And if you see hoary-headed sinners, that have served the devil all their days, serving him still, why then would you make their desperate madness a reason for giving your youth to the devil? God will not inquire of you what they did, but what you did. If your friends, if your relatives, are all the servants of sin, O! be ambitious to be the *first* in your family, that shall find the way to heaven. Pray for them; perhaps some of them may follow; but if they should not, it is better to go to heaven without ungodly relatives, than to go to hell with them.

Obj. 3. Perhaps, my young friend, such is your humble lot in life, that you have to object,

I am poor, and possess but little knowledge. I work hard all the week, and if I do not make Sunday a day of recreation, I can never take my pleasure. I see too my superiors in riches and knowledge, giving themselves little concern about religion, then why should I mind it?

Ans. You should regard religion as your chief concern, because you are not to follow the example of the great and the noble, but that of the blessed Saviour, who was in this world a man of poverty and sorrows. You are told, in his word, "that not many wise men after the flesh, not many mighty, not many noble are called;" and that it is "the poor" that "have the gospel preached to them." They often hear it gladly, when the rich and great scorn and neglect it. And though you may have no day for recreation except the Sabbath, yet what will be the end of that pleasure, which is gained by profaning that holy day? It will be everlasting bitterness and despair. Is not your soul worth more than your body? and endless ages than a few short sorrowful years? If you knew the pleasures of religion, you would think "a day in God's house better than a thousand" days of mirth elsewhere; and though you may be poor in this world, would find that delight in prayer and communion with God, which you never found in all your sinful sabbath-breaking pleasures; and which those of the great and noble, that know not God, never obtained from all their riches and honours.

Obj. 4. Religion it is true is important; but this is not to me a suitable season for following it : when I have a convenient time I intend to inquire for the ways of God.

Ans. And what time will be more convenient than the present? Will it be so when the cares and burdens of the world, or perhaps of a young and rising family, are pressing on you? Will it be so, when the pains of disease and the languors of sickness are overpowering all your faculties? or when the infirmities of age make the grasshopper a burden? Ah no. Least of all will it be so when you come to die. Often have I heard the sick and dying declare, that if they had not sought the Lord before, they could not have sought him then. But perhaps you think that as life advances, your appetite for sensual pleasures will grow less; and that you shall embrace religion with less difficulty then than now. Alas! you are dreadfully deceived. " You might as well expect to drown a fish by putting it into water, as to extinguish sensual desires by following sensual delights." If you could scarcely cure a cold, would you expect to cure it when become a confirmed consumption? If it be hard for a captive to break a single chain, will it be easy for him to escape when loaded with more than double fetters? So conversion is made more difficult by delay. Think then of no more convenient time. None can be more so; all will be less so than the present. Remember, Felix said, " Go thy way for this time, when I have a more convenient season, I will call for thee ;" but that **more convenient season never came, and Felix** was undone. God tells you of no season more convenient than the present. "Now," says his word, "is the accepted time, behold, now is the day of salvation."

Obj. 5. I might attend to religion, but I have little leisure, and have much else to mind.

Ans. O my young friend! whatever else you may have to mind, the salvation of your soul should be your first concern. If you were sure of gaining a crown and a kingdom; what would this be compared with gaining a crown of glory, and an endless life of blessedness in heaven? To enjoy this, and escape the damnation of hell, is of ten thousand times more consequence to you, than to gain the whole world, if you were sure you could do it. The apostle Paul counted *all things loss* that he might *win Christ;* nor does he now repent of his choice. Would a dying man say, "I have so much else to mind, that I cannot find leisure to take the medicines, that, under God, may raise me from this bed of sickness?" Would a condemned criminal say, "I have so much business to attend to, that I cannot find time to apply for my pardon, or to accept it if offered?" And shall a perishing sinner say, "I have no leisure to escape from hell and seek for heaven?" What will all your studies, or labours, or cares come to if your soul be lost? You would think a condemned criminal distracted, who would eagerly attend to other things, and slight the pardon offered him, though the hour of execution might be at hand. You would say to him, "Secure your life first, then you may follow other concerns with comfort." But what is the loss of life compared with the loss of the soul? What is the folly of the man

who might trifle in view of the gallows, compared with his who trifles on the edge of hell?
Secure your soul first: Seek first the kingdom
of God and his righteousness, and all other
things will be added unto you. Mind this one
great business. Let that one work be done, without which you are undone for ever; and then
you may comfortably attend to the other business of life. Delay is injustice to the God of
heaven; and insulting treatment to his holy Majesty, to put off attending to what he enjoins,
while you are busied with mere worldly trifles.
If ten thousand pounds and a fine estate were
offered you, would you say, "I have too much
else to mind, to think of this offer now?" And
when God offers you Christ, and salvation, and
heaven, will you neglect a Saviour, and everlasting blessings, for things, for which you would
not neglect a few hundred pounds or shillings, if
offered by a fellow creature?

Obj. 6. I see no need of such strictness; and
cannot think it necessary to make so much ado
to get to heaven.

Ans. You are by nature corrupt and blind,
and it is not what you may see, but what the
eternal God declares that should be your guide.
Your Judge will not inquire at last whether you
fancied it right to be in earnest in seeking the
kingdom of God, but whether you listened to his
decisions. He says " strive to enter in at the
strait gate. Labour for the meat which endureth to everlasting life." You think probably
that a little formal religion will be sufficient, but
he says to such, " Thou hast a name that thou
livest and art dead; I know thy works, that thou
art neither cold nor hot: because thou art luke-

warm, and neither cold nor hot, I will spue thee out of my mouth." If you speak of making too much ado about religion, will you stand to your own words at last? Will you say on your death-bed, that the most prayerful and religious person that ever lived, was too earnest in getting to heaven? Do saints in glory, think they made too much ado to get there? and that they might have reached it as well with less care and pains? Do lost souls in hell, *now* think, as they once did, that heaven was not worth so much care and thought? Do they think you can make too much ado to flee from the everlasting burnings? O, could you see that world, to which you are hastening; could you know what it is to stand before the eternal God, and hear your sentence from his lips; and could you taste but for *one short hour* the joys of the blest, or the miseries of the damned; you would think no care, and labour, and pains, and diligence could be enough, in making your own salvation sure. Then if you saw saints, as eminent as Paul himself, around you, you might say to them, "O, how slow is your progress! how formal your prayers! how cold your zeal and love, to what theirs should be, who have such an eternity before them!"

Obj. 7. I love the pleasures of the world; and when should I enjoy them except in youth! I cannot give them up.

Ans. But has not God declared, that living in pleasure is being *dead while we live?* 1 Tim. 5, 6. What will the end of your delights be? The pleasures of the world end in bitterness and gall. Often do they leave a sting behind even here, and will sting the guilty soul with everlasting remorse hereafter. The paths of worldly pleasure conduct to endless pain. **Remember** that unhappy lover of pleasure, whom the Lord describes, in Luke, 16. He loved the delights of the world, and had them too; but died and awoke in hell. Ah, dismal end of a pleasant course! How short, how wretched is that pleasure, which ends in such bitter and eternal sorrow! And cannot you give up the sinful delights of a foolish world? you must give them up, or must lose your soul. If you will not part with them now, you must at last part with them all, and lose God and Christ, and heavenly glory for them. If you choose them as your portion, remember you choose damnation with them.

Obj. 8. I might follow religion; but it is such a melancholy thing, that I fear it would destroy all the comfort of my life.

Ans. My young friend, what is real religion? Is it not the knowledge of God? and the enjoyment of his love and favour? This constitutes the happiness of angels. And is that which makes them happy, a melancholy thing? How you condemn yourself, and prove yourself to have *a carnal mind* which *is enmity against God,* while you look on his service and love, as a source of gloom and dissatisfaction! But while you think religion melancholy, it is dreadfully plain that you are not fit for the enjoyment of heaven, where every pleasure is religious. Who are they that charge religion as unhappy? Are they those who have tried what comforts it can afford? No; they will tell you, they never knew what comfort was, till they found it in the paths of peace and piety. Who is it then? It is a poor, foolish, distracted world; that speaks evil of what it knows not. Would you believe a thief, that might be extolling the advantages of robbery, and representing honesty as contemptible and mischievous? And why will you believe a world that is at enmity with God, when it extols the way of destruction, and represents the path of piety as base and contemptible?

It is true the most pious Christians have some sorrows peculiar to themselves; but their sorrows spring, not from the religion they possess, but from the want of more; and even in their tears of humble grief, there is more true satisfaction, than in the foolish laughter and noisy merriment of the sons of pleasure.

It is true also, that such an exercise of mind as deep repentance, may embitter some of the first parts of their way, who are turning from the world to God. But is it not better to be troubled for sin here than in hell? Is it not better to repent of sin in time, than to grieve for it to eternity? To feel even the bitterest pangs of penitential sorrow for days or weeks in this world, than burdened with sin to lie in misery for ever and ever?

Obj. 9. I cannot embrace religion, for all my companions are averse to it; and were I to follow it, I must lose the friendship of them all.

Ans. Yes, if you follow religion, you must *come out from the world, and be separate from them;* and if they will not forsake the ways of sin, you must forsake them. But is their love to you so great, that you should ruin your soul on their account? Are you not grieving and losing better friends while you are pleasing them? They did not make you an immortal being. They have not crowned your life with comforts. It is your God that has done this; and will you slight your God for them? They did not redeem you. No one of them has groaned, and wept, and hungered, and thirsted, and bled, and died for you; but this, the Lord has done; and will you prefer them to him? No one of them can cheer you in sickness; comfort you in death; make even the gloomy grave the passage to eternal day; befriend you when help is needed most; and welcome your departed soul to glory and to God: but all this the Lord would do; and should not you prefer him and his friendship to theirs? If they can make up to you the loss of a Saviour; if they can give you a place in heaven; and save you from the pit of destruction; then cleave to them. You know they cannot: if now companions in sin, unless you or they repent, you will soon be companions in hell.

Obj. 10. Religion would expose me to the scorn and ridicule of my companions and friends.

Ans. And what is the ridicule you fear? Is it so serious an evil, that to avoid it you should run into perdition? Were not the blessed Saviour and his apostles scorned and derided by the world? Was not he insulted with profane mockings, even in his dying moments? And did he endure such contempt for you, and will you refuse to endure a little contempt and derision for him? But if you are afraid of following Christ lest you should be laughed at, think which is worst, the silly laugh of dying men, or the eternal frown of the eternal God. Will you choose the last for the sake of missing the first? Is it not better to enter the way to heaven, though all the world were to deride and despise you for doing so, than to take the way to hell, though all the world were to applaud your choice? Will you, to avoid the scorner's laugh, lose God, and Christ, and glory? Surely, if you do, angels may pity, and devils deride such folly.

Obj. 11. Whatever advantages may flow from religion, yet it has many difficulties.

Ans. And has not sin its difficulties, and its sorrows too? Is not *the way of transgressors* often *hard?* and always ruinous? If religion bids us sacrifice much, does not sin lead many to sacrifice more? Do not youthful lusts hurry some to the gallows, and multitudes to the grave? How many do they sink from plenty to beggary! On how many others do they entail infamy or disease, where health might have been enjoyed! How many sleepless nights and painful days do they occasion! How many fears lest secret sins should come to light! and how many contrivances to conceal from detection, those crimes which lie open in the sight of God! Do the lewd, and the drunken, and extravagant, find no difficulties attendant on their crimes? Yes, my young friend, such are the difficulties of the ways of sin, that it often ruins reputation and health; blasts every pleasing hope; destroys the body, and damns the soul. Many have suffered martyrdom for Christ; but where one has been a martyr for religion, thousands have been, in effect, martyrs to sin. Excess in iniquity has shortened their days; and they have sacrificed their all in this world, and in that which is to come. And though religion may have some difficulties, yet it is easier to overcome these, than to be lost for ever; especially as grace and strength from God and Christ are promised; and as the further any one goes in the ways of religion, the easier they will become. In a little while too all the Christian's trials will cease. A few days or years are the moment for his conflict, but eternity the measure of his rest.

Obj. 12. Though I may not have just such a religion as you recommend, yet I have more than many round about me. I see some that go not to a place of worship once a year, while I attend one frequently, and I hope I shall fare better than they.

Ans. If many have not even the outward forms of piety, and you have nothing but those forms, you are only taking a different road to the same wretched abode as they. If they choose destruction in one way, you should not choose it in another. You will not be judged by comparison with them. The Lord declares "you must be born again." He does not merely say you must excel your ungodly neighbours, or never enter eternal rest, but, "Verily, verily, I say unto thee, Except a man be born of water and of the Spirit, he cannot enter the kingdom of God. Marvel not that I say unto thee, Ye must be born again." If you go on in your negligent course, will it comfort you, when cast into hell, to think, that you fare as well as those ungodly creatures that may be perishing by thousands round you? Whatever others are, let it be your concern to be a Christian in sincerity; and whatever others do, let it be your first business to make sure of the kingdom of heaven.

Obj. 13. It is true, I have not much religion, but I hope to repent at last. The thief on the cross in his last extremity found mercy; and why should I despair? They who went at the eleventh hour received as much, every man his penny, as they who were called at the first.

Ans. It is true God is merciful, but he is also just. Now is the day of mercy, and now he says, "Let the wicked forsake his way, and the unrighteous man his thoughts; and let him return unto the Lord, and he will have mercy upon him, and to our God, for he will abundantly pardon." But his word discourages their presumptuous hope, who neglect him now hoping to find mercy at last. "Then shall they call upon me, but I will not answer; they shall seek me early but they shall not find me." As for the case of the thief on the cross, his situation was peculiar; he hung dying by the Lord of life; and God at that hour would glorify his Son. You can never be placed in his situation, and therefore have no ground from it to hope for mercy at last. It would be more reasonable for you to expect a translation to heaven without dying, because Enoch and Elijah thus went to glory, than it is to hope for God's mercy on your death-bed, because the dying thief was pardoned. You read in the word of God of two that went thus to heaven; but from the creation of the world to the death of Christ, a period of above four thousand years, you read but of one who found mercy in the hour of death. As for a hope of heaven, because those who went at the eleventh hour were admitted, it is a hope founded on delusion. Even if the parable were to be thus interpreted, it would afford no encouragement for delay. For they who went at the eleventh hour, went *as soon as they were called. They were not called till the*

eleventh; and listened as soon as they were; bu
you are called now. The day was not quite gone
with them; they had *one hour* to labour for their
Lord; but you on a sick-bed would have none.
Nevertheless, it is proper to add, that the parable is wholly misinterpreted when thus applied.
That the reward mentioned does not mean the
blessings of eternity, is extremely evident from
ver. 11 and 15; where some are represented as
murmuring, and as having that evil, or malignant
eye, which is the effect of an envious temper; but
such murmurings and dispositions will not be
found among the blessed; and consequently the
parable has no reference to their future state.
The 16th ver. also speaks of many as being rejected. But this will not be the case of any, that
receive the promised crown. The intent of the
parable seems briefly this: the early labourers
denote the Jews, who were soon called into the
vineyard of God; the latter ones, the Gentiles,
who were called much later to the enjoyment of
spiritual privileges and blessings; and the murmuring of those called soon into the vineyard,
expresses the malignant murmurings of the Jews,
when the Gentiles were called to partake of equal
privileges with themselves. Many instances of
this envious disposition are recorded in the New
Testament.

Obj. 14. Would you have me believe that all
are going to destruction, who are not acquainted with that divine change in which you state
religion to consist? Few seem to know any
thing of that; are few only to be saved?

Ans. My young friend, this is not what I
would make you believe, but what the eternal
Judge declares. He assures you that *his flock*

is small; that the way of *life is narrow,* and but *few* travellers in it. His word says, "If any man be in Christ, he is a new creature; old things are passed away; behold, all things are become new." "Verily I say unto you, except ye be converted, and become as little children, ye shall not enter into the kingdom of heaven;" "Many are called, but few are chosen." Numbers are no proof of safety. God's judgments will not be turned aside, because the number that choose ruin is great. "The wicked shall be turned into hell, and all the nations that forget God." If nations are unacquainted with religion together, together they must perish. Numbers perished in Sodom for one that escaped. Hundreds of thousands of the Israelites died in the desert, for one that reached the promised land. Millions perished in the deluge, for one that was saved in the ark.

Obj. 15. There are so many different kinds of religions among Christians, that I hardly know which to choose.

Ans. And would you therefore choose none? But you mistake : among real Christians there neither is, nor ever was more than one religion. All that are Christians in sincerity, though they may vary in some minor points, unite in the most important. They all believe in *repentance towards God: and faith in our Lord Jesus Christ:* he is the only Saviour to whom they all look. They all are *born again by the Spirit of God.* They all live to the glory of God; and walk in the ways of holiness. They all *lay up their treasures in heaven;* and, as pilgrims, go through this

Luke, xii. 32. Matt. vii. 14. 2 Cor. v. 17. Matt. xviii. 3; xxii 14. Psalm, ix. 17.

world aspiring to a better.   In this world persons wear clothes of different colours, or a different shape, who all possess similar limbs, and
a similar form. They speak different languages ;
and have been born in different lands ; but they
all belong to the same race; all are descended
from the same parents. So in religion, true Christians may be distinguished by a variety of smaller
differences, but they are all related to the same
Parent ; they are all begotten again by the same
Spirit. An army may have many regiments,
and these composed from different nations, and
wearing different uniforms; but the same leader
guides them ; they form but one army still. En-
list, my young friend, into the army of the Saviour ; and as to the particular regiment to which
you should attach yourself, make his word your
guide. In other words, embrace religion, and
let the scriptures teach you what denomination
of real Christians to join.

Obj. 16. I have heard of so many crimes committed by persons who professed religion, that
I am disposed to think all who make such a
stir about religion are alike, and are hypocrites
at heart.

Ans. What if they were ; would that set aside
death and judgment, to which you hasten ?
Would it unmake heaven and hell, one of which
must be your eternal dwelling ? Would it render the favour of God less valuable, or his anger
less dreadful ? Would it excuse your neglect of
him ? You are not to answer for them, but for
yourself. But perhaps the crimes that have giv-
en you disgust, were those of persons, sincere in
heart, but unhappily drawn, in an unguarded moment, into sin, which has since cost them many

a week of bitter grief. Now if this were the case, should their unhappy fall be a reason with you to neglect your God? Should you cut your throat because they have cut a finger? If you saw a man slip his foot into the sea, would you make that a reason for throwing yourself head-long, with a millstone round your neck, into the mighty deep? O, do not then, because some, in the main sincere, may by sin have wounded their own souls, cast yours into the pit of eternal per-dition.

Obj. 17. If God have elected me to eternal life, I shall be saved, and if he have not, it is in vain for me to give myself any concern respecting it.

Ans. You most probably know that with res-pect to the ground of this objection, there is a wide difference in the opinions of those that re-ally *love the Lord Jesus Christ.* Nor is it your business to trouble yourself with inquiries into the decrees of God, but to listen to what he en-joins; and he now commandeth ALL *men* EVE-RY WHERE *to repent.* God's foreknowledge as much extends to all the concerns of this world, as to the state of souls in that which is to come. But what would you think of the farmer who might say, "I will not sow my fields; if God de-sign me a harvest, I shall have it." Or of a man fallen into the sea, who might say, "I will not get out; if God have decreed that I shall not be drowned, he will take me out." You would not argue, "I will take no food; and though I am but twenty, if God have decreed that I shall live to sixty, I shall live as well without it as with it." Do not then let Satan delude you to neg-lect an immortal soul by an excuse so frivolous and foolish, that you would not, for the same, deny your perishing body even the food of a single day. Without inquiring into the secret things of God, remember these are his decrees, " He hat believeth and is baptized, shall be saved; but he that believeth not shall be damned." " Except ye eat the flesh of the Son of Man, and drink his blood, ye have no life in you." "He that believeth on the Son, hath everlasting life; and he that believeth not the Son, shall not see life; but the wrath of God abideth on him." "Except ye repent, ye shall all likewise perish."

Obj. 18. I do not see that early religion comes to much : many that once professed it have forsaken it, and become worse than ever.

Ans. You must be sadly blinded by ignorance, prejudice, and sin, if you do not perceive that it is early piety which is commonly the most eminent, even in the present world. Some instances of this were mentioned in chapter 9, and many might be added ; for most who adorn religion are converted young. It is true, a young hypocrite may prove an old apostate. If men in youth wear religion as a form or mask, they will probably cast it aside; and then be more profligate than ever. One devil might appear to have left them, but seven to have taken possession of them : but not thus is it with the possessors of real, youthful piety. Their path is that of the just, shining more and more unto the perfect day.

Obj. 19. But I do not believe that God will be so strict as he is represented. Nor do I believe that he will be offended with me for following my pleasures, and gratifying the inclinations of the nature he has given me.

Mark, xvi. 10.   John, vi. 53.   iii. 36.   Luke, xiii. P

Ans. So then your objections come to infideli-
ty at last. You do not believe what God declares; for he in his own word represents himself
thus righteously strict; he there assures you that
the *end* of a life of vanity is *eternal death.* You
do not believe God, but listen to the tempter in
preference to him. Thus was the world at first
ruined. The tempter said to our parent, " Ye
shall not surely die." The lie was believed, and
they were undone. As for following the inclinations of your nature, you might safely do so,
if your nature were what it was, when man came
from his Creator's hands: then were his dispositions holy; but now your nature is corrupt and
fallen; its dispositions *earthly, sensual,* and *devilish.* The heart is deceitful above all things, and
desperately wicked, as is shown Chap. 2. § 4. It
would be as safe for a man, in a fit of raging madness, to follow the suggestions of his disordered
mind, as for you, in your fallen state, to follow
those of corrupt nature.

Obj. 20. After all that can be urged, I am determined not to relinquish my pleasures, and become a poor melancholy creature. I will venture eternity. I will have my own way.

Ans. Alas! if these are your feelings, it is your
own way, and the downward road; it is not
God's, nor will it lead you to him. But if you
have your way, depend upon it, by and by he
will have his. You have your day of sin, and
your Judge will have his day of retribution.
And *what will you do in* that *day of visitation!*

CHAPTER XXII.

THE YOUNG READER FURTHER URGED TO MAKE NO DELAY IN GIVING HIMSELF UP TO GOD.

§. 1. IT is related, that a pious minister of the 17th century, having finished prayer, observed a young gentleman just shut into one of the pews, who discovered much uneasiness, and seemed to wish to get out again. The minister felt a peculiar desire to detain him, and turning towards one of the members of his church, who sat in the gallery, he asked him aloud — "Brother, do you repent of your coming to Christ?" "No, Sir," he replied : "I never was happy till then : I only repent that I did not come to him sooner." The minister turned towards the opposite gallery, and addressed himself to an aged member. — "Brother, do you repent that you came to Christ?" "No, Sir," said he : "I have known the Lord from my youth up." He then looked down upon the young man, whose attention was fully engaged, and, fixing his eyes upon him, said, "Young man, *are you* willing to come to Christ?" This unexpected address from the pulpit, exciting the observation of all, so affected him, that he sat down and hid his face. The person who sat next him encouraged him to rise, and answer the question. The minister repeated it — "Young man, *are you* willing to come to Christ?" With a tremulous voice he replied, "Yes, Sir." "But *when*, Sir?" added the minister, in a solemn and loud tone. He mildly answered, "Now, Sir." "Then stay," said he, "and hear the word of God, which you will find in 2 Cor. vi. 2: *Behold,* NOW *is the accepted time; behold,* NOW *is the day of salvation.*" By this sermon he was greatly affected: he went into the vestry, after service, dissolved in tears. That unwillingness to stay, which he had discovered, was occasioned by the injunction of his father, who threatened, that, if ever he went to hear the fanatics, he would turn him out of doors. Having now heard, and being unable to conceal the feelings of his mind, he was afraid to meet his father. The minister sat down and wrote an affectionate letter to him, which had so good an effect, that both father and mother came to hear for themselves. They were both brought to the knowledge of the truth; and father, mother, and son, were together received with universal joy into the church.

Does this young man now repent that he listened *immediately* to the message of God? Far from it. God rewarded his immediate compliance, by bringing his parents also to the knowledge of the truth.

§ 2. Already have you been entreated to make the same choice; and have you done so? or are you still for putting it off a little longer? O! if you are, be assured that delay is one of the most successful of Satan's infernal stratagems for ruining immortal souls; hell, it is to be feared, is filled with delayers. Multitudes that did not intend to live and die neglecting Christ, yet have been persuaded to delay a little longer, and still a little longer, till death overtook them unprepared. Not merely then do I beseech you to give your youth to God, but to do so without delay: consider the dreadful evils of delaying.

While you delay, your life is going; every sabbath leaves you one season of mercy less. Your heart is hardening; and every day there is less hope of your conversion than there was the day before. While you delay, you are grieving the Spirit of God, and tempting him to leave you for ever; and, if he should, you will be undone for ever. The oftener he has called, the seldomer he will call. The oftener you have slighted, or quenched, the impressions he has made on your heart, the less probability there is of your ever partaking of the grace of God. While you delay, you continue in your lost and wretched state; all your sins are upon you. You linger on the brink of hell. You put off seeking mercy, but cannot put off the approach of judgment. Alas! your *judgment lingereth not, and* your *damnation slumbereth not.* You lie down at night with no security that you shall not awake in hell before the morning dawns. You rise in the morning to pursue your business, or your amusements, with no certainty of being out of endless misery when the evening comes. What would you think of a man playing with a weed while drowning, instead of accepting the help that should snatch him from destruction? Alas! how ruinous would be his folly! but, O! how much more ruinous is yours, while you put off attending to those things which belong to your everlasting peace! An hour improved or lost may be to you more than a thousand worlds.

While you delay, you let Satan have his ends; it is enough for him, if you will but put off turning to Christ; for he knows full well, though you forget it, that death will soon put this off for ever. While you delay, you live without one real blessing; you have no hope of glory; no interest in God; no place in heaven. You insult the Most High, who bids you to seek him today. You are ungrateful to his beloved Son, who did not delay to come and die for wretched men, when the appointed time arrived.

§ 3. Consider also that many are eternally shut out of heaven, and eternally shut up in hell, through delaying to turn to God. Some years back, I repeatedly visited an aged man,. who was ill. He had spent nearly fourscore years without God in the world; but then professed penitence. He unexpectedly grew better, and a little space was added to his life; but apparently added in vain. When his health was restored, he seemed to serve the same hard master again, as he had always served. But illness soon returned; and it was understood that he died miserably. I knew another person, that seemed much in earnest in inquiring for spiritual blessings; but, ah, delay! after a time he grew careless. God now visited him with a painful affliction. I saw him at that time; he seemed sensible of his sin and folly, and penitent for it. At length divine mercy favoured him once more with health; but when health returned, the serious impressions of illness, fled away. Again he grew careless of his God. Again he delayed; but, ah! not for a long period: illness soon returned. His soul was filled with distress and misery, and death summoned the unhappy criminal to the bar of his God. Shall I relate another anecdote? A young person called upon an aged man, ill, and hastening to the grave; the youth spoke of the blessed Saviour and the precious gospel: for a few minutes he listened with serious attention, then burst into a flood of tears, and exclaimed, "Ah! my young friend, had I thought on these things thirty or forty years ago, what a happy man might I now have been, but now (wringing his hands) it is too late; hell must be my portion for ever."

> "And shall I say, "'Tis yet too soon
>   To seek for heaven, or think of death?'
> A flower may fade before 'tis noon,
>   And I this day resign my breath.
>
> If this rebellious heart of mine
>   Despise the gracious calls of Heaven,
> I may be harden'd in my sin,
>   And never have repentance given."

§ 4. The word of the Most High says, "To-day if ye will hear his voice, harden not your hearts;" and that is a most important question, "Wilt thou not from this time cry unto me, My Father, thou art the guide of my youth?" Can you, will you, hesitate to say, "Great God, thou shalt be the guide of mine?" What! hesitate whether to seek God as your Father, or to have no interest in him! What! hesitate whether Christ shall be your Saviour, or Satan your tormentor! whether heaven or hell shall be your inheritance! whether angels or devils shall be your companions! If you will delay, consider well what you are about. Try if you can make a memorandum to this effect: "That, having weighed the importance of true religion, you yet resolve to pay it no attention at present;—that you resolve, for some years more, to plunge deeper and deeper in the service of the devil;—that though your present path conducts to hell, yet that you will not so soon leave the way to hell for that to heaven; — that, though living every day on the goodness of God, you resolve to spend at least some years more in insulting him, in forgetting his love, in abusing his mercies, and in tempting him to cut you down as a cumberer of the ground, to send you to perdition; — that though the blood of the Saviour was shed to redeem you, yet that you will spend some years more in all manner of ingratitude to him, and in doing what you can to defeat the end for which he died; — and that having done all this till, if God spare you, all the best and prime of life is past, that you will then profess to forsake these evil ways; will declare that you are very sorry for what you have so *wilfully* done; and that you then will offer to God the wretched dregs of a life spent in serving the devil." Could you commit to writing such horrid resolutions as these? If you could not, O! do not, by your actions what you would not profess by your words; for, remember that " actions speak louder than words."

§ 5. Rather be persuaded this day to cast yourself at the Saviour's feet. Happy then would this day be to you. Happy would be this year. Happy is the day to the condemned criminal, in which he finds forgiveness; but happier far would be the day to you, that brought you to the blessed Jesus for mercy and life; that led you to him for deliverance from all your soul-destroying sins. Inexpressibly happy would be the day to you, in which God received you as his child, in which Christ and heaven became your own. O! if this day you would, in sincerity, cry to God, " *My Father, thou art the guide of my youth;*" if you would this day look to the Lamb of God, and commit your soul to his care; long would

G r 3

it be a memorable day to you; you might remember it with pleasure on a sick-bed, in your
dying hour, and in the eternal world.   Then, at
some future period of life, you might say, " Alas!
I gave my youth to the world, to sin, and folly,
for too many sinful years!   But, O! I remember
the day when God turned my feet into the paths
of peace.   Blessed day! it has been the source
of a thousand comforts to me.   I was a poor,
thoughtless creature, but God met with me, and
pitied my dying soul."   If this, or any other little volume like this, were made the means of awakening your mind, you might have to add, " With
a careless heart I began to read even of those
things which belonged to my everlasting peace;
blessed be the name of the Lord that I laid the
book down with feelings so different from those
with which I took it up."

O, be persuaded now to yield yourself to God;
and then next new-year's-day shall find you
walking in the way to heaven, or landed there.
In either case, how blessed a change would the
grace of God have made in your condition!
Should you be spared for future years, how happy an alteration would it be, though you began
the year in sin, long ere it ended, to have found
forgiveness for all your sins;—though you began it a child of wrath, before it ended to be a
child of God;—though you began it without any
part in one spiritual blessing, ere it ended, to be
able to say, "God and all his love, Christ and all
the riches of his grace, and all the sweet promises
of Scripture, and all the glories of heaven, are
mine!"   But, perhaps, before even this year shall
conclude, your mortal course may finish.   If it
should do so, and none can tell that it will not.

how infinitely important is it for you, without an hour's delay, to flee to Christ; for then, how happy a year would even this, though your last year, be to you! How changed next new-year's-day would your state then appear! O, happy change! to have begun the year on earth, and ended it in heaven; — to have begun it with man, and ended it with God; — to have begun it unacquainted with the ways of peace, and ere the year concluded, to have found the way, have fought the battle, and received the prize; — to have begun it a thoughtless, prayerless creature; and, before it ended, to have learned to commune with God below, and to have begun communion with him above; — to have begun it far from peace, and Christ, and heaven; and, ere it ended, to have found salvation, and to be a companion of angels and saints in the regions of glory. May the God of all grace make you, from this hour, a child of his own in and through Christ the Lord! *Amen.*

CHAPTER XXIII.

BRIEF ADDRESSES TO SEVERAL CLASSES OF PERSONS; AND A FEW DIRECTIONS TO THE YOUNG CHRISTIAN.

TO THE IRRELIGIOUS CHILDREN OF PIOUS PARENTS.

§ 1. MY young friends, much of what has been here said to all, applies with peculiar force to you. You have peculiar privileges; and your youthful sins are proportionably greater and heavier than those of others. God has laid you under especial obligations to live to him; and, if you perish, your ruin will be far more dread-

ful than theirs, who have been brought up in
the midst of ignorance and sin. Alas! you
have lived in the midst of spiritual privileges;
yet had them all in vain. You have been
brought, from your infancy, to the house of God,
yet gone there in vain, or worse than in vain;
you are, perhaps, almost hardened in careless
neglect of what you have heard so long, to so
little purpose. You have heard of mercy, yet
have no part in it. You have heard of heaven,
yet have no title to its blessings. You have
heard of Jesus, but not sought him as your Saviour. You have heard of God, but not chosen
him as your Father. Young as you are, for
how many years have the prayers of your parents ascended to God for you, but they are not
yet answered. For how many years have you
seen others coming forward to devote themselves
to God, and yet you have not done so. They,
who were once the vile and the profligate, enter
the kingdom of God; but you go not in. You
have probably seen many, who had not sat under the gospel a quarter of the time that you have
done, forsaking the world to follow Jesus. You
have probably seen many that had been brought
up in the abodes of ignorance, by parents that
are going to destruction, forsaking the way of
their parents, to come to Christ; yet you, children of the kingdom — you, nursed as it were,
in the house of God — you, whose parents would
rejoice to lead you with them in the path to
heaven, yet you refuse to go. Are you happy?
Do you not often feel an inward sting? or have
you resisted God so long, that he has left you
to hardened hearts? If this be not the case, do
not you feel that you are still in an awful state?

Can novels, or vain companions, drive the thoughts of your condition quite away? Do not you feel that something is wanting? That something is religion. Perhaps you have pious parents in heaven. Would you not join them there? There is but one way to do so: make their God and Saviour yours. Perhaps your parents are still on earth, sorrowing over their ungodly children. Shall God guide them, and Satan you? Heaven be their abode, and hell yours? Will you so live as to be sure, ere long, to lose them for ever? Alas! you are amongst the most guilty of mankind; and your sins the most inexcusable. Your neglect of Christ is peculiarly wicked and dreadful. Your future account will be awfully strict, and inexpressibly terrible, when all your abused mercies are brought forward in the judgment against you, to show the aggravations of your sins, and to double your condemnation. O! lay up then a better portion for futurity, than the bitter fruits of such youthful sins. When you see those, who have had none of your peculiar advantages, pressing into the kingdom of God, O! let it stir up you to deplore your past folly, and to enter in at the strait gate. In pity to yourselves, choose religion; have compassion on your own highly-favoured souls. You would not make a fellow-creature wretched for a month; do not, by abusing your privileges any longer, make your own souls doubly wretched for eternity. You may be happy; and will you not? You might glorify God, as many, who never had half your privileges, are doing, by lives devoted to him; and will you not? O, listen to the persuasions that have been addressed to you! Yield to God, and be happy.

But, perhaps, you, who read these lines, have felt at times the importance of religion. Once you seemed about to enter the way of life; yet, alas! the pleasing hope was blasted, and you became careless again. O, once more *consider your ways!* After all your awful delays turn to God, and the past shall be forgiven and forgotten. But if you will not, if you will quench the Spirit still, O, remember, though you may forget the tears you shed, the desires you expressed, the impressions you felt, yet God forgets them not. They all stand recorded against you; and you, hereafter, may feel the truth of the remark, that "slighted convictions are the worst death-bed companions."

§ 2. TO THE CHILDREN OF IRRELIGIOUS PARENTS.

You, my young friends, have not had all those advantages which many have enjoyed. You, perhaps, have been almost nursed in crimes; and to the evil propensities of your hearts, has been added the fatal influence of their evil example, who should have taught you better things. Yet, notwithstanding all the guilt of your lives, remember, that God is no respecter of persons; and, if you listen to his voice, none will be more welcome to his kingdom than you. To have lived so long in the midst of ignorance, has made yours a pitiable state. But God is willing to receive you, and to number you with his children. If you give your youth to Christ, he will not love or bless you the less, because you may not have one friend on earth travelling in the way to heaven. All the blessings promised the young Christian, you, by coming to Christ, may obtain. Consider not then what your friends or relatives are, but what God would have you be; and what, on a dying bed, you will wish to have been. Perhaps you have to say, "I have been taught to serve Satan, to profane the sabbath, to laugh at religion, and undo my own soul ;" yet, if you have to make this sad complaint, O! be persuaded to add, "But I will listen to these in-instructions no more. If I cannot take my friends with me to heaven, I will strive to go myself. If I cannot save their souls, I will seek salvation for my own." Many, that like you, have been trained up in vice and folly, have for-saken the paths of sin; have turned to God; have honoured religion; have been distinguish-for their piety on earth; and shine in glory for evermore. And would not you be like them? you may. Yield yourself to Jesus, and you will.

§ 3. TO IRRELIGIOUS PARENTS.

If the importance of early religion is so great, how much should your affection for your chil-dren, urge upon you to improve every means, for bringing them to a knowledge of it! How great is your guilt while you trifle with your own salvation, and, by your example, teach your chil-dren to trifle with theirs! Ancient heathens pre-sented their offspring to be burnt alive, as offer-ings to that horrid idol Moloch. And do not you, in reality, act a still more shocking part, if you train up your offspring, in that way, which will make them slaves to Satan here, and sink them to hell hereafter? Where is your pity for your children, if you have no pity for their im-mortal souls? And where is your pity for their souls, if, by your example, you teach them to profane the sabbath, and to neglect God, and Christ, and heaven? You would be filled with horror at the thought of being their destroyers; yet, which, at last, will appear the greater cruelty, to destroy the bodies of your children, or, by your sinful negligence, to sink to damnation their immortal souls? O, as you love your offspring, show yourselves their real friends by teaching them to seek the friendship of their God.

§ 4. TO THE YOUNG CHRISTIAN.

I may now, my young friend, with pleasure address you, who are a partaker of those spiritual blessings, which are so vast, that their worth can never be unfolded, except in the realms of everlasting day. Happy are you, and, if faithful unto death, you will soon be unspeakably happier. Allow me to suggest to you a little affectionate advice.

Direction 1. Be thankful: you have peculiar reason for gratitude. Look around you, and see what multitudes die in sin! what thousands float down the torrent of iniquity, that bears them to perdition! And why are not you one of the number? It is the grace of God that has made you to differ. Perhaps you are poor; you are employed in the factory, the fields, or the mill; and many others are employed around you, who are unacquainted with the blessings of religion; and why are not you, like them, poor for both worlds? Why have you riches that will endure, when those of this world perish?

> " 'Twas the same Love that spread the feast,
>   That sweetly forc'd you in ;

Else you had still refus'd to taste,
And perish'd in your sin."

Perhaps you are placed amidst wealth and splendour, but you have learned to seek more enduring riches. If so, you have double cause for gratitude. Few that are in such circumstances find the safe, the narrow way.

Direction 2. Be prayerful. Cherish a spirit of devotion. There can be no religion without prayer. The word of God says, " Pray without ceasing. Be careful for nothing ; but in every thing, by prayer, and supplication, with thanksgiving, let your requests be made known unto God. And the peace of God, which passeth all understanding, shall keep your hearts and minds, through Christ Jesus. Pray to thy Father which is in secret ; and thy Father, which seeth in secret, shall reward thee openly. Ask, and it shall be given you ; seek, and ye shall find ; knock, and it shall be opened unto you ; for every one that asketh, receiveth ; and he that seeketh, findeth ; and to him that knocketh, it shall be opened."

Have stated times for devotion. At the very least, begin and end every day with God. You cannot justly expect to keep religion alive in your heart with less than this. Take time from sleep, sooner than want time for prayer. Watch against formality in your devotions. It is heartfelt, not cold, though studied prayers, that are acceptable to God. Cherish a devotional spirit, and, besides your intercourse with God in stated seasons of prayer, often be looking up to him ; and ever go to him in the name of Jesus. Remember that, in the hour of prayer, God, in a

1 Thess. v. 17.   Phil. iv. 6, 7.   Matt. vi. 6; vii. 7, 8.

peculiar manner, is present with you. Go into your closet, or down on your knees, for prayer, with as much reverence as if you beheld the great and blessed God. Could you ascend into heaven, every morning and evening, to offer your devotions to the Most High, and then return again to earth, what a life of holiness would you lead! what fervent prayers and thanksgivings would you offer! O! consider that you are as much before the heart-searching God now as you would be then, and that he as much knows your desires and hears your requests.

Direction 3. Be humble. "Be clothed with humility." Wear it as a garment; let it appear in all your intercourse with God and man. *Pride goeth before destruction.* Nothing would give Satan more advantage against you than pride. This would make you self-conceited, and unwilling to be reminded of your defects; and the next step to this is ruin. Remember what you were — a child of wrath; — what you are — a frail, defective creature; — and what you should be — holy as a saint in heaven — *perfect as your Father in heaven is perfect.* When you compare yourself with what, according to the declarations of the Lord, you ought to be, you may cry out with one in former times, "Blessed Jesus, either these are not thy words, or we are not Christians;" and, while this is the case, you should cherish humility.

Direction 4. Cleave to Jesus. Make him your all in all. Let his death be your hope, his life your pattern, his promises your encouragement, his precepts your guide. Watch against every thing that would lead you to rest your hopes on any foundation, except Jesus crucified. Remember that you always were, that you still are, and ever will be, at the best, but an unprofitable servant. Keep in mind that the Lord has said, *Without me ye can do nothing.* Apply to him for strength, and grace, and every good. Consider that *you are not your own;* that you are not to live to yourself, but to Christ; and that the governing desire of your heart should be, that the Lord Jesus Christ may be magnified by you, in your life and death.

Direction 5. Follow holiness, and live to the glory of God. Christianity is a religion all heart and soul; and you having embraced it betimes, have the best opportunity for exemplifying its power. The slothful servant is a wicked servant. The fruitless tree is a cumberer of the ground. Jesus expects more than the leaves of a fair profession; he expects the fruits of holiness. When he compares the divine word to seed, he represents it, in his real disciples, as producing *thirty, sixty, and even a hundred fold.* Though more in some than others, yet much, even where least. You have much to do for the glory of God, for the honour of Christ, for the welfare of others, and the benefit of your own soul. Though your situation should be ever so humble, though you should even have but one talent, yet by the silent, but powerful eloquence of a life of constant holiness, you may do much to recommend the gospel.

Direction 6. Improve every help for growing in grace. With this view, attend some place of worship, where the gospel is faithfully preached. Make those your friends who are the friends of

John, xv. 5.   Phil. i. 20.   1 Cor. vi. 19, 20.   Matt. xxv. 26.
Luke, xiii. 7.   Mark, xi. 13, 14.   Matt. xiii. 8

Christ, and whose converse and counsel will help you onward to heaven. By all means seek admission into the church of Christ. You have no right to the honourable name of Christian, till you are a member of it. Be not satisfied with merely hearing of Jesus, but confess him ; avow yourself on the Lord's side, and openly take part with his people. Search the scriptures ; read them daily, with prayer, for divine illumination, and the divine blessing. Read such practical works as Baxter's Saint's Rest, Doddridge's Rise and Progress, Freeston's Directions, &c. &c.*

Direction 7. Live above the world. Consider it your chief business on earth to glorify God, and get safe to heaven. Confess yourself a stranger and pilgrim upon earth ; and keep eternity and heaven in view. Thus strive to entertain no more regard for the world, than you will have for it, when in death you are leaving it for ever. " Pray, as for eternity ; hear, as for eternity ; live, as for eternity ; obey, and do every thing as for eternity."

Direction 8. Be faithful unto death. The young followers of Jesus are exposed to so many snares, that, while the aged Christian rejoices over them, he may, excepting over a few who seem to be too firmly rooted to be shaken, rejoice with trembling. Irreligious connexions are among the most fatal snares. Alas ! there is too much truth in the severe observation ; " How few young professors are there, that will not forsake their Christian friends and their

---

* A Guide for Young Disciples, by the Author of this book, is especially designed to instruct and animate young Christians in their way to heaven. 384 Pages, 18mo. Price 3s 6d.

Redeemer, for an ungodly wife or husband." Watch against all the snares that would en- tangle your feet; and all the *fleshly lusts that war against the soul.* Keep in view the blessings promised to those who persevere. When the world tempts you aside, think of Peter's words: *" Lord, to whom shall we go? thou hast the words of eternal life!"* I once knew a poor man, who mentioned to me how much happiness he had found in religion, in the early part of his Chris- tian course. Peace with God made his life pleasant. The night and the day were alike cheerful; and fear and grief fled far from him. But words to this effect were suggested to him, and run in his mind: " What need is there of so much ado about religion?" For a time he resisted, but at length yielded to the tempter. He went backwards, and Satan triumphed. And now farewell to peace; his comforts were gone. Distress haunted him; he could not lie down at night without fear of waking in eternal torments before the morning came. He found it a bitter, as well as a guilty thing to forsake his Redeemer. And, though he was afterwards restored to God, he stated that he did not find that degree of happiness which he had experi- enced before his fall. *Hold fast,* then, *what thou hast, that no man take thy crown.*

§ 5. A PRAYER FOR THE YOUNG CHRISTIAN.

Great and most compassionate God, with what pleasure should I approach the, since thou hast taught me to call thee my Father, and hast con- descended to become my God. Thy love to me has been as unceasing as the flight of time; and

O! thou hast taught me to indulge the ecstatic hope, that thou wilt be my portion in a better world, when time, with all its periods, is no more. I bless thee, my God; I praise thee for what I am, and what I have, and what I hope for. I am, I trust, through thy grace, a child of thine, though once I was thy enemy. For ever be thy love adored, for softening my hard heart, for enlightening my benighted mind, for leading me to Jesus, and giving me every good in him. O my Father! the praises of all the inhabitants of heaven, through ten thousand ages, would not sufficiently extol thy love to me: and alas! how mean are my feeble offerings. O my Saviour! I owe thee a debt which I shall never be able fully to acknowledge. Train me, O my God! for that world, where I shall praise thee in sweeter strains, "while immortality endures." Let me keep that world in view; and lead me forward, till thou shalt fix me safely there. Ever let gratitude dwell in my heart, and praises flow from my lips. Let prayer, as it is my highest privilege, ever be my dear delight. While I am pursuing my pilgrimage to eternity, may I daily, and often in the day, hold sweet communion with thee, O Lord. To thee may I flee in every hour of temptation or grief, to tell thee all my heart; and show thyself the hearer of my prayers. Let me be *clothed with humility.* Let me manifest this grace, in all my intercourse with mankind. May I feel my defects, reach at higher holiness, and lie, with a lowly spirit, at the foot of the cross. May I abide in Christ, as the life of my soul, the foundation of my hopes, the source of my comfort, and my all in all. While I trust in his death, may I imitate his life; and, by consistent holiness, adorn the gospel I profess. Let thy word be dear to me. May its treasures be hidden in my heart; and when I search its sacred pages, may it be with a humble, teachable mind; and may thy Spirit deign to be my instructor. May thy house and ordinances be the delight of my soul; and may I live on earth looking forward, with longing desires, to thy house above. Let me confess myself a stranger upon earth, have my affections set on heaven; and feel that all which worldly men esteem important, is a trifle to me, who hope soon to appear in thy presence above. My God, for Jesus's sake grant these blessings, and this one more request: Keep me faithful unto death; and, when I have done and borne thy will here, with robes washed in the blood of Jesus, may I enter thy kingdom, and unite in the triumphal song — *Salvation to our God, which sitteth upon the throne, and unto the Lamb, for ever and ever!* Amen.

THE END.

Printed by Thomas Richardson, Derby.

CONTENTS.

BY THE AUTHOR OF THE PERSUASIVES,

A GUIDE

FOR

YOUNG DISCIPLES OF THE HOLY SAVIOUR,

IN THEIR WAY TO IMMORTALITY.

(FORMING A SEQUEL TO THE PERSUASIVES.)

384 pages 18mo. 3s. 6d. extra boards.

"The principal object of the Author of this judicious and admirable publication, is to impart suitable advice and instruction to the young Christian in his passage through the present world to the heavenly kingdom. The contents of the work admirably accord with its title. We have seen no work which more richly merits a place in the library of every youthful Christian. The work is divided into 19 chapters upon a vast variety of important subjects, interspersed with many interesting anecdotes; the whole forming a compendious system of theology. We most cordially recommend it to the attention of our readers. We think it likely to be extensively useful."

Congregational Magazine.

"Though written for young disciples, it especially refers to persons who are advancing to riper years, by whom the chapters on the choice of companions, marriage, family duties, domestic piety, and the right improvement of the sabbath, are worthy of especial attention. We are at a loss to mention a work containing so much matter at so cheap a price as that before us, and hope many will derive lasting benefit from its perusal."

Christian Guardian; or, Church of England Magazine.

"It is all that young disciples need as a body of doctrinal and practical divinity. It is a suitable book for ministers to put into the hands of inquirers after truth, nor are there any serious persons, whatever their age or standing in the church, but might obtain from it edification and comfort. We recommend it with the utmost confidence and cordiality to all our Readers." *Baptist Magazine.*

"It is not possible to read much in any part of the work, without feeling the vehemence of its exhortations to zeal and diligence in the pursuit of salvation. We cordially recommend it to all our Readers, but especially to young disciples." *General Baptist Repository.*

"Mr. Pike has rendered most important service to young persons by his excellent books, designed for their spiritual benefit. He has just views of Christianity, and enforces its truths and duties with great simplicity, earnestness, and affection. His Guide for Young Disciples, and Persuasives to Early Piety, are full of holy unction."

Wesleyan Methodist Magazine.

"We have seldom seen so much excellent matter compressed in so small a compass. We think it can scarcely be possible to read this book without benefit. Christian parents should put it into the hands of their beloved children, and follow the gift with their fervent prayers, that this excellent Guide may direct them in the way of Peace."

Home Missionary Magazine.